'HOOPS HOTBED'
ON THE
HUDSON

—

RICHARD KANER

Acknowledgement

We at 'Hoops Hotbed on the Hudson' gratefully acknowledge the support of countless coaches, players, administrators, members of the press, fans, other contributors (and, of course, those colorful characters) who share our love of Hudson basketball.

This doesn't ever happen without you.

Cover design by Sue Rinaldi
Interior design by Jacquie Parker

Photos Courtesy of:

ESPN Images
CBS Sports
NFL
UNC Athletic Communications
Richmond Athletic Communications
Syracuse Univ Athletic Communications
George Washington Athletic Communications
U.S. Air Force Athletic Communications
Albio Sires Elementary School
St. Peter's Prep
Seton Hall Athletics
Montclair State
Joe Shine
Secaucus H.S.
Bayonne H.S.
Harrison H.S.

For information: SPI,156 E. Cedar St., Livingston, NJ 07039
The Library of Congress Cataloging - in - Publication Data has been applied for.

ISBN 978 - 8 - 218- 32664- 7 (softcover)

http://www.hoopshotbed.com

'Hoops Hotbed on the Hudson' is dedicated to two doctors, each a big part of my life.

Dr. Norman Kaner, my brother and the first person I ever remember
espousing the high level of Hudson basketball.

Dr. Elnardo Webster, my first basketball client and whose magnificent performance
in the 1968 NIT generated 'Hoops Hysteria on the Hudson.'

While no longer with us, both tremendously influenced this project.

"

Having coached in high school in
North Jersey, I can attest
to the fact that Hudson County was
ALWAYS AWESOME BABY
in producing so many
STARS
over the years.
The **PRIDE** and **PASSION** for
high school hoops in Hudson County
was as good as it gets.

Dick Vitale, Legendary Broadcaster / Hall of Famer

"

Photo: Courtesy of ESPN Images

DR. ELNARDO J. WEBSTER

MARCH 6, 1948 - MARCH 22, 2022

In our family's embrace, Dr. Webster was more than just a basketball legend who graced Hudson County hoops with his talents, playing for the iconic teams like Lincoln High School and St. Peter's University. He was more than his memorable journey through the NBA with the Memphis Pros, the New York Nets, and Serie A in Italy. He was, first and foremost, a devoted husband, a loving father, a cherished uncle, and a doting grandfather.

Our memories of him are imbued with his unwavering commitment to making a difference, particularly in the lives of children from our inner cities. He believed fervently in the transformative power of education and hope and left an indelible mark on all those he touched.

As we navigate this period of mourning, we find comfort in the knowledge that Dr. Webster's legacy will live on through the cherished memories we hold dear. The values he instilled, the love he showered upon us, and the indomitable spirit he embodied will forever shape our lives. His memory continues to be a profound source of inspiration for our family.

We want to express our deep appreciation to each and every one of you who has contributed to honoring Dr. Elnardo J. Webster's life. Your support, kind words, and gestures provide solace during this time of loss.

In warmest regards,

Sandra Webster & Family

loving memory

CONT
ENTS

"Charlie Brown was a great player, teammate ,
coach and friend. His basketball career was marked by
so many accomplishments. He was unselfish and devoted
to playing as a team. His statistics speak for themselves with
the number of wins while playing and coaching at
Jersey City State College (JCSC) now known as New Jersey
City University (NJCU)."

- ED PETERSEN -

GENESIS OF 'HOOPS HOTBED'

This wasn't just a spur-of-the-moment project, rather my first thoughts about what has become "Hoops Hotbed on the Hudson" dates back more than a half-century.

In the summer of 1957, I attended Claire Bee's basketball camp as a camper. Later, in 1958, I worked as a camp waiter.

Claire Bee was a coach at Long Island University Brooklyn, and ran what was the predecessor to Howard Garfinkel's legendary Five Star Camp.

Located at New York Military in Cornwall, New York, the camp attracted a "Who's Who" of high-school basketball elite. Each week featured a prominent coach on site to conduct a clinic and give a lecture.

Coaching luminaries included North Carolina's Frank McGuire, Kentucky's Adolph Rupp, St. John's Lou Carnesecca and Holy Cross/Dartmouth's Doggie Julian. The staff featured collegians who relished the competitive games every evening at the camp.

Besides myself, other Hudson campers included Bill Madden (All-County caliber at Stevens Academy), Arthur Ader (my Lincoln teammate) and George Campen (who also played at Stevens).

Over the the eight-week summer session, the "Hudson and other North Jersey guys" would often discuss the highly-rated and highly-recruited players in camp who went to school in New York City, Long Island and Connecticut.

Invariably, the conversation would lead to the comparison of those players with the ones we had played with, against or seen in our own environs.

Madden, after competing against many of the top players in camp, made the initial assessment that Hudson players were every bit as good or better than most in the camp.

Some scoffed at Madden, as if to say, "Of course he's partial," or What did you expect?," favoring his hometown players."

In my opinion, that was never the case. Anyone who knew Bill knew he was a guy with high moral standards who would never knowingly promote a false narrative.

He'd then begin a comparison, such as, "I'd definitely take Vinnie Ernst (eventual 1961 NIT MVP with Providence) over this guy and that guy," or "Bill Raftery and George Blaney are definitely more complete players than A, B and C." Also, Mike Rooney, sharp-shooting guard, earned Madden's acclaim as compared to others at his position.

These were casual comments and not heated conversations, but as far as I was concerned, it was the seed that grew into this book.

After my 1963 graduation from St. Peter's College in Jersey City, I had various jobs in marketing, with several companies, such as Proctor and Gamble, Hooper Research and RCA. I was also getting my feet wet part-time in the field of basketball player representation, brought about to a large extent by the signing war between the American and National Basketball Associations.

It was 1969 when I decided to go "all-in," embarking on what has become a half-century career in the field of sports management and marketing. Over the course of those 50 plus years, I've been fortunate to attend 44 Final Fours, 43 Portsmouth Invitational Tournaments, seven Euroleague Final Fours as well as a number of Big East Tournaments, NBA playoff games and Vegas summer leagues. Discussion of the prowess of Hudson County basketball grew over time at various events around hotels, gyms, bars and restaurants when games weren't scheduled.

It wasn't surprising that the emerging dominance of St. Anthony (Jersey City) as a national power, along with the individual college and pro (NBA and overseas) success of their former players were a major factor in substantiating the claim of Hudson hoop superiority.

During that period, I was convinced a book recounting the rich and colorful basketball history of Hudson would be both interesting and informative.

Eventually, I began to develop an outline of subjects that should be included. I discussed the theme with a number of former Hudson County players and coaches, all of whom strongly believed in the concept.

I was encouraged to move ahead with the project.

Move to June of 2013. It was definitely a Saturday night. I was driving home after a party at the home of the sister of Father Earle Markey, celebrating his 50th year as a Jesuit priest.

Listening to one of the sports stations, there was an interview with Derek Whittenberg, one of the stars of North Carolina State's improbable 1983 team which won the NCAA Championship against the heavily-favored Houston Cougars in Albuquerque.

Whittenburg was discussing a documentary in the works, highlighting the success of his high school alma mater, DeMatha (Hyattsville, Md) and coach Morgan Wootten.

That struck a chord with me. I was even more convinced that the success of St. Anthony, coupled with all the many other Hudson basketball standouts, truly was worthy of a book.

To the winter of 2016. I was in the midst of several other sports-related projects when I scheduled a series of interviews with Tom Heinsohn, Togo Palazzi and the aforementioned Father Earle Markey (that's three of the pantheon of greats in both Hudson County and Holy Cross).

I not only came to realize the plethora of Hudson County stars who continued both their education and basketball careers in Worcester (Mass.) with the Crusaders, but also the interesting fact that nine players on the rosters of the 1947 (NCAA) and 1954

(NIT) championship teams were still alive, including Heinsohn and a guy named Bob Cousy.

Believing that a Holy Cross documentary would be favorably considered by a national sports network, I then switched gears, concentrating on the Holy Cross story.

'College Basketball's Purple Reign' never made it to one of those outlets. It was, however, broadcast by NBC Sports Boston in 2019, and was subsequently honored with three national "Telly" awards as well as two Boston/New England Emmys.

I then returned to my roots, gathering some of the very interesting stories concerning Hudson hoops and its extraordinary impact on basketball in America. You're about to read what I and those who tirelessly contributed to this project have outlined in supporting the claim on Hudson's basketball superiority among other similarly sized geographic areas. I strongly feel readers will view the story to follow as interesting, informative and entertaining whether you're from Hudson County, Carolina or Timbuktu.

It is with great pride we present 'Hoops Hotbed on the Hudson.'

Enjoy!

– Rich Kaner

INTRODUCTION

Hudson County is the smallest county geographically in New Jersey, with a current population estimated at about 700,000. Consisting of 12 municipalities (Jersey City, Hoboken, Bayonne, Union City and North Bergen are the best known), the county was named after English explorer Henry Hudson, as was the body of water separating it and Manhattan Island.

'Hoops Hotbed on the Hudson' recounts the area's rich and colorful basketball history. What's little-known, or at the very least insufficiently recognized, is that over the past 80 years, Hudson has produced more top-level players, per capita, than any other similarly sized area in the country.

The story becomes even more impressive and compelling when examining the remarkable achievements of Hudson hoopsters in any number of sports-related endeavors and professional careers, sports or otherwise.

The following groups of players as well as many others throughout the book contribute toward making a powerful argument for Hudson to lay claim to the superiority of Hudson basketball among similarly sized geographic areas.

Players from Hudson County who excelled throughout their college and professional careers:

• Tommy Heinsohn – After a stellar career at Holy Cross, a key performer on eight Boston Celtics NBA Championship teams; also guided the Celtics to two titles as coach. One of only five in the Naismith Hall of Fame as both player and coach.

• Bobby Hurley Jr. – Point guard and star of Duke's 1992 and 1993 National Championship Teams, five-season NBA career and currently head coach at Arizona State.

• Terry Dehere – Seton Hall, Big East Player of the Year in '92-'93 – his 2,494 career points still stand as a Seton Hall and Big East records; six seasons in the NBA.

• Nick Galis – Following Seton Hall, "Nick The Greek" became one of Europe's greatest scorers. An inaugural member of the FIBA Hall of Fame in 2007, 10 years later inducted into the Naismith Hall of Fame.

• Elnardo Webster – St. Peter's, star of '68 NIT with a 51-point game and 29-point effort in upset of top seeded Duke; led Italian League in scoring.

• Mike O'Koren – University of North Carolina, eight seasons as NBA player, 11 as NBA assistant coach.

• Vinnie Ernst – the flashy playmaker directed Providence to two NIT Championships ('61 & '63) and was Tournament MVP in '61.

• Jim Boylan – Marquette 1977 National Championship Team plus 20+ year NBA coaching tenure.

• Togo Palazzi – Holy Cross, 1954 NIT Championship Team and Tournament MVP, fifth player selected in the NBA draft (Celtics), had an eight-year pro career.

• Kyle Anderson - A major contributor to a pair of undefeated seasons and state titles at St. Anthony. Following a standout career at UCLA, the 1st pick of the Spurs eventually signed lucrative free-agent contracts in 2018 with the Memphis Grizzlies and in 2023 with the Minnesota Timberwolves.

• Jackie Gilloon - "The best guard and most entertaining player of his era" according to Hall of Fame Coach Bob Hurley. "Over the '70s, '80s and '90s, the point guard by which all others were compared." Scored 1,340 career points which was then a Memorial school record. Three-time First-Team All-County, twice All-State and in 1974 named to the Parade All-America Team. At the University of South Carolina. He scored 1,125 points and set a then a career record of assists with 533. Gilloon played professional basketball for four years in Argentina.

• Jim Spanarkel – Duke, five seasons as NBA player, currently color commentator for CBS, Fox Sports.

• Tony Nicodemo - 1st 1,000-point scorer in Jersey City public school (Ferris H.S) history who continued prolific scoring with season and career records at St. Michael's (Vt.) College.

• Mike Rooney – Snyder H.S., one of the greatest shooters and most passionate players ever in Hudson County. Upon leaving Snyder in 1961, was the most prolific scorer in Jersey City history.

• Mickey Winograd - Lincoln H.S. (J.C.), Duquesne Univ. star player on '54 NIT runner-up and '55 NIT Champs.

• Gerald Govan – St. Mary's (KS), one of six players to have participated in all nine ABA seasons, appearing in 681 regular-season games (fourth highest) and third highest in career rebounds.

• Tommy O'Keefe – Georgetown, 1st 1,000-point scorer in school's storied basketball history, coached alma mater 6 seasons (.577 winning %).

• Louis King - A 2018 McDonald's All-American at Hudson Catholic. After one season at Oregon, has played parts of four seasons in the NBA.

• Rafael Addison – All-Big East at Syracuse, six seasons in NBA, three in Italian League.

• Hank Finkel – Dayton All-American had nine-year NBA career, six with Boston ('73-'74 NBA champion Celtics had strong Hudson County presence in Hank [Holy Family H.S.] and aforementioned Coach Heinsohn).

B **Hudson County players who excelled in their basketball careers and went on to achieve success in other sports-related endeavors:**

• Paul Tagliabue – Georgetown and after successful law career, served 17 years as NFL Commissioner.

• Bill Raftery – LaSalle and former N.J. high school scoring record holder, now one of the leading color analysts in sports broadcasting, currently with CBS and Fox Sports.

• Bob Hurley Sr. – Premier H.S. coach in the U.S. after building St. Anthony into national power. One of only three high school coaches enshrined in Naismith Hall of Fame.

• Fred Barakat - Assumption two-time Division II All-American, Fred was the most successful coach in Fairfield history (160-128). He enjoyed a distinguished career as Assistant Commissioner of the ACC and was its Director of Men's Basketball.

• Jack Nies – St. Mary's (Kan.), went on to a 31-year career as an NBA referee, officiating in over 2,000 games.

• Fred Shabel - Vice-Chairman, Comcast-Spectacor, a diversified sports and entertainment firm that has achieved great success and enormous growth during his 27-year tenure. Previously served as head coach, Univ. of Conn. (71-29 in 4 seasons) and athletic director, Univ. of Pennsylvania.

• Chuck Wepner – Bayonne High School, gained national fame as a heavyweight boxing contender; the "Bayonne Bleeder" went seconds shy of 15 rounds in a 1975 championship fight vs. Muhammad Ali.

Hudson County players who went on to achieve success in non-sports endeavors:

• Mayor Albio Sires – The shores of Cuba to the hardwood of St. Peter's to eight terms in Congress, with a pair of tenures at city hall. Although he was honored with the town of West New York renaming his old stomping ground of P.S. 4 "The Albio Sires Elementary School," perhaps the late author Harry Golden said it best in describing his storied career..."Only in America."

• Jim Spanarkel – Perhaps the top candidate for most versatile among former Hudson hoopsters. Although maintaining a full schedule as a TV basketball analyst of college games on CBS and Fox Sports, Jim's primary activity is senior vice president of investments for a major brokerage firm.

• Fr. Earle Markey, S.J. – Following an outstanding career at Holy Cross (64-15 in 3 varsity seasons), was a high choice of Boston Celtics in '53 NBA Draft but chose instead to enter the priesthood. Returned to St. Peter's Prep as principal and college alma mater as vice president of student affairs as well as serving on boards of trustees at Fordham, St. Louis U. and Holy Cross. Recently celebrated his 30th anniversary as a Jesuit priest.

• Leon Gast – Scrappy southpaw out of Snyder High School who garnered the 1996 Academy Award for Best Documentary Feature ("When We Were Kings").

• Lou Brown – His career at North Carolina was short-circuited by implication in the infamous 1961 betting scandal; resurrected his life by earning a Ph. D. teaching at University of Wisconsin and becoming a world renowned authority on educating children with learning disabilities.

• Jerry Walker - After a stellar career at St. Anthony and Seton Hall, Jerry co-founded Team Walker, a non-profit that offers various academic and athletic programs to the children of Jersey City. Elected as a Hudson County Commissioner, he currently serves as the Vice-Chairperson of the Board of Hudson Commissioners.

• Tommy Smith – Extremely quick guard who finished St. Peter's Prep and College as career scoring leader. His 24.8 pt. average as a senior made him 5th highest among NCAA Division I scorers as well as number one in field goal pct. (56%). Eventually became better known as Mayor of Jersey City (1977-81).

The saga of Hudson County basketball has been greatly enriched by each group and there's sufficient proof in the ensuing pages.

Congratulations

to all who have contributed to the success of
'Hoops Hotbed on the Hudson'
and Hudson County basketball.

It's where I learned to love the game 'in perpetuity.'

Regards and Best Wishes,

Dan Silna

RICH KANER

THANK YOU FOR THE OPPORTUNITY TO SUPPORT YOUR RESEARCH ON
"HOOPS HOTBED ON THE HUDSON"

THIS HAS BEEN A TRIP DOWN MEMORY LANE.
BASKETBALL DEVELOPS CHARACTER AND LIFE TRAITS.

RICH, YOU ARE A TRUE PROFESSIONAL AND A GENTLEMAN.

YOUR FRIEND,
STEVE RICCIARDI

GRASS ROOTS PROGRAM
ST. MICHAEL'S SPORTS ASSOCIATION

1957 —————————————————————— 2023

TO ALL THE VOLUNTEERS & SUPPORTERS OF THE PROGRAM

*Thank you for your time and effort in teaching the game of basketball
and life, without your volunteer efforts the success of the program
over 66 years would not have been achieved.*

IN MEMORY OF FRANK MCGOVERN - OUR GUIDING LIGHT AND FOUNDER

'GRAZING IN THE GRASSROOTS'

Hudson County's hoops hotbed didn't just happen. It was a mixture of boys and girls who loved to play, coaches who lived to teach … and venues aplenty.

We have witnesses.

"There were rec gyms, playgrounds, CYOs and grammar schools where the kids played basketball."

"There were also mentors in the neighborhoods. Good people, and in many cases, the only guidance these kids had so they wouldn't get sucked into street life."

Are you gonna argue with Bob Hurley Sr.?

"It was a mixture of the kids—boys and girls—who loved to play, and the self-sacrifice of the coaches.

Coaches, both paid and unpaid, who, according to Hurley, instilled/demanded the fundamentals "by imitation and repetition."

"Dribble, pass, shoot, rebound, defend."

…and not to mention the protocol.

"The after-school culture had younger kids ('biddy ball') playing first, then the older ones."

Hurley, he of the 26 (St. Anthony) state championships, five undefeated teams and one Naismith Hall of Fame (Class of 2010) induction, doubles as unofficial historian of Jersey City roundball.

"There used to be (college) programs flush with Jersey City guards," Hurley said. "D(ivision) I scholarships all over the place."

Exhibit A…"I remember (former St. Anthony standout, Seton Hall All-American and six-season NBA vet) Terry Dehere's mother allowing him to stay out as long as she heard the basketball."

The decline, per Hurley, started in earnest over the last decade.

"Many Catholic schools closed (including St. Anthony in 2017) due to declining enrollment, also the rec and summer leagues. The places that remain aren't open as late, and the inner city doesn't have a sufficient number of kids."

Then, there's the instant-gratification affliction.

"Rick Pitino used the term 'microwave society,' and he's not alone. Just about all the coaches I know, myself included, have (had) those kids who expect(ed) short-term success without working. It's the AAU culture, where the best ones get identified early, which disenchants others."

Hurley, however, presents the flip side.

"It was my experience that the biggest successes were the late bloomers, kids who loved it more, kids who wanted to be pushed a bit more."

"I miss those times. I miss those kids."

—

By, Frank Drucker

EVOLUTION OF GIRLS BASKETBALL IN HUDSON COUNTY

Adrienne Goodson playfully slapped at a lightweight exercise sitting ball as she attempted, with only some success, to try to control dribbling it around the lane before the start of a girls basketball practice at Bayonne High's auxiliary gym.

She grabbed it and repeatedly heaved it to the basketball rim with giggles, knowing that it was far too big at two feet in diameter to fall through the netting.

Goodson continued playfully dribbling and shooting the large ball with laughter, while her teammates were shooting basketballs at other rims. It was one of the few times in her career she hit an ice-cold shooting streak.

Going into the early 1980s as a ninth grader, Goodson was just embarking on her storied hardwood journey that would cement her legacy as Hudson County's most decorated female basketball player.

Moments later, coach Jeff Stabile entered the gym and started the practice, players snapping to attention to begin arduous conditioning, practice drills and, eventually, intrasquad scrimmaging.

"She's going to be a good one," Stabile said, looking at Goodson, who was the heir to stardom previously enjoyed by her predecessor, Sharon Ross, in the late 1970s.

Title IX was enacted less than 10 years earlier, in 1972, establishing gender equity in sports. That particular day in Bayonne, it was the girls team's turn to use the auxiliary gym while the boys team practiced in the main gym, part of the routine of switching gyms each day.

Girls who played at any of the five all-female parochial schools in Hudson County at the time did not worry about alternating gyms, although the St. Dominic Academy gym had lockers set back from the sidelines.

Goodson, a consensus high school All-American,

went on to Old Dominion University, where she played on its 1985 national championship team. After that, she played for nine seasons in the WNBA – including a 2002 All-Star selection – and now serves as a consultant to the NBA overseeing the women's pro league.

Goodson's era was a time of both change and unprecedented, explosive growth in the girls' game. Along with the five parochial all-female school teams, there were six co-ed parochial ones with girls teams as well as 15 public schools. That's 26 girls teams in a county of 46 square miles.

By the 1990s, McNair Academic in Jersey City added a 27th team to the fold.

However, all four of the Jersey City co-ed parochial schools subsequently closed, including St. Anthony. It had its own acclaimed history of girls basketball to go along with the nationally-heralded boys' team which earned coach Bob Hurley a spot in the Naismith Basketball Hall of Fame. St. Anthony shuttered in 2017, as severe as any loss to Hudson County high school sports.

The all-girls Academy of St. Aloysius closed in 2006.

JEFF STABILE

Holy Family Academy, another female-only school, closed in 2013, while co-ed St. Joseph's (WNY), went in 2009.

St. Michael's (UC), another all-female school (formerly co-ed), was also among the 'parochial casualties,' along with Sacred Heart Academy in Hoboken. Marist, an all-male school which became co-ed, closed in 2020.

Union City's two schools – Emerson and Union Hill – merged in 2008.

That was one of several changes dramatically altering the landscape of girls' basketball. In order to avoid the same fate of many other local parochial schools, the previously all-boys Hudson Catholic went co-ed, with its first girls' team in 2009 as part of the newly created Hudson County Interscholastic Athletic League.

It now included Kearny (first time), and also welcomed back the St. Anthony girls team (independent the previous two decades).

With the old HCIAA – and its tournaments – gone, that season featured a true Hudson County tournament,

JAMES TURNER

including Kearny, St. Anthony, Harrison, Weehawken and Secaucus.

While earlier generations were denied the opportunity to see how Jack Rodgers' great Harrison teams would have fared against the best in Hudson County, this generation has seen Secaucus, class of the NJIC, compete (and succeed) against the best in the county.

Secaucus is 367-70 in 16 seasons under coach John Sterling. In 13 county tournament appearances, Secaucus has advanced to the title game five times, winning it twice. In 2023, Secaucus won its first ever state sectional title and reached the Group 2 state final.

Just two hours after Secaucus' state finals appearance, Bayonne, under coach James Turner, won its first state championship, defeating Cherokee in the Group 4 final.

Coach Maureen Wendelken

Pat Quilty

Cathy Myers   Alice Schmidt

Pat Colosurdo

Montclair State
1977 - 1978 Final Four

The Bees of Bayonne, who started four sophomores, became just the fourth Hudson County team to win a state title, joining St. Anthony (1984), Harrison (1991) and Marist (2001). This decade has also seen Union City, under former St. Anthony great Carlos Cueto, win consecutive sectional titles in 2022 and 2023, their first in any girls sports and Lincoln, under Tom Best, reached consecutive state finals in 2019 and 2020, bringing back a level of success the Lions hadn't enjoyed in generations.

Hudson County alumni and fans who played, coached or even attended high school girls contests may remember the old six-on-a-side format transitioning to the standard five players and other changes.

Those six-on-a-side teams included two on offense (only in frontcourt), two on defense (only in backcourt)

and two 'rovers,' who were allowed to play on both ends of the floor.

There was a post player offensively (for rebounding), plus a shooter against two defenders. Those defenders were usually taller players on the opposing team.

players on both teams at both ends of the floor, with 10 seconds to advance the ball over half-court.

That change to mimic the boys' game was a prelude to the aforementioned Title IX, a federal gender equity mandate enacted by Congress a year later.

St. Dominic's Louise 'Loukie' Melleno earned stardom in those six-aside bygone days, as well as a caricature in The Jersey Journal. In the 1960's and 70's, the paper's cartoonist captured images and heroics of local stars, though only a few subjects were girls.

Melleno put a name and a face on the game. She was one of the first female athletes widely - recognized beyond Jersey City and amassed 1,600 career points. Loukie went on to a collegiate career at Caldwell University in the early 1970's, leading her team in scoring all four years while earning Hall of Fame selections at both the college and the county.

Another former St. Dominic star, Angela Zampella, also had widespread acclaim in both baseball and basketball. At St. Joseph's University in Philadelphia, she was nationally- ranked in free throws and assists.

As the ladies received greater opportunities to continue their careers in college, fans in the mid-1970's remember All-County first-team selections Pat Colasurdo (Holy Family), Alice Schmidt and Cathy Meyers (both of St. Anthony) and Pat Quilty

(St. Dominic Academy) who went on to play at Montclair State, coached by Hudson County legend Maureen Wendelken.

In a Cinderella run, Montclair St. reached the national semifinals in 1978, ultimately losing to UCLA (it then won the third-place consolation game). This was before the NCAA established three different divisions.

Schmidt was the runner-up for the Wade Trophy, awarded annually to the best female player in the nation.

Some other former local girls' basketball stars went on to coach at high school and colleges, helping the future generations advance their own games.

Wendelken, Schmidt and Holy Family's Pat Longo are recognized as the leading female coaches to come out of Hudson County. Schmidt's stops included St. Dominic Academy, Marist and Montclair State, with two stints at New Jersey City University. It was there where she spent 27 years, 11 as the school's distinguished director of athletics.

Schmidt is the winningest women's basketball coach in NJCU history, with 108 wins. She died in 2020 at the age of 63.

PAT LONGO

While Wendelken brought Montclair State to national prominence, she was simultaneously leading Holy Family to a remarkable 238-45 record, which included a 44-game winning streak at the all-girls school. Eventually the demands of coaching both teams became too much as Wendelken offered the Holy Family job to one of her former players, Longo, in 1978.

Already a pioneer in women's coaching, Longo, who was also the first ever softball coach at Saint Peter's College, coached at her high school alma mater for 35 seasons, winning 568 games until the school closed down.

It was those early years of Title IX when girls in Hudson County and around the nation not only endured a more physically-demanding game with five players, but did so as equals to their male counterparts.

Bayonne coach Stabile often alluded to Title IX as a benchmark raising the game.

Stabile, Harrison coach Rodgers and former Marist and St. Anthony coach Bill DeFazio often praised the commitment and work ethic of girls, which enriched their teams' success...

JACK RODGERS

JOHN STERLING

...and their dedication that might've surpassed the boys.

It wasn't long before fans and critics realized that as the girls' game 'shrunk' to five players, females not only were resilient, but they didn't mind pushing the pace. That was in sharp contrast to some boys' teams and their strategies to slow tempo.

Offenses among the ladies were sophisticated – 'back-door' plays and 'high-low' half court sets enhancing opportunities to score. Players like Hoboken's Tara Mitchell and Kim Lee (St. Anthony) were dynamic, using crossover dribbles to rouse crowds and lose defenders.

In 1987, the three-point line was drawn on courts across the country, largely to give losing teams a better opportunity to rally.

Of course, the shot also enabled teams to increase early leads and take command of the game. It also accelerated the scoring of prolific individual shooters.

Milestone moments of players scoring 1,000 career points were met by a stoppage of play and a presentation of the game ball. There were also flowers and celebratory balloons with the star, her parents, coaches and teammates posing for photos. It was a requisite shoot by The Jersey Journal photographer, appearing in the next day's paper each time it occurred.

The late Jersey Journal sports editor Jack Powers gruffly ordered his staff to no longer assign photos to a feat that eventually was commonplace. "Show me a player who doesn't score 1,000 points," he said.

Now that 1,000 career points has morphed into 2,000, photographers were back at it.

As of this writing, nine Hudson County girls have reached the plateau. Despite tougher defenses, that sorority figures to increase.

The following girls scored 2,000 points in their high school career:

NAME	SCHOOL	CLASS	POINTS
KIM MCDONOUGH	HARRISON	1998	2,760
KIM LEE	ST. ANTHONY	1990	2,387
TARA WALKER	MARIST	2001	2,376
ADRIENNE GOODSON	BAYONNE	1984	2,333
AMANDA ULRICH	SECAUCUS	2019	2,224
GINGER QUINONEZ	HARRISON	2001	2,187
MILLICENT GERTRUDE	DICKINSON	1989	2,151
JODY HILL	HARRISON	1990	2,098
MILLY COLLAZO	SACRED HEART ACADEMY	1994	2,033

–

By, Wayne Witkowski

(Jason Bernstein also contributed to this story)

Fr. Earle Markey, S.J.

Terrific Basketball Player

Committed Educator

Revered Jesuit Priest

Dear Friend

Extraordinary Career and...
an even more Extraordinary Man

We the undersigned
applaud those accomplishments...

Steve Anderson | HC '76

Bob Cousy | HC, '50

John Ferguson | HC '61

John Gearan | HC '65

Tom Lally | SPP, '73 - HC '77

Joe McVeigh

Anthony Romano | SPP, '73

Bruce Sabbatini | SPP, '72 - HC '76

Dan Shaughnessy | HC '75

Ron Statile | HC '69

Gary Walters

John Wendelken | HC '65

IV
—

INSIGHTS OF
MARQUEE HUDSON COUNTY PLAYERS

Discussion of their Hudson County Development and Experiences

SANDY ADER
Dickinson, 1955

Most of us in the early '50s came from families of modest means. Most of us did not have the funds to send kids to college. Therefore, most of us needed to get scholarships. And basketball, in a city environment, was a way to get the scholarship, if you were good enough. There was a tradition in Hudson County of being in the schoolyard, but those were our summer camps. A pair of Chuck Converse canvas sneakers, PS 27 outdoor court or PS 23 outdoor court, (and) the Marion Section of Jersey City, that's where our summer camps were. That's where we played hoops from sunup to sunset with a bottle of Hoffman Ginger Ale to give us some liquid refreshment until we went home to have dinner.

And so, Saint Peter's Prep was the No. 1 rated school in the area. It got most of the press, It was a kind of an elitist, where Roy Leenig would sit up in the balcony, have tournaments, and handpick the kids from the Catholic elementary schools to come to Saint Peter's Prep.

We didn't have that luxury at Dickinson, and Hudson County basketball was pretty hot. There were very good teams. The public schools plus the Catholic schools. My class of 1954–55, we won the city championship.

Hudson County was a hotbed for hoops in the '50s. All of us in high school would have different nights at different places. It was very ecumenical. I played for Grace Lutheran Church. I played for Mount Carmel CYO. I played for the Jewish Community Center of Jersey City. We just looked for games to play (in) and teams to be on. Many times we did it with alias names because our coaches didn't want us to play with independent teams, in case we would be subjected to injuries.

We should have probably spent a little more time doing our homework, but we were always playing hoops nights and weekends. (On) Saturday mornings in the Mount Carmel Area, PS 23, there was (a) huge turnout (of) good players from all over Hudson County to play ball.

And the ticket, the college scholarship, was what we all worked toward. The competition was very keen in high school and all the schools. Everyone. We were all gym rats.

So the per capita, I guess it's a small county. In the '40s and '50s, for sure, there was tremendous, tremendous activity (and) very competitive groups. The stands were always packed with kids. Basketball was big in the high schools in Hudson County. And we didn't have any giants. I must say also that at that time it was almost all Caucasian.

There were very few black basketball players in Hudson County at that time. These kids were in the schoolyards all the time playing ball. They'd shovel off the snow and shoot hoops. So all the city boys were highly motivated to get the scholarships.

RICK APODACA
North Bergen 1999

You don't necessarily need a passport to read the story of Rick Apodaca, but it certainly would not hurt.

Mentioning he's the all-time leading scorer in Hudson County boys basketball (those 2,206 points were amassed at hometown North Bergen H.S. by 1999) is just the beginning of the itinerary.

It was the record of none other than Bill Raftery whose record Apodaca broke, the final game of his career (state semifinals against Teaneck). In the small-world category, Apodaca also played AAU ball with Bill Raftery Jr.

"Bill Raftery congratulated me after I set the record. That was nice."

Then, off to Hofstra, where Apodaca earned a place on the All-America East rookie team before leading the then-Flying Dutchmen in scoring (17.7 points/game) as a junior.

A self-inflicted, derailed senior season notwithstanding, Apodaca (1,422 career points at Hofstra) was about to embark on his 16-season (2000-2015). 18-stop hoops travelog.

With the help of the good folks at Wikipedia, we can't help but notice the success in his 'ancestral' home of Puerto Rico, where he represented the island country in any number of international competitions.

"Playing there also in the summer helped my game," he said.

Apodaca and his mates acquitted themselves quite well against some of the best players ("including Steve Nash") and teams in the world, medaling often and stunning the United States, 92-73, at the 2004 Olympics (Athens). The loss was the Americans' first since NBA players were allowed to compete back in 1992.

(A pre-existing foot injury hampered Apodaca's participation in Athens, and he played just one minute against the U.S.).

There were subsequent pro league stops in Puerto Rico, Poland, Italy and Turkey, while not overlooking the U.S. Basketball and National Basketball Development Leagues (the latter a forerunner to the 'D' and 'G' leagues).

"I was always one who saw myself as an international player," Apodaca said. "I didn't have the (court) vision to play in the NBA, "I wasn't overly athletic. Rather, I was a shooter and could mentally control a game."

Apodaca had a 2003 tryout with the Orlando Magic, "but lost a 10-day contract when I broke my toe."

"Probably the best thing about me was that I wasn't afraid of anything," he said. "Those were some very tough places. I didn't have a lot of guaranteed contracts during my career.

"I was forced to earn it, which was fine with me."Nowadays, the 43-year-old Apodaca is sort of a transportation entrepreneur. Dividing his time between North Jersey and Puerto Rico, he owns the private aviation company My Jet Charters as well as the island's Vanderhall Motor Works (three-wheeled autocycles) franchise.

It's not surprising that while no longer traversing the globe to play basketball, he's still moving.

-

By, Frank Drucker

NAME	SCHOOL	CLASS	POINTS
NORM CALDWELL*	CROYDEN HALL	1973	2,302
RICK APODACA	NORTH BERGEN	1999	2,206
RAY LUCAS	HARRISON	1991	2,198
BILL RAFTERY	ST. CECILIA (KEARNY)	1959	2,193
ROSCOE HARRIS	MARIST	1992	2,051
RICHIE O'CONNOR	ST. MICHAEL'S (UNION CITY)	1969	2,025

*Jersey City native, played as a freshman at Holy Family and then transferred to Croyden Hall

JIM BOYLAN
St. Mary's, 1973

I have thought of Hudson County basketball as top level, producing year after year of quality basketball players. I think that it's a hotbed of basketball. Always has been in my lifetime. I would stack Hudson County up against any other similar sized place in the United States.

When I was in the eighth grade, I played at the CYO on Bergen Avenue. I played for the St. Paul of the Cross' grade school team. It was always an exciting, exciting time to go to the CYO and play on Saturdays. Games started early in the morning and continued all through the day.

And when you went into the gym, the energy level was just super high. They had a great biddy basketball program for the young kids, and Hudson County biddy all-star teams always did very well in national competitions. There was a guy, Joe Polito, and he was a superstar of the biddy basketball league and star of the Video All-Star team, which was the pinnacle for young players to make that team and to travel in the days when there wasn't an AAU program.

I made that team a couple of years later, and it was a great honor.

When I was playing in the CYO league, a man walked up to me and introduced himself as Bill Kuchar, the coach at St. Mary's High School. He looked at me and said, "I'm going to offer you a scholarship to go to St. Mary's."

The most formidable players I played against were Michael O'Koren, Jim Spanarkel, and Jim McDonough.

O'Koren was starting as a freshman, and you could see his amazing talent. Another guy who really understood the game at an early age, had unbelievable movement without the basketball, knew how to use his body, and knew how to get his shot. He was the consummate team player, as we saw later at North Carolina University (and) as he continued to play that way under Dean Smith.

My emphasis is that I believe that Hudson County basketball is based on that. It's based on team play. Even in the schoolyards, the guys played a team game. If someone was open on a fast break, you gave them the ball. And if you didn't give them the ball, your teammates would say something to you.

So, it wasn't about just going out and trying to score as many points as you possibly could. It was about playing the right way. I think that's what's been drilled into players in Hudson County for decades. You have to play the game the right way. You have to respect the game, you play it as a team, and you make your team better.

A lot of that comes from the schoolyards, where if you lost the game, you had to sit out. So, you never wanted to lose the game.

We had guys in the schoolyard who demanded respect from you, and that respect was based on playing the game the right way.

I think that's what's been instilled in the essence of Hudson County basketball: to play the right way, play as a group, and make the right play, instead of thinking about trying to score, your own glory, and your own point scoring.

I think Hudson was such a hotbed because, given the urban environment that we lived in, basketball courts were everywhere, and you would find a basketball court in your neighborhood. You went to the schoolyard, you hung out there all day long, and you played whatever sport season it was. If it was football season, you played football on the basketball courts. If it was baseball season, you might be playing stickball on the basketball courts.

I know I'd go to the schoolyard, and the place would be packed with kids. There would be 100 kids at the schoolyard. And so, competition was very thick. If you wanted to play in the games on the courts, you had to win. And so, in order to stay on the court, you had to win. You had to play a team game.

I would get up early in the morning, leave my house by about 7 a.m., and just to go to the courts and have a little bit of court time, kind of by myself. There might be one or two other guys there. I could get some shots up instead of playing with 100 kids around. I'd make believe I'm Walt Frazier, or make believe I'm Earl Monroe, Bob Cousy, or someone like that.

BOB FAZIO
Emerson, 1973

I started playing basketball in the sixth grade. I was tall for my age, and Nick Mastorelli, a legendary guy from Hudson County, he was my biddy basketball coach. So, we played for the biddy championship of the United States back in 1968. First time I went on a plane, we played down in Augusta, Georgia for the national championship, and while we were down there, Martin Luther King was assassinated. So, it was really, really crazy.

Unfortunately, there was a height requirement, and it was five-six. I grew an inch (in three weeks) between when we won the state title to when we played the game. I'm out warming up after getting measured, they call me back in, and they tell me I'm disqualified. Nick Mastorelli got into a fist fight with the Texas coach. It was crazy as a young kid, but I was disqualified. I wasn't allowed to play. We didn't win the national championship, and I remember that was my first taste of life and politics and how upsetting it was to me. It was sad on many levels and very, very difficult for me to process. I came back, I graduated (from) grammar school, and I go to Holy Family.

It was an introduction (to) Hudson County basketball and how competitive it really was. Al Baldini was very instrumental. Holy Family closes after my freshman year. So, I now wind up at Emerson High School and played for Hank Morano, another legendary coach

from Hudson County. Hank had tremendous influence in my life, along with Pep Novotny and Vito D'Orio, two other legendary people from Hudson County.

So, I played at Emerson for three years, and I was very lucky the state of New Jersey allowed me to play (in) the NJSIAA my sophomore year. Most of the teams wanted me to have to sit out for the year, and we appealed it on financial hardship with my family. We won the appeal, and I was able to play my sophomore year. So, I played three years at Emerson.

I played a lot at Gilmore schoolyard in Union City. That's where I grew up, and the likes of Danny Calandrillo and Mike O'Koren and Jimmy Spanarkel would come up there. You would wait seven and eight games in order to play one game at Gilmore. It was unbelievable, and once you lost the game, people got on that bike and they went to the next schoolyard. It was unbelievable.

That's really where I grew up, and just great players that would come in and out of that school yard. We called it The Gilmore Gardens. So, I would play all day long until I was exhausted.

When you look today, (at) all the AAU teams, parents driving kids to play dates, and all that crap, we did conflict resolution back in the schoolyards and figured out games. You didn't call a foul. You had to earn every bit of that scoring opportunity to go to the

next game. We learned so many things about life (in) that schoolyard. I just think that we were all competitors, and we all thought we were better. South Hudson thought they were better than North Hudson. North Hudson always felt (there were) politics with The Jersey Journal (favoring South Hudson). They always got the upper hand, we were always like the stepsister. There was that war, that rivalry, and that sibling rivalry between North and South.

JIMMY FOSTER
Hoboken, 1970

I started playing basketball at the Hoboken Recreation Center. It was organized. You had officiating, and that was just teaching young kids at the age of 10, 11 (and) 12 to dribble the basketball and (to play) defense.

Not a whole bunch of jump shots because we were little. We were lucky we could reach the rims. However, a lot of basketball playing was outside at the parks. Lot of three-on-three, four-on-four, (and) five-on-five. And as we got older, we were learning from guys like John Wendelken, who would supervise and coach us.

Remember, we are similar to New York City. We are an urban community. And as I said to you earlier, basketball's a street game. You could always pick up a basketball game anywhere in Hudson County. I remember a lot of kids coming out of Weehawken High School because I grew up with them who never played college ball. Or if they played college ball, it was for a limited period of time. And then, they went on to other things.

GERALD GOVAN
Snyder, 1959

I went to Public School Number 14, and I played on the grammar school team. Actually, I was probably one of the younger guys on the team because we won the city championship two straight years that I was there. We got sweaters and all that kind of stuff, but I didn't start. There were guys better than me, older than me. They were better than me. It was just a nice thing.

I thought I was going to be a baseball player until I found out I couldn't hit the curve ball. But I played all the sports. When you're a kid, you play them all.

At that time in Jersey City, the public schools had a citywide thing, and we were in different divisions. The other parts of the city had the same thing. In the finals, we played 23 schools for the (grammar school) championship. In high school, I always had a little job. I wasn't playing. I (started) to think, when (would) I play?

Actually, my junior year, I wasn't playing. The coach at Snyder was Jerry Degman. He had this thing. Right after the basketball season, the varsity season, he'd have these intramurals. That was pretty much his way (of getting) other players.

I played in the intramurals right after school, and the guys on the varsity, they would be the referees. I guess some people told him, "Oh, there's a big tall guy, Govan." He (told) me, "Hey man, you need to play some ball, if you like it."

I did like it. I played, and I'd go to school at night. Recreation opened up the gyms at night, and we played and whatnot, but I had not played since grammar school or anything.

I just think that the kids here in Hudson, they just seemed to be tough. You learned how to play and were tough about it.

I just think that the kids in Hudson County are tough.

TOM HEINSOHN
St. Michael's (UC), 1952

I was born in Jersey City, and until the fourth grade, I lived in Jersey City. I moved to Union City.

So, I didn't know the first thing about basketball. In fact, my father thought basketball was a sissy game. But when I moved there, there was a schoolyard at the Gilmore Grammar School, and they had two backboards against the building on pipes. One they called the JV Court, and the other one they called the Varsity Court.

You played three-on-three, which I still believe is the best way to learn the game of basketball. I was fortunate enough (that), when I moved there, (I ran) into a guy who was playing college basketball at Villanova with the great Paul Arizin, a Hall of Famer I played against in the pros. He would practice in the summer after working.

It was Perry del Purgatorio, and I would shag the balls for him. As a consequence, he started to teach me the game.

So, this was the fifth grade. I started to go to the JV Court, and I couldn't get into the games. Finally, somebody didn't show up one day. They needed somebody, and I ended up playing. It was very, very competitive, three-on-three games in the schoolyard. It was winners stay up, losers go home. Most of the time, what they would do, because there were oodles of people

waiting to play, is you'd go to another schoolyard, see what the heck was going on there, (and see) if you could play. It was a real hotbed of basketball. It was that you either make a decision to shoot yourself or use the other two guys to have a play and see who was open.

So, you got the fundamentals of any offense that you would be able to play in later on, or in any game. And then, I started to grow, and I got this opportunity to go to St. Michael's High School. By the time I was a sophomore, I guess I got to be pretty good.

And there was a guy, Al Murdo was his name, who owned a place called the Woodshed, which was a bar up the street from where I lived. These were all ex-pro players playing in the Eastern League. I played with them, and against them, and I played for the Woodshed AC. I played for the Lincoln Hotel. I played for the Jewish Y, where you had to be Jewish to play there. I changed my name so I could play.

I played on a team with my cousin, Eddie Matson, who played at Emerson High School and was in the same year as me. He was a pretty good player.

But anyway, I learned a lot of basketball just playing in those semi-pro leagues because I was playing against advanced players compared to the high school teams. So, by the time I got to my senior year with Pat Finnegan as coach, we developed a pretty good basketball team. Our main rivals were Demarest High School and St. Peter's Prep.

And so, we beat Tony Radovich, who was (a) great offensive player at Demarest. We lost to St. Peter's Prep. But we ended up going over (to) New York, and we won the Metropolitan Catholic Championship, which involved all the Catholic high schools from the whole New York area.

And then, we went to a tournament in Newport, Rhode Island. We were going to play in the final game, and I got sick the day before. I had the flu, but I played. We lost to All Hallows. There was a guy named Joe Liebler who played on that team, and he ended up as my roommate at Holy Cross for four years.

I wanted to go to a Jesuit college, and so, (I) looked at Georgetown, Fordham, and Holy Cross. Georgetown didn't really have a very good basketball program in those days. I played in a North-South high school game sponsored by Converse Rubber, and I made the All-America Team, which was the only All-America high school team.

I could have gone to any college in the country based on that, but I had already made up my mind that Holy Cross was the place to go because they were the most honest with me. I thought (that) I wanted to be a doctor, and they said, "Well, if you're going to pursue that, we'll have to take back the offer because we don't think you can do both." I talked to different people on how difficult it was to do pre-med and play basketball.

When I went up to Holy Cross for a visit, Earl Markey was there. He was the guy that showed me all around, and he's just a terrific person. And so, we talked about going to medical school and all the other stuff, and he leveled with me.

At Holy Cross, we won the Sugar Bowl Tournament. We beat Bob Pettit and LSU down in New Orleans. And so, we ended up No. 2 in the country. We lost to Connecticut, which got the bid to go to the NCAA. But we were the powerhouse for many years in New England. But Togo Palazzi graduated, and then, the team wasn't the same without him. We didn't have the replacement or the punch equal to Togo.

Well, I will tell you about Hudson County in my era and growing up there. It was such a hotbed of basketball because of this three-on-three mentality, and the high school coaching was pretty good.

The seventh or eighth man on some of these high school teams were getting scholarships to play basketball and turning out to be contributors on those teams. The whole county had exceptional basketball, but Union City in particular. It was really, really a hotbed because Emerson High School really established the sport, and all the kids wanted to play for Emerson.

When I went to Holy Cross, some of the players that got recruited from Massachusetts towns were there, and they were supposed to be the best and this and that. They wouldn't have made the JV teams in Hudson County.

EARLE MARKEY
St. Peter's Prep, 1949

We did not have a gym to practice in, so we practiced outside. And when it was warm enough or not so utterly cold, we could play outside in the school yard, and that would last for a couple of weeks. And then, we'd go indoors. In my sophomore year at least, we played in the Cullen Memorial Auditorium when the Saint Peter's College was not practicing and when the varsity was not practicing.

So, we didn't get so much time, but we did practice. Third year we were not very good. We were worse (in our) third year because we didn't have a gym to practice in. We tried to practice in the Jersey City Boys Club, which was a comical disaster. We would go and practice there and the kids in the Boys Club would show up and when we'd scrimmage, we'd run down to one end of the court, and the Boys Club kids would run to the other end of the court.

And then, when we went back to the other end of the court, they scattered. So, it was just crazy. And we had a poor record. We were a poor team, but we enjoyed playing, and we did practice around the students' lockers and locker room. Where all the lockers were there'd be a letter and a number above the lockers, and we'd pick out one of them and use it as our target for shooting.

So, obviously everything was geared towards academics, very little geared towards basketball. However, in our senior year, somebody at St. Peter's Prep said, "Look, we have to have a gym, and we don't even have a gym around here."

We were one of the many schools that did not have either a gym or a recreation facility. And so, they began to build it and raised money for it. Now today, it's not a great looking building, but in those days to us, it was a palace. It was built nicely. I'd say 400 or 500 people could sit in the stands. The floor was immaculate, and it was kept that way. The locker rooms were pleasant. Everything was nice.

After that, we had a Jesuit priest, who was kind of a character, but he was a bright man and he saw what was going on. He introduced Hudson County to the Grammar School Invitational tournament. The next thing you know, the next year he brought in the better grammar school teams from around Hudson County and wound up bringing in some of the finest young high school players, including George Waddleton and Jerry Vayda.

KIM McDONOUGH-HURANGA

Harrison, 1998

She's Hudson County through and through.

Kim McDonough-Huaranga, Harrison Class of '98, is the leading scorer (2,760 points, boys or girls) in the history of the county.

However, to suggest that any accomplishments are/were limited to the hardwood would be a disservice to both her and Hudson.

McDonough-Huaranga hadn't played any sports before trying basketball in the third grade. "My father (Tom) ran a rec league, so that's how it started.

"I found I enjoyed it, and I excelled at it," she said.

There were five years of AAU ball (starting in the seventh grade) which also honed her skills.

At Harrison, "I had a chance to play under (Hudson County Sports) Hall of Famer Jack Rodgers. He had 600-plus wins with a tradition of excellence."

McDonough-Huaranga, herself a member of the Hudson Hall of Fame, is also quick to point out she's not the only one in the family with a milestone at Harrison. "My brother, Tommy (Class of 2002), is a 1,000-point scorer."

Choosing a college, McDonough-Huaranga visited any number of Metro Atlantic Athletic Conference (MAAC) schools, but St. Peter's in Jersey City "checked all the boxes. It was close to home, a small community while getting a Jesuit education.

"Playing at a Division I school was definitely an adjustment," she said. "I had to work harder to earn a place. People were surprised I didn't average as many points in college, but everyone at that level is a scorer. I had to be a role player as well."

A torn ACL (junior year) led to a medical redshirt and subsequent fifth season of eligibility,

There were three MAAC tournament titles and three NCAA tournament appearances with the then-Peahens, coached by Mike Granelli.

Reinforcing the subject of this missive is exponentially smarter than the author, McDonough-Huaranga owns an undergraduate degree in elementary education and American studies, along with a graduate degree in administration supervision.

"Right after playing, I did volunteer teaching (fourth grade) at a Jesuit school in Arizona, then went back to New Jersey."

Nine years of teaching (Washington Middle School) history takes us to 2012, when McDonough-Huaranga returned to Harrison High, beginning a decade as the school's vice principal and (first female) athletic director.

McDonough-Huaranga is currently vice principal in charge of early childhood development in the Harrison preschool program.

"As an administrator, there's so many more details than when I was playing," she said. "Planning the events, getting the kids where they need to be, working with the parents and coaches."

With a son and a daughter both playing high-level sports, those "small" details are near and dear.

How about the growth of the women's game?

"I didn't have any interest in going overseas to play," McDonough-Huaranga said. "It was near the end of my college career when the WNBA was beginning.

"It's been phenomenal to see what's happened, big-time women's basketball and role models right in the area. My daughter and I watched the (New York) Liberty play in Brooklyn. It was a sellout.

"There are limitless opportunities, certainly ones that I never had.

"Looking back, it's not the scoring record that I remember. Basketball has given me an education, friendships and a career, along with the gift of travel and the tools to succeed.

"Now, as I coach my daughter, I have the chance to give back to the game with the next generation."

–

By, Frank Drucker

ALEX MIRABEL
Dickinson, 2002

I came over here from Puerto Rico when I was about 12 years old. I grew up in Hudson Gardens, and at the time, Gary Greenberg was in charge of the Boys Club. So, we had leagues. We played all day in Hudson Gardens, and then they used to have the bus pick us up to play in the league. And before you know it, that summer when I was turning 13, he grabbed me, and asked me to play on the AAU team with Donald Copeland. So then, I started playing with Donald Copeland. We had really, really good players. Most of them went to St. Anthony.

Soon after that, I went to Dickinson High School. I played three years varsity. Out of the four years I was there, we made it to the finals three times and we won it twice. We won it my sophomore year and my senior year.

Being in the inner cities brings the best out of you. You got to be a tough guy. You can't just walk (onto) the court and just not be a tough guy. So, you're kind of fighting for your life. And back then, when I played, we used to go to Lincoln Park.

We had to wait like 30 (or) 40 minutes to get into a game. And you didn't want that soft stuff. If you get hit, you call foul. As (a) young guy, they'll probably just throw you (off) the court and (say), "Nah, you can't play with us." Even playing in Hudson Gardens was a really tough environment. You're playing against men. But it's the grittiness of it in Hudson County, and it's very similar to New York City, Philadelphia, and those top cities. It's really good basketball. And we care about it. We're very passionate.

JACK NIES
St. Peter's Prep, 1955

There've been many 'hotbedders' who have come out of Hudson County (if not, we wouldn't have bothered with this book), but few certified whistleblowers with more credibility than Jack Nies.

The native of Jersey City and graduate of St. Peter's Prep, it was reffing at the high-school level where Nies first honed his craft.

Then, an Eastern League gig before getting hired by the NBA.

Over a 31-year career (1978-2009), No. 35 compiled a refereeing resume of more than 2,000 regular-season games, another 150 in the playoffs, 10 Finals games and two All-Star contests.

Nowadays, he's Nies the Sailorman, and it was on the high seas where he opined about Hudson County and beyond.

"Gerald Govan, Robert McLaughlin and Bill Raftery, all of them in Audubon Park (Jersey City)," Nies said. "They were just so many good players back then.

"That's the thing, just failing to keep the local kids at home in college. Guys such as Tommy Heinsohn (to Holy Cross), Mike O'Koren (North Carolina) and Jim Spanarkel (Duke) to start. They were tremendous players who left.

"It's been my belief that if major Jersey basketball programs, such as St. Peter's, Seton Hall, Rutgers and Fairleigh Dickinson, did a better job at that, there's no doubt they'd be nationally ranked (more frequently)."

Nies was self-deprecating regarding his own prowess.

"I played defense, once held Sonny Hill (the 'Mayor of Philadelphia Basketball') to 55."

...and what about that 1987 Legends Classic (at the All-Star Game) in Seattle?

"Bob Cousy was dribbling at the foul-line extended, and may have taken a few steps.

"The other bench is screaming 'that's a travel,' and I just turned and said, 'I don't call a walk on a legend.' "

There wasn't an argument.

-

By, Frank Drucker

BOB O'CONNOR
St. Aloysius Coach

We agree the contribution of Hudson County is unusual. Players played and practiced to emulate the success of previous players playing with college scholarships.

This fostered good play... CYO leagues provided organized competition. It promoted competitiveness... The open freelance style of play with the center open developed ball handling. Players were allowed to develop in all phases, dribbling, cutting and passing. They were not confined to roles. It developed a well-rounded player.

New York college basketball stimulated interest...

The playing style in Hudson wasn't brute force, but more about fundamentals...There were no activities like hunting, fishing and golf to diminish the basketball pool.

MIKE O'KOREN
Hudson Catholic, 1976

At Hudson Gardens, there were a lot of buildings around. Right in the middle was one called the rink. And I probably first started playing basketball then because the Jersey City Housing Authority would have teams. You'd go down and play the other projects.

And then, a friend who lived in the back of the projects, Ron Steinmetz, who coached at St Joe's Grade School, saw that I was a little tall and got me to try out for the St. Joe's grade school team. I was influenced by him. And my brother, Ron, got involved with that, wound up playing, and just took it from there.

It was pretty simple, but it was fun going to play around in the Jersey Housing Authority because there were a lot of good teams out there. You had Marion Gardens, you had Curries Woods, (and) you had Booker T. Washington. It was like playing on the road in the ACC going down to play in some of those places. So, it got me accutomed to what I was going to experience later on in life.

At the University of North Carolina, the reporters after a game would say, "Wow, that was some atmosphere at Cameron Indoor Stadium, in Raleigh at Reynolds Coliseum, at Virginia, (and) at Clemson at Little John Coliseum," (where) everybody was just on top of you dressed in orange." They asked, "Were you bothered by the crowd, the noise, and the fans?"

I said, "You've got to be kidding me. What are you talking about? Did you ever play at Lincoln? Did you ever play at Ferris High School in Jersey City? Did you ever go to Dickinson? You ever play at Dt. Peter's Prep or St. Mary's, where there were 500 people in a 250-seat gym?"

And I said, "This is nothing compared to playing where I played in high school." And I mean that. I've told that story several times. It helped you playing over at those schools. The only big gym we ever had really was Marist, and that would be packed, too, when we played out there. So that helped, that really did. To play on the road in some of these high schools, that helped me in college.

JOE PALERMO

Over the course of some six decades in coaching, teaching and "good guy-ing," 97-year-old (this past Sept. 12th) Joe Palermo has left his mark as a Hudson original.

He isn't in the County Sports Hall of Fame (Class of 2001) without reason.

At then-Demarest (now Hoboken) High School, Palermo was a multi-sport star. Then, after a distinguished collegiate career at St. Michael's (Vermont) College, coaching was his passion.

At a variety of colleges, both girls and boys, both as head coach and assistant, Palermo's teams won titles at any number of levels.

Among those he coached were Bill Raftery (varsity, St. Cecilia's [Kearny]) and Bob Hurley Sr. (frosh, St. Peter's College [Jersey City]).

Both gentlemen are Naismith Hall of Famers. Coincidence? There's no shot.

"He had seven children and taught school," Raftery said of Palermo. "Very competitive, but was concerned about the future.

"He was a great offensive mind, understood what opponents tried eliminating, too.

Substitute "great" with "terrific," as in "terrific offensive mind," and you get the assessment of Hurley.

"He was quiet, but forceful when necessary.

"He had his sons at practice when they were young, which was something I could relate to with my sons."

Palermo also "really gave his players freedom, as long as they dug in defensively," Hurley Sr. said.

Palermo, now a resident of Lake Tahoe (Nevada), recently returned to his Hudson roots. Sharing a meal with Richard Kaner (publisher of this book) and Anthony Nicodemo Jr., Palermo was effusive in his praise of Hurley Sr. and Raftery.

Admiration was indeed a two-way street.

MIKE ROONEY
Snyder, 1961

I started (playing) basketball at St. Aloysius Grammar School. They ran a biddy league, and a guy named Brennan ran it. That exposed me to basketball.

I would go to Bayside Park, and I'd stay there and shoot the ball until like one o'clock in the morning. Some guy was studying for the Bar, and he would call the cops. The cops would come and take my ball.

What happened the next day at school? The police station was right next to Snyder High School. I would go to the police station and tell a sergeant or lieutenant that I was robbed last night by a policeman, and I wanted to press charges. The cop would say "Listen, you nut. If you don't go to sleep at 10 o'clock, we're going to put a bullet in this basketball. Here's your ball. You got to go to bed at 10 o'clock."

At that time in Jersey City, most of the kids that went to school played in these leagues, like recreation leagues and biddy leagues. They were more advanced than other kids. When I was around, everybody in Jersey City went to a Division One school. It was because they had a feeding system. We were playing basketball when we were 8 years old. So, by the time we got to high school, that's all I did was play basketball. I told you I was in Bayside Park at one o'clock in the morning, taking jump shots. I became a very good shooter. And at that time, AAU basketball was just starting.

The feeding system, in other words, there were gyms all over Jersey City. Even when I started, I was terrible, but I got better. And then, the CYO would be on Saturday. We (were) just playing basketball with that. They don't have that now. Now, gyms aren't even open. They got people shooting each other. It's a tough thing.

We always had problems in this city, but we worked around those problems. Basketball was the thing.

RAFTERY / SPANARKEL

"Why is Hudson County basketball so good?" can best be answered with, "Who's so good in Hudson County basketball?"

Well, your honor, let's swear in a couple of impeccable sources who happen to double as duly-certified, damn good participants.

"Playing in Hudson County, there were North and South divisions, and the South was so competitive."

That assessment came courtesy of Jim Spanarkel, Hudson Catholic Class of 1975.

"The public and Catholic schools each had their own identity. Back then, many of the best players didn't leave.. Now, with AAU, it's different."

What was the "secret" to the success of Hudson basketball?

"Well, in Jersey City, there's about 300,000 people. Kids were able to play and learn sports without having to go anywhere else."

Spanarkel subsequently starred at Duke, part of the Blue Devils' improbable run to the 1978 NCAA title game, before a five-season career (first-round selection) with the nascent Dallas Mavericks.

Harkening back to Hudson, "There were great players everywhere, including Mike O'Koren with me at Hudson Catholic, Jackie Gilloon (Memorial [West New York]) and Tommy Wise (Bayonne), just to name a few.

"I also had the chance to play against Elnardo Webster in the summer league. Right then and there, I learned I needed to get stronger if I was going to compete."

Spanarkel was also quick to credit his high-school coach and "my second father," Rocky Pope. "He taught me discipline."

Alluding to the differences between today and yesteryear, "It was the early days of the (3-point) line, We didn't even think about that shot, but the math behind it has changed the game.

...which in itself is somewhat strange since, according to Spanarkel, "80 to 90 percent of the players are stronger than we were."

Now, in the paint, there's less happening.

Spanarkel is now dutifully ceding the witness stand to an-other gentleman who swears to tell the truth and nothing but the truth.

"Basketball was all we had, morning until supper," Bill Raftery, St. Cecilia (Kearny) '60, said. Owning the Garden State scoring record (more than three decades) and a Jersey school title, Raftery went on to a terrific collegiate career at LaSalle.

..though not before his foundation.

Start with Vinnie Ernst (St. Aloysius, who later starred at Providence), Frank Nicolletti (St. Peter's Prep, Dave Bing's Syracuse roomie) and Joe Palermo (coach at Demarest [now Hoboken] High School).

"Joe was special. He was a gentleman. He had seven children of his own, but was concerned about the future of all of us.

"He was a great offensive mind as a coach, because he knew what the opposition tried to take away."

When it was his turn to be a leader of men, Raftery "coached some great Hudson players (at Seton Hall), including Nick Galis (Union Hill) and Danny Calandrillo (North Bergen)."

"Nick was one of the greatest international players, a Hall of Famer (Class of 2017). Danny was there in the early 1980's, at the beginning of the Big East, as good a scorer as anyone."

Opining about what was in Hudson County's basketball water, "We were able to compete against teams that were better, even some colleges. There was a toughness, an attitude."

Perhaps the Chamber of Commerce can use that.

DAN SILNA
Co-Owner, Spirits of St Louis (1974–'76)

My brother Ozzie was 11 years older than me and was in a basketball league in Hudson County. I was the team mascot. I was probably 5- or 6-years-old. And I would lead the team out onto the court dribbling a basketball, and I'd get to get up to the hoop. I couldn't make a layup. I would take the ball, throw it over my head to the guy behind me, and he'd make a layup. That was my first exposure to basketball.

There was a time that baseball dominated the sports scene, and a lot of great athletes played baseball. And then, basketball started to come into its own in the '50s. It took a little while. I think one of the great changes for basketball was when African American players were allowed to play the game. I still remember Willie Naulls, and (he) changed the game dramatically. I remember, also, when I was a kid, the biggest guy on the team was probably 6'5", 6'6".

I remember going to the schoolyard playing stickball and basketball. Yeah, basketball's a street game. You don't need 18 guys to play basketball. You could play three-on-three, and it was fine.

And by the way, one on one, I still don't consider that basketball. Basketball's a team game. It's not an individual one.

ALBIO SIRES
Memorial, 1970

I learned to play the game in Washington Park. I just picked it up. My first organized competition was in the 8th grade at PS 4.

The one who taught me the most was Charlie Swenson, my freshman coach at Memorial.

I patterned my game after Jerry West. I used to go to the park and pretend I was Jerry West and release the ball fast.

Richie O'Connor (St. Michael's U.C.) and Jimmy Foster (Hoboken) were the toughest players I faced in my high school career.

Other players in the county I was impressed with were Mike Rooney and Jackie Gilloon, who played at Memorial after me. Rooney was such a great shooter that if they had the three-point shot when he played for Snyder, he would have scored three thousand points. I know a lot of people would agree with me that Jackie Gilloon was the Pete Maravich of Hudson County.

My greatest memory was winning the county championship in 1970 when we defeated Dickinson, which was undefeated at the time.

I used to hang out at Memorial Park on 57th Street. I practically lived there. At 10PM they would close the park and I'd be bouncing the ball while walking toward my home and my mother would usually meet me halfway and say she was worried about me returning so late. I told her I was 6'4" and would be OK. She then would say she could not be at ease until I returned home safely. I appreciate that more than ever.

I never thought I would be going into politics. A friend ran for commissioner and he was against the administration and I became persona non grata. I had always wanted to be a coach at Memorial High School but that situation made it seem unlikely for the time being.

Basketball taught me a lot. I learned not to give up on anything.

At St. Peter's College, I didn't play as much as I wanted. The fast break was not my style of play. It didn't fit my type of game.

GEORGE COOK
IS MY
HUDSON COUNTY
HOOPS LEGEND
MORE IMPORTANTLY
HE IS MY
FATHER AND HERO

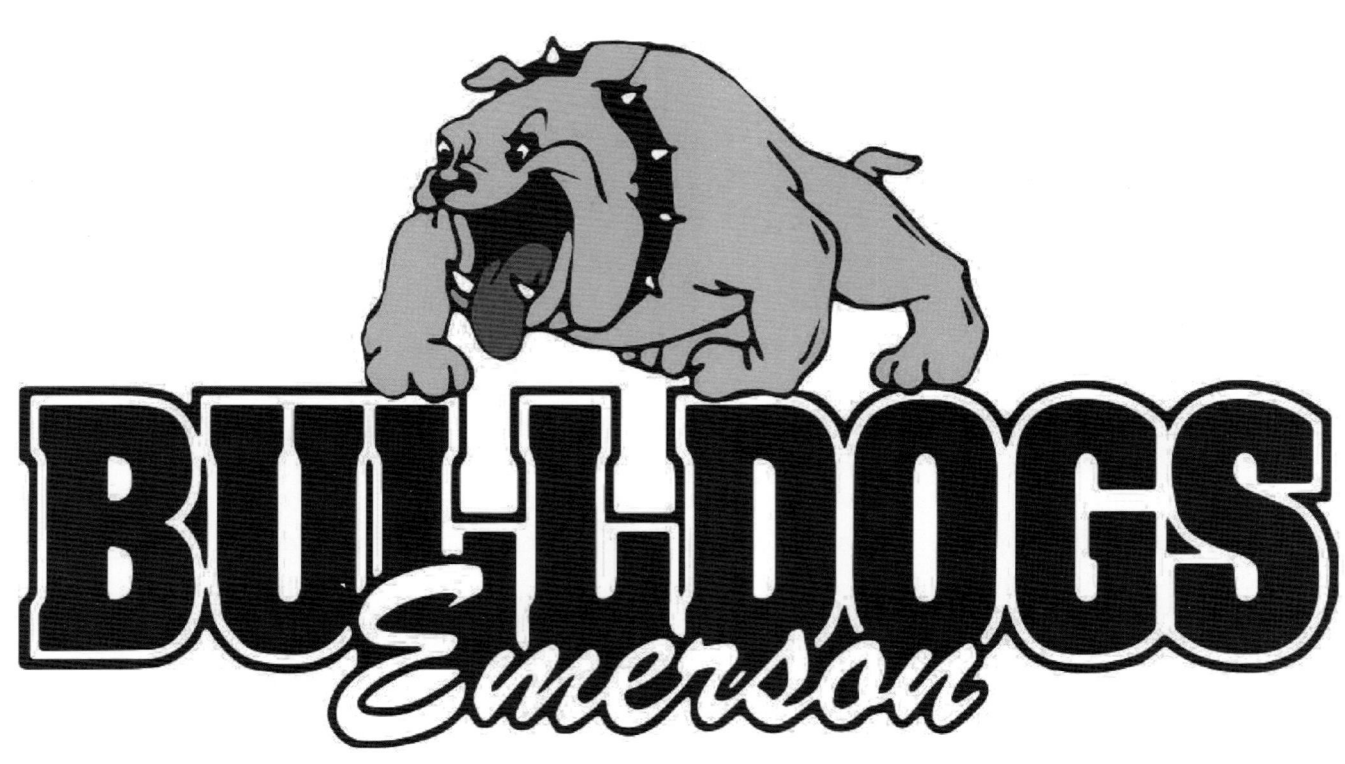

ADAM COOK
EMERSON HIGH SCHOOL
CLASS OF 1963

V

ALL DECADE TEAMS

The selection of players for this section was compiled by a committee of long-time Hudson County basketball observers which included coaches, journalists, administrators and former players. Although the high school performance of each player was a major element, the entire body of work of a player's career was taken into consideration.

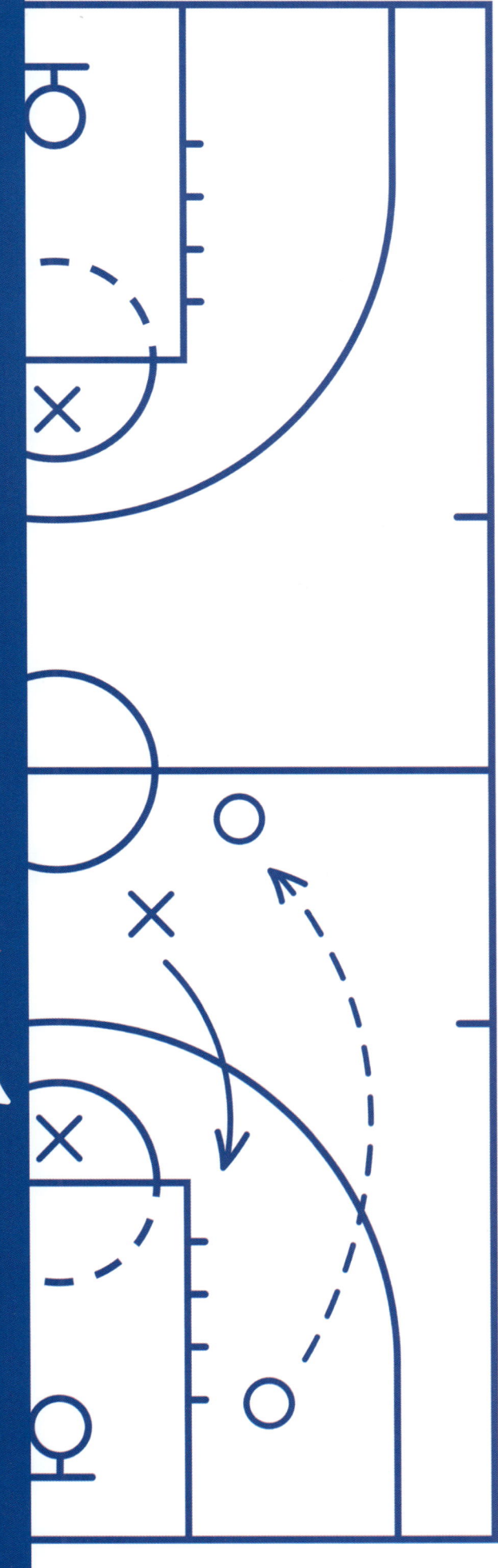

Harry Brooks, Emerson, 1950 An All-State basketball and baseball player at Emerson, where he established the then career record of 1,468 points. At Seton Hall, he scored a career total of 856 points, and in his senior year, averaged 15 points per game to lead the team in scoring. During his three years of play at the college level, the Pirates accumulated a record of 69-15 and won the 1953 NIT Championship. As captain of the 1954 team, Brooks won MVP of the Dixie Classic and an All-East Selection. He continued his career at the pro-level in the Eastern League (later known as the CBA) for six seasons.

Bob Budd, Dickinson, 1949 Continuing his strong development as a low post 'big man', Bob advanced from the 1947-48 Second Team to First Team in 1948-49. His season's scoring totals in city and county competition were just under leader Tex Silverman's marks. Bob was also a top retriever and had unusual agility for a player his size. Budd carried Dickinson to second place in both city and southern division races and was largely responsible for the Rams finishing 2nd to Emerson in the HCIBL Jamboree.

John Clune, St. Peter's Prep, 1950 Most people remember John Clune for his time as athletic director of the Air Force Academy, but he had a spectacular high school career in basketball for St. Peter's Prep. He earned All-State honors, led the team to a state championship in the 1949-50 season and graduated as the school's all-time leading scorer. At the U.S. Naval Academy, he received All-American honors, scored 1,561 points in 70 games and became the program's all-time leading scorer – a record that was broken by David Robinson 30 years later. After he passed away in 1992, the Air Force Academy renamed its basketball facility "Clune Arena" in his honor.

Harry Donovan, Union Hill, 1945 Harry Donovan graduated from Union Hill High School with 680 points in the 1944-45 season, which at the time was the county scoring record, averaging 18.8 points per game. At Muhlenberg College, he was the first player to be named four times to the All-Pennsylvania Team and was an honorable mention All-America in his senior season. He scored 1,527 points there and went on to play for the Knicks in the 1949-50 season.

Dan Gabbianelli, Weehawken, 1940 A unanimous 1941 All-County selection, Weehawken's Dan Gabbianelli was the school's first ever four-letter winner, earning varsity letters in soccer, basketball, baseball and tennis. Gabbianelli's game was described by The March 13, 1940 Jersey Journal as follows: "Gabbianelli is in a class by himself as a scoring threat and ball handler. One of the shiftiest players in the state, he led the county league in scoring (17 ppg.) as well as handing out assists." Gabbianelli continued his career at Georgetown, where he was one of the leading performers on the Hoya team that finished second to Wyoming in the 1943 NCAA Basketball Championship at Madison Square Garden.

Emil Hudak, Bayonne, 1944 A 1944 graduate of Bayonne High, Emil was ranked the top basketball player in the state. The 6-2, 200-pound forward was named to the All-State team for three consecutive times. Hudson County's leading scorer in 1944, Hudak continued his impressive career at Dartmouth where he excelled in both basketball and baseball. The March 4, 1943, write-up of the All-County team sums up Hudak's game very succinctly: "Undoubtedly, one of the best players in the state, it was his sparkling all-around ability that literally brought Bayonne its fifth divisional title in a row. He not only is one of the best marksmen in Hudson's ranks, but also is a splendid playmaker, unselfish team player, strong defensive man and just about tops in getting the ball off the backboards."

Bob Kirk, Kearny, 1944 As a result of becoming the most prolific scorer in county history, Bob advanced from All-County Second Team honors in 1942-43 to 1st team in 1943-44. His offense sizzled with his signature leaping left-handed lob shots on his way to a near 20 point average and a total of 537 points for the season, the most any Hudson player ever made in one campaign. He continued his basketball career at Upsala before embarking on a career with the Kearny Board of Education.

John Macknowsky, Lincoln, 1941 As a senior at Lincoln in 1941, he led the county in scoring and earned All-County and All-State honors. His college career at Seton Hall was interrupted by Navy service, but he returned to the game after the war. The sharp-shooting guard led the Pirates to a 24-3 record in 1946-47. He continued his career in the NBA with the Syracuse Nationals, earning Second-Team All-Rookie honors and achieving a career play-off scoring average of 10.5 points per game. A wrist injury prematurely ended his promising career in his fourth season with the Nationals.

John Mahnken, Memorial, 1942 Often referred to as the best player to ever compete on the court for Memorial, the 6-8, 215 lb center was the leader of a team that won four county championships in each of his four seasons (1939-42), two state championships and two runner-ups in state finals. His size and a remarkable hook shot made him very difficult to guard in the low post, and on defense, he was a particularly good shot blocker. A four-time All-State selection, his 1,650 points at Memorial, his career 16.8 average and individual high game of 38 points were county records when he graduated. As a freshman at Georgetown in the 1942-43 season, Mahnken led the Hoyas to a 22-5 season – their best record in program history at the time – and to the NCAA Championship game, where they fell to Wyoming at the Old Garden. That season, Mahnken was named a First Team All-American, the first Georgetown player so honored and the only such First Team All-American until Eric "Sleepy" Floyd in 1982. World War II interrupted his college career, and upon returning to the game, he transitioned into the NBA, playing the 1945-46 season for league champion Rochester. He played a total of eight seasons in the NBA, four of which were for the Boston Celtics.

Earle Markey, St. Peter's Prep, 1949 One of the all-time hoops greats at St. Peter's Prep, Earle Markey captained Prep's "Firehouse Five" that became the first South Hudson team to win the county championship and clinched a state Catholic championship. That year, Markey earned individual All-County and All-State honors. At the collegiate level, Markey was a three-year starter at Holy Cross and led the Crusaders to a composite 62-11 mark from 1950-53. A fourth round draft choice of the Boston Celtics, Markey instead opted to join the Jesuit Order. Recently, he celebrated his 60th year as a Jesuit priest.

Tommy O'Keefe, St. Peter's Prep, 1945 A star backcourt player at St. Peter's Prep, Tommy O'Keefe was one of a long list of Prep alums at Georgetown. Counting on playing for Elmore Ripley at Notre Dame, he committed to playing for the school, but after one year, Ripley left ND for a job with the Hoyas and O'Keefe followed. O'Keefe was the leading scorer in his junior and senior years and the first Hoya 1,000-point scorer. After a brief career with the Baltimore Bullets and military service in the Korean War, he returned to Georgetown as an assistant coach and was elevated to head coach in 1960-61. During his tenure there

Harry Brooks

John Mahnken

Earle Markey

through the 1965-1966 season, two of his star players were Hudson County products – future NFL Commissioner Paul Tagliabue and sharpshooter Jim Barry.

Togo Palazzi, Union Hill, 1950   At Union Hill, Togo Palazzi was recognized as one of the top prep basketball players nationwide. At Holy Cross, he led the Crusaders in scoring three years and in rebounds two years. In the 1954 NIT, Holy Cross defeated favorite Duquesne, thanks in large part to Palazzi's 77 points on his way to earning MVP laurels. No surprise when he was selected fifth in the first round by the Boston Celtics, Palazzi played a total of six seasons in the NBA – two with Boston and four with the Syracuse Nationals. At one time, he was the co-record holder for most points in one quarter by an NBA player (24 with Syracuse at the Boston Garden).

Dario Pia, Emerson, 1945   A top performer both offensively and defensively, Pia, assigned to guard country scoring record holder Harry Donovan in the four Emerson-Union Hill struggles in 1945-1946, held him well below his usual heavy output of points. As a near unanimous selection for the 1946 team, the Jersey Journal declared Dario's "knack of successfully guarding the opposition's best scorers and his court generalship" as major factors in being a near unanimous selection for his second consecutive All-County First Team selection in 1946.

Larry "Tex" Silverman, Snyder, 1949   After a standout career at Snyder, Tex Silverman enrolled at George Washington University, where he was a three-year starter for the Colonials as they compiled a record of 41-27. Upon graduation in 1953, he was drafted by the NBA's Rochester Royals (now the Sacramento Kings), but before he could pursue a career in the pro ranks, he was drafted again – this time by the U.S. Army, an offer he could not refuse. After serving two years of military service, the New Jersey native began a successful career in real estate sales. Silverman made a very generous donation to the GW Department of Athletics and in honor of his sizable contribution, the University named the Smith Center playing surface, "Tex Silverman Court".

Tommy Smith, St. Peter's Prep, 1945   Although he is better known as the former mayor of Jersey City, at one time, the name Tommy Smith was strictly associated with basketball stardom. Following a stellar career at St. Peter's Prep, Smith helped usher in the golden years of St. Peter's College basketball. As an exceptionally quick 6-0 guard who could shoot or drive to the basket equally well, he graduated as the Peacock's leading scorer with 1,304 points. An area draft choice of the New York Knicks, Smith played briefly for the team in a couple of pre-season games, and continued his basketball career in the Eastern League for two seasons.

Togo Palazzi

Mickey Winograd

George Blaney, St. Peter's Prep, 1957 It would be difficult to find a more "complete" basketball talent than George Blaney, whose career as both player and coach over five decades is marked by excellence at every level. At St. Peter's Prep, he led his team to the Hudson County Championship in his senior year and was named Hudson County Athlete of the Year. He went on to Holy Cross, leading the Crusaders to back-to-back 29-win seasons and earned All-New England honors. He recorded a 357-276 coaching record in a 22-year career at Holy Cross that resulted in three NCAA Tournament appearances, five NIT berths and seven 20-win seasons overall as head coach, notching 459 career victories. In 2000, he joined the staff of Jim Calhoun at UConn and went on to serve as associate head coach for two of UConn's national championships – one under Calhoun in 2004 and one under Kevin Ollie in 2011.

Harry Brooks, Emerson, 1950 An All-State basketball and baseball player at Emerson, where he established the then career record of 1,468 points. At Seton Hall, he scored a career total of 856 points, and in his senior year, averaged 15 points per game to lead the team in scoring. During his three years of play at the college level, the Pirates accumulated a record of 69-15 and won the 1953 NIT Championship. As captain of the 1954 team, Brooks won MVP of the Dixie Classic and an All-East Selection. He continued his career at the pro-level in the Eastern League (later known as the CBA) for six seasons.

Warren Buehler, Bayonne (Sweeney), 1952 While at Bayonne, Warren Buehler was a standout basketball and baseball performer. On the hardwood, he was a two-time All-County and All-State player for the Bees in 1951 and 1952, leading Bayonne to the Group IV State Title in 1951. Buehler averaged 18 points per game as a junior and 23 points per game as a senior. After Bayonne, he attended Georgetown, where he continued to play both sports. When he graduated in 1957, he was the school's all-time leading scorer with 1,319 points. Starting in 1959, he served as a teacher, vice principal, principal and superintendent of schools in Weehawken. He was also the coach of the Weehawken High varsity basketball team that captured the 1967 Hudson County Championship and went to the finals of the Group IV state tournament.

John Clune, St. Peter's Prep, 1950 Most people remember John Clune for his time as athletic director of the Air Force Academy, but he had a spectacular high school career in basketball for St. Peter's Prep. He earned All-State honors, led the team to a state championship in the 1949-50 season and graduated as the school's all-time leading scorer. At the U.S. Naval Academy, he received All-American honors, scored 1,561 points in 70 games and became the program's all-time leading scorer – a record that was broken by David Robinson 30 years later. After he passed away in 1992, the Air Force Academy renamed its basketball facility "Clune Arena" in his honor.

John Crotty, St. Peter's Prep, 1956 Despite being slowed by a sophomore year injury, John Crotty went on to establish himself as one of Prep's all-time great basketball players. In naming him for First team All County, the Jersey Journal proclaimed: "Crotty was probably the county's best defenseman and conversely, anyone trying to cover John, usually fouled out. His driving game, hustle and 20-point average made him a must-selection." Crotty has been long remembered for his running one-hander 8 feet past half court as time was running out that resulted in a win over Memorial for the County Championship. He entertained numerous college scholarship offers but decided on UNC, which won the 1957 NCAA Championship during his tenure.

Vinnie Ernst, St. Aloysius, 1959 Vinnie Ernst started young and attained stardom as an eleven year old when he led the Jersey City CYO team to the World Biddy Championship in Scranton, Pennsylvania. Next stop was St. Aloysius where he led the Cardinals to two Parochial B state titles and won All-State honors on his way to compiling over 1,300 points and what would have been a record number of assists if they kept that stat back then. At Providence College, the 5'8" wizard with the ball helped the Friars capture NIT titles in 1961 and 1963 as well as Ernst garnering the 1961 MVP award. To this day, Ernst continues to hold Providence's single game assist record of 17.

Hank Finkel, Holy Family, 1960   After his high school career at Holy Family in Union City, the seven-foot Hank Finkel had a great freshman season at St. Peter's College, he transferred to the University of Dayton, where he scored 1,968 points and was an All-American. He was drafted by the Los Angeles Lakers and Philadelphia 76ers, but chose to stay in school. He wound up playing nine years in the NBA and was a member of the Boston Celtics' 1974-74 World Championship team.

Gerald Govan, Snyder, 1959   Gerald Govan didn't have a stellar career at Snyder High School, but blossomed at St. Mary's of the Plains College in Kansas, where as a junior, he led the nation in rebounds with 24.7 per game and was named Small College All-America. He chose to play in the Italian League rather than with the St. Louis Hawks who drafted him, but in 1966, returned to the U.S. to play for the New Orleans Buccaneers in the ABA. He played for over nine seasons. Not known for scoring but he was a ferocious rebounder, shot blocker and hustler. Only one of six players to have participated in each of the original ABA's nine seasons, he appeared in 681 regular season games (4th all-time) and retired as the league's second all-time leading rebounder behind Mel Daniels.

Tom Heinsohn, St. Michael's (UC), 1952   Perhaps Hudson County's greatest player, after a stellar career at St. Michael's (UC), Tom Heinsohn recorded 1,789 points at Holy Cross, averaging 22.1 points per game. Posting an average of 15.5 rebounds per game, Heinsohn totaled 1,254 rebounds in his college career. After being selected as a territorial pick of the Boston Celtics in 1956, Heinsohn started his career off with a bang by earning 1957 NBA Rookie of the Year Award and being a key cog in his first of eight NBA Championships as a player. He became the Celtics head coach in 1969-70 on his way to two NBA Championships as a coach (1974, 1976). Later, he had a long and successful career as a Celtics broadcaster. One of five individuals who are double inductees as a player (2006) and coach (2015).

Tony Nicodemo, Ferris, 1955   In a city well known for its basketball greats, Tony Nicodemo became a Hudson hoops immortal when he became the first public school player (and fourth overall) to score 1,000 points. In 1955, the 5'9" sharpshooter set a scoring record in the Jersey City Interscholastic League and led the county with a 26.7 average. Nicodemo continued his court excellence at St. Michael's College in Vermont as he gained national recognition with an eye-popping, record setting 49 point effort in an NCAA College Division Tournament game followed by a clutch 31-point performance which propelled St. Michael's into the 1958 Final Four. A charter member of St. Michael's Hall of Fame, Nicodemo's No. 13 jersey has since been retired.

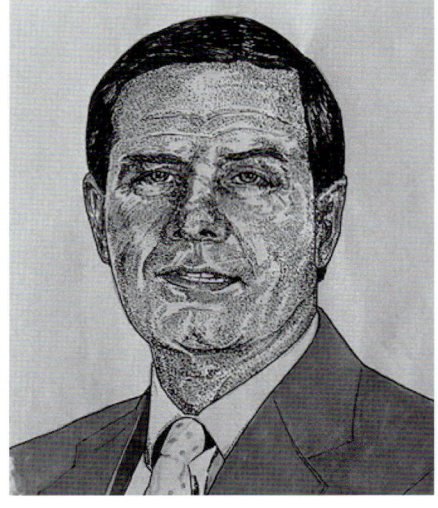

George Blaney

Vinnie Ernst

Tom Heinsohn

Bill Raftery, St. Cecilia (KY), 1959 Bill Raftery is best known as one of the leading analysts and color commentators in sports broadcasting for college basketball and the NBA, but his own basketball career was just as exceptional. At St. Cecilia High School, he was All-State and 1959 Mr. Basketball USA, and he led his team to the New Jersey State Championship in his senior season. Scoring a total of 2,192 points in his high school career, Raftery held the state record in points scored for 35 years. After a great college career at La Salle University, he coached at Fairleigh Dickinson-Madison and Seton Hall. While at the helm of Seton Hall's basketball program, he led the team to two National Invitational Tournaments before embarking on a Hall of Fame sports broadcasting career, where he currently is the lead color analyst for CBS' NCAA Basketball Tournament coverage.

Tony Radovich, Hoboken (Demarest), 1952 The "Hoboken Hurricane" was a point-a-minute man for Demarest, averaging 32.7 as he poured in 753 points in 23 games. No surprise that Tommy Heinsohn considered Radovich the "toughest player I faced in the county." A starter for North Carolina as a sophomore and junior, Radovich was also a member of their NCAA Championship team in 1957 – his senior year. On January 11, 1955 Tony and Lennie Rosenbluth became the eighth Tar Heel pair to score at least 30 points in the same game, scoring 30 and 32 points respectively.

George Ramming, Union Hill, 1956 A two-time All-County First Team player, George led Union Hill to the county championship in 1955 and back-to-back state titles in 1955 and 1956. The Jersey Journal claimed, "Nobody, but nobody, could match him in the slot." Moving on to Dartmouth, he achieved All-Ivy First Team honors in his senior year when he also banged in 39 points in a game against Boston University, the highest scoring game, to that point, in Dartmouth history.

Paul Tagliabue, St. Michael's (UC), 1958 After leading St.Michael's (U.C.) to the runner-up position in the 1958 County Championship, Paul Tagliabue selected Georgetown from the many schools that pursued him. Paul's association with his alma mater can simply be described as "Georgetown Royalty" – three year starter averaging 11.4 points and 7.6 rebounds, team captain, class president, recipient of the Duffey Award as the school's outstanding student-athlete and formerChairman of the University's Board of Directors. His law firm, Covington and Burling, represented the NFL, which paved the way for his being named NFL Commissioner and served in that prestigious position for 17 years.

Hank Morano

Paul Tagliabue

Bill Raftery

George Waddleton, St. Peter's Prep, 1953 One of the great high school players of his era in Hudson County and St. Peter Prep's first 1,000 point scorer, George Waddleton was also a phenomenal all-around athlete. The leading rusher on Prep's football team, Waddleton was also the starting shortstop on the baseball team and a standout cross-country runner. Moving on to Holy Cross, Waddleton helped the Crusaders to an overall three season record of 53-24 with the team advancing to the 1955 NIT and 1956 NCAA Tournament. Waddleton led the team as a senior captain with a scoring average of 18.5 points per game, including a career-high 29 points against NYU.

Mickey Winograd, Lincoln, 1952 After earning All-County and All-State honors, Mickey moved on to Duquesne University. His steady playmaking and defensive skill were key elements in the Dukes qualifying in three consecutive seasons for the NIT at Madison Square Garden, then considered a more prestigious tournament than the NCAA. The 1954 team was a runner-up to Holy Cross and the 1956 team lost to Louisville in the quarterfinals. Duquesne defeated Dayton in 1956 for their first NIT title, and Mickey shined in the final as he held his foe, Jack Sallee, who had scored 77 points in three previous tournament games, to a mere two points.

Jerry Vayda, St. Peter's Prep, 1952 The catalyst for Prep's 1951 Parochial A State Championship and 1952 state and county titles, Jerry Vayda was the first recruit of new coach Frank McGuire at North Carolina. Vayda led Carolina in 1954, the first season in the ACC, at 17.1 points per game and was second behind Lennie Rosenbluth a season later at 14.5 points. Scoring 1,187 points as a Tar Heel, he finished his career third in scoring at UNC behind only Al Lifson and Lennie Rosenbluth. Vayda was the first Tar Heel to earn All-ACC honors in all three varsity seasons.

Harry Anderson, Weehawken, 1968 Harry Anderson was the first Weehawken High School player to score 1,000 points and in 1967 as a junior helped the team to its only HCIAA championship. In his senior year, he averaged 30.9 points per game, which included a 50-point game against Union Hill and which was a county scoring record at the time. After a stellar year at Jacksonville University, he returned home following a death in the family and scored 984 points during his three years at St. Peter's College.

Jim Barry, St. Peter's, 1961 One of the most prolific scorers in Prep history, Jim Barry was a three-year starter who was named First Team Catholic All-State each year. Barry held the Prep's scoring record (1,219 points) at the time of graduation. At Georgetown, he set three freshman team records. As a sophomore, he scored 29 points in his first varsity game, and had eight games of 30 or more points, finishing among the nation's leaders at 22.6 points per game. Despite knee injuries, as a junior, he averaged 19.1 points and was the ninth best free-shooter in the nation (86.6%). Although knee injuries relegated him to playing off the bench in his senior year, Barry still set career records for points and average. In 2007, Barry was named one of the ten greatest players in Georgetown history, along with the likes of Patrick Ewing, Alonzo Mourning, Dikembe Mutombo and Allen Iverson.

Mike Boylan, St. Peter's Prep, 1969 Mike Boylan had a stellar career at St. Peter's Prep, leading his team to second place in the 1969 Parochial A State finals. He was hailed by highly-regarded Prep coach Jerry Halligan as "the best all-around player I coached in fourteen years." Boylan had an uncanny knack for blocking shots and intimidating the opposing team's defense, while leading Prep in scoring at 19 points a game. He continued his career at Assumption College, where the school enjoyed their most productive three-year run on the hardwood, including Regional Championships in the 1971 and 1972 NCAA College Division Tournament as well as a third place finish in the 1973 tournament. Boylan was named 1973 College Division Player of the Year and, upon graduation, began a 25-year career with Wilson Sporting Goods, where he eventually was named its Global Business Director/Golf Division.

Ron Dabney, Dickinson, 1967 Ron Dabney was one of the greatest basketball players in Dickinson High School's history. Skilled all-around player with a nice shooting touch and very mobile for a guy his size. Twice named First Team All-County, Dabney finished his career as the second leading scorer in Jersey City history with 1,524 points, trailing only Mike Rooney. He continued his career at St. Louis University.

Keith Hochstein, St. Peter's Prep, 1964 Keith Hochstein was named First Team All-County and All-State Parochial in his senior year at St. Peter's Prep, which he attended from 1961 to 1964. At the College of Holy Cross, he was named New England College Basketball Player of the Year, was honorable mention All-American and Northeast Regional All-American in his senior year. A center at 6'4" he scored 22 points in a game against Kareem Abdul-Jabbar, and he was inducted to the Holy Cross Hall of Fame in 1984.

Harry Laurie, Lincoln, 1963 After a stellar career as a guard at Lincoln, he was recruited by Loyola of Chicago the year they won the NCAA championship. After his freshman year at Loyola, Harry transferred back home to St.Peter's where he helped spark the Peacocks to two NIT appearances and was the Most Valuable Player in the Met Conference as a senior. Played a brief time (9 games) with the Pittsburgh Condors of the ABA and then joined the Allentown Jets of the Eastern League and was a key contributor on their 1970 championship team.

Ted Martiniuk, Emerson, 1968 Following in the footsteps of his older brother Frank, who was First Team All-County in 1966 and later a 1,000-point scorer at Vermont, Ted Martiniuk was named honorable Mention All-County in 1967 followed by a First Team selection in 1968. Martiniuk led Emerson to the North Hudson championship in the 1967-68 season, before they dropped a 69-68 decision to Bayonne in the championship game. Continuing his career at St. Peter's College, Martiniuk recorded career averages of 19.3 points, 5.2 rebounds and 4.3 assists per game.

Frank Nicoletti, St. Peter's Prep, 1962 Frank Nicoletti scored over 1,200 points in his varsity career at the Prep and left St. Peter's as the second highest scorer in school history. Prep was undefeated, 12-0, in County play during his senior year and repeated as County champs. Finishing the regular season with a 22-1 record that season, Nicoletti was First Team All-County and All-State as well as Dell Second Team All-American. After Prep, he went on to play three varsity seasons at Syracuse University on a team that included Naismith Hall of Famer Dave Bing and Jim Boeheim, head coach for Syracuse. After working twenty-five years for a number of top law firms, Nicoletti started his own firm in 1995 in New York City where he continues to practice today.

Jim Barry

Mike Boylan

Ted Martiniuk

Richie O'Connor, St. Michael's, 1969   Richie O'Connor earned All-County honors at St. Michael's from 1966-1969, and at the time, joined Jim Barry as only the second player in the annals of the Jersey Journal All-County team to be voted first team over three consecutive years. He scored over 600 points in his senior season for an average of 25.1 points a game on his way to finishing with a career total of 2,025 points. O'Connor was an invaluable floor general and rebounder, leading St. Michael's to the Parochial B state finals, where they fell to St. Anthony in 1969. He led Duke to the 1971 NIT and later transferred to Fairfield, where he also led the Stags to the 1974 NIT. After college, he enjoyed a successful career as an accomplished sportswriter.

Craig Ross, St. Mary's, 1969   In the illustrious basketball history of St. Mary's, Craig Ross is the all-time leading scorer with 1,628 points and that came before the three-point basket. After making Second Team All-County in 1968 as a junior, the 6'3" guard/forward was named to the first team in 1969. Ross helped St. Mary's win its first Parochial B state championship as a sophomore in 1967 and then capped his career with a second Parochial B title in 1969. With his career total of 1,628 points, Ross surpassed Mike Rooney as the top scorer in Jersey City history, averaging 28.7 points per game in the 1969 season and scoring 679 points. He was held under 20 points in only three games all year. He also led the Ramblers in rebounds for the season.

Mike Rooney, Snyder, 1961   Mike Rooney was selected First Team All-County in both 1960 and 1961, and Snyder was a perennial contender in the South Hudson Division thanks to the phenomenal, deep outside shooting of the 6-2 guard. Snyder dropped a 59-58 decision to St. Michael's (UC) in the 1960 Hudson County Finals. Upon graduation in 1961, Rooney was the all-time leading scorer (1,608 points) in the history of Jersey City scholastic basketball, and that was in the pre-three-point shot era. Rooney averaged 9.8 points per game as a sophomore at St. Bonaventure before transferring to Oklahoma, where the Jersey City native averaged 9 and 6.5 points per game in the following two seasons. After completing his college eligibility, he played for several years in the Eastern League and continued his scoring prowess with game highs of 50 and 57 points.

Vince Roundtree, Lincoln, 1969   Vinnie Roundtree was a First Team All-County selection for 1969, leading Lincoln to its first county championship as well as a runner-up berth in the Group III state finals. Coach Bob Hurley compared Roundtree's style to NBA superstar Charles Barkley. A ferocious rebounder and inside threat, the 6'5" Roundtree competed and often won the rebounding battle against much taller opponents in high school and at Rutgers. In three years at Rutgers, Roundtree averaged 9.5 points and 5.6 rebounds per game. As a senior in the 1973-74 season, Roundtree was third in scoring and second to the late Rutgers star Phil Sellers in rebounds.

Mike Rooney

Aron Stewart

Elnardo Webster

Harvey Smith, Snyder, 1967 Harvey Smith achieved First Team All-County honors in 1967 at Snyder High School. He is widely regarded as one of the top shot blockers of his era. After transferring from Cleveland State, he played one season at Long Island University in the 1971-72 season, averaging 11.7 points per game and 8.3 rebounds, shooting 55.5 from the field and 74.4 from the foul line. A three-term Jersey City councilman who spent four years as City Council president and later acting mayor following the untimely death of Mayor Glenn Cunningham.

Aron Stewart, Lincoln, 1969 Aron Stewart didn't make the varsity at Lincoln and only started one game as a senior. At Essex County CC his 36.6 ppg in his sophmore season led all junior college players in the nation and earned him First Team All - America honors. He continued his high scoring performnces at Univ. of Richmond where in two season he registered a 28.1 average on his way to 1,237 career points and Southern Conference Player of the Year in 1973.

Danny Waddleton, St. Michael's (UC), 1960 No surprise this 5'11" outstanding playmaking guard made First Team All-County in consecutive seasons (1959 and 1960) as he led St. Michael's to the Hudson County championship in 1960 with a victory over Snyder after suffering losses in the championship games in 1958 (Bayonne) and 1959 (St. Peter's Prep). Waddleton continued his career at St. John's, where he played for Hall of Fame coach Joe Lapchick and his assistant Lou Carnesecca. As a sophomore during the 1961-62 season, Waddleton helped St. John's to a 21-5 record and a berth in the NIT, where they beat Holy Cross and Duquesne before finishing runner-up to Dayton. A teacher for many years in the Jersey City Public School system, Waddleton took over as the head coach at Dickinson High School in the late 1970s and quickly turned around a basketball program that had hit rock bottom.

Elnardo Webster, Lincoln, 1965 Fans who attended the 1968 NIT at Madison Square Garden or spoke to friends and relatives that were there still talk in awe of one of the greatest back-to-back performances in tournament history – Webster's 51 point performance against Marshall followed by his 29 point,10 rebound game against top-seeded Duke as the "Run Baby Run" Peacocks defeated the Blue Devils 100-71 and ran them right back to Tobacco Road. Webster continued his scoring prowess in Italy where he was the league's leading scorer in 1970 and then played a season in the ABA. After basketball, Dr. Webster went into the education field and acquired a national reputation for his exemplary work in developing after-school and summer programs.

John Wendelken, Hoboken (Demarest), 1961 At Demarest-Hoboken High, Wendelken was not only a four-year starter for both basketball and baseball teams, but also earned All-State honors in both sports as a senior. He graduated class valedictorian and the basketball team's all-time leading scorer with 1,456 career points. Wendelken continued his excellence on the hardwood for Holy Cross, where he was named All-New England three times and New England Player of the Year in 1965. Drafted by the NBA's Baltimore Bullets, Wendelken played briefly in the Eastern League before beginning a career as a high school teacher and coach.

Tom Best, Lincoln, 1979 One of Lincoln's all-time greats, Tom Best made the jump from an All-County Honorable Mention in 1978 to First Team in 1979 – the year he hit a buzzer-beating shot to defeat St. Anthony. At Lafayette College, he was East Coast Conference Rookie of the Year and the next year was All-ECAC and 10th in the country in field goal percentage. Upon transferring to St. Peter's College, he earned First Team All-MAAC and First Team All-Tri State. Later, Best coached the Lincoln girls basketball team to multiple county championships.

Jim Boylan, St. Mary's, 1973 Jim Boylan's standout career at St.Mary's was highlighted by the team's 1972 Parochial C state championship. He continued his excellence on the court as he led Assumption College to the 1974 and 1975 Final Four of the NCAA Division II Tournament with the team finishing both seasons as the nation's No. 3. After transferring to Marquette, the Golden Eagles defeated North Carolina in the 1977 NCAA national championship game where Boylan scored 14 points. Following his collegiate career, he chose to continue his game overseas and played five seasons in Europe, the last four as player/coach for Vevey, which secured its first Swiss Championship with Boylan at the helm and on the court. He returned to the States in 1986 to embark on a 25-year NBA coaching career highlighted by being a member of Cleveland's staff when they captured their first NBA title in 2016 as well as two stints as Interim Coach for Chicago (2007-2008) and Milwaukee (2012-2013) for a total of 106 games.

Dan Callandrillo, North Bergen, 1978 Dan Callandrillo's 'Cinderella' career at North Bergen was highlighted by four North Hudson titles, two county championships, a Group IV state crown, a county single season scoring record of 853 points and a 62 point game. On to Seton Hall in his soph year which was the charter season of the Big East Conference, Callandrillo led the conference in scoring and as a senior, averaged 25.8 points per game. In 1982, Dan was named Big East Player of the Year, UNICO National Athlete of the Year and was the recipient of the Haggerty Award as the metropolitan area's outstanding player.

Darryl Charles, St. Anthony As smooth as any Hudson guard in the 1970's, Darryl Charles led St. Anthony to back-to-back Parochial C State Championships in 1973 and 1974, with a two-season record of 57-2. Achieving First Team All-County honors in 1974, Charles was an efficient playmaker who also exhibited good shot selection and strong defensive skill. He went on to play for La Salle University for two seasons before transferring to George Washington University for his final two seasons.

Don Fanelli, St. Joseph (WNY), 1972 Perhaps the greatest all-around athlete to ever come out of St. Joseph (WNY), Don Fanelli was a two-time All-County First Team selection in both football and basketball. During the 1970-71 season, he guided the Blue Jays to a 27-1 record, capped by Hudson County and Parochial B State Championships. His 36-point effort in the county finals against perennial power St. Peter's Prep was one of the greatest championship game performances in Hudson County history. Fanelli went on to captain the Cornell football team, and as a senior, he was the nation's leading rusher until a knee injury knocked him out of action for the remainder of the season.

Bob Fazio, Emerson, 1973 One of the most celebrated basketball stars to ever come out of Union City, Bob Fazio was a two-time First Team All-County selection. In one year at Edward Williams College, he led the nation in scoring among junior colleges, averaging nearly 35 points per game and earned First Team JUCO All-American honors. Upon transferring to St. Peter's College, Fazio became one of the most prolific scorers in the school's history as he led the Peacocks in scoring and rebounding for three straight seasons, ending his career

Dan Callandrillo

Bob Fazio

Jimmy Foster, Hoboken, 1970 Following a career at Hoboken High and Becker Junior College, Jimmy had a breakout season in his senior year, leading UConn to a 19-8 record, including a 82-70 win over St. John's in the 1974 NIT. His three three-point plays – the "old-fashioned way" as there was no three-point shot at the time – broke up the game in the final minute. Foster was nothing short of consistent, averaging 16 ppg, 3.6 ast, & 48.8 from the field. Foster played two seasons in the ABA with St. Louis and Denver, and he continued his career in the Italian League.

Nick Galis, Union Hill, 1975 After an outstanding career at Union Hill under coach Bill McKeever, Nick Galis starred for Bill Raftery at Seton Hall University. The 6'0" shooting guard capped his collegiate career by winning the prestigious 1979 Haggerty Award, given annually to the Metropolitan Area's top college basketball player, as he averaged a lofty 27.5 points per game in his senior year. Galis made 50 percent of his field-goal attempts during his career at Seton Hall, including 57 percent as a senior, and was an 82 percent free-throw shooter. After getting drafted in the fourth round pick in the 1979 NBA Draft by the Boston Celtics, he starred for 16 seasons in Europe and played for the Greek National Team, earning praise as Europe's greatest scorer ever. Galis was an inaugural member of the FIBA Hall of Fame in 2007 and was inducted into the Naismith Hall of Fame in 2017.

Jackie Gilloon, Memorial, 1974 One of Hudson's all-time great guards, Jack Gilloon scored 1,340 points during his career at Memorial High School, which at the time, set the school scoring record. He made First Team All-County for three consecutive years and All-State twice. In 1974, he was named to the Parade All-America Team. At the University of South Carolina, he scored 1,125 points and at the time was the all-time leader in assists. He played professional basketball in Argentina for four years.

Luke Griffin, St. Mary's, 1976 Nicknamed "Cool Hand Luke," after the Paul Newman character in the movie of the same name, Luke Griffin was just that as the 6'0" guard led St. Mary's to great success and a Parochial C state championship in 1975. Griffin's playmaking was a key factor in his selection to All-County First Team in his junior and senior seasons. Continuing his career to St. Joseph's (PA), Griffin played in 107 games for the Hawks and averaged nearly five assists per game while scoring 7.4 points a game for a career total of 797 points. His 523 career assists still ranks third all-time, and the Hawks also made it to the NIT in Griffin's senior year.

Mike O'Koren, Hudson Catholic, 1976 Mike O'Koren and Jim Spanarkel put Hudson Catholic basketball on the map, leading the Hawks to the HCIAA title in 1974-75. The following year, with Spanarkel graduated, O'Koren led Hudson to the Parochial A championship. At the University of North Carolina, he was named to the

Jim Boylan

Mike O'Koren

Jim Spanarkel

All-ACC and All-NCAA Tournament Teams. He was a three-time First Team All-America and a first- round draft pick of the Nets. He played eight years in the NBA as well as 11 seasons as an NBA assistant coach.

Albio Sires, Memorial, 1970 On his way to scoring a career total of 1,130 points, Albio shot his jump shot over every possible defense in compiling a 25.7 average. Sires hooped in double figures every game his senior year, had highs of 43 and 40 and was a strong force under the boards. After three varsity seasons at St. Peter's, the Cuban-born Sires eventually became the 1st Hispanic mayor of West New York and then moved on a political fast track as Speaker of the N.J. Assembly and 8 terms in the U.S. House of Representatives before returning to his prior and current position as mayor.

Jim Spanarkel, Hudson Catholic, 1975 Jim Spanarkel earned honor after honor at Hudson Catholic: All-State in both basketball and baseball and All-America in basketball as a senior. The honors continued at Duke University. In his final two seasons there, he was named team MVP, All-ACC, All-America and Academic All-America and was a baseball letter winner. In his junior year, he sparked Duke to the Final Four. After his five season NBA career, Spanarkel has enjoyed success in his dual role as stockbroker at Merrill Lynch and TV color commentator with CBS and Fox.

Darryl Strickland, Ferris, 1976 Darryl Strickland was a First Team All-County player for Ferris in 1976. The 6'4" Strickland was a top-notch defender and one of the most athletic wings of his time in his senior year, averaging 21 points per game with 14 rebounds per game. After playing one year at Fairfield University, he averaged 10.8 points per game in two seasons at Rutgers.

Kerry Walker, Dickinson, 1970 One of Dickinson High School's greatest players, Kerry Walker was a First Team All-County player in 1970 after getting Honorable Mention honors the year prior. He scored 321 points in his senior year, second in the South Hudson scoring race. During his three years at Boston University, he averaged, a consistent 17.5, 17.3 and 17.3 points per game.

Mel Weldon, Ferris, 1970 Regarded as one of the "quickest players to ever play in Hudson County," Mel Weldon led Ferris High School in scoring for two years and was a First Team All-County and Honorable Mention All-State selection. After winning an NJCAA National Championship at Mercer County Community College and earning tournament MVP, he was a three year starter at Boston College, where he made First Team All-New England and was later inducted into the college's Hall of Fame. After graduation, he played professional basketball in Venezuela.

Rafael Addison, Snyder, 1982 Rafael Addison didn't become a varsity starter at Snyder H.S. until his junior year, and in his senior year went from starter to star. He made All-County that year and led the Tigers to the Section 1, Group IV title. An outstanding shooter and solid all-around player at Syracuse, he scored 1,876 points and earned Big East 1st team honors in 1985 and later was named to Syracuse's All Century Team. Addison went on to play six seasons in the NBA and five seasons in Europe (Italy/Greece).

Robert Arnold, Bayonne, 1986 A dominating inside scorer and rebounder for Bayonne, Robert Arnold made the jump from Honorable Mention in 1984 to earning First Team All-County honors in 1985 and 1986. As a junior in 1985, Arnold helped the Bees to the runner-up position in the Hudson County finals. "Most ferocious offensive rebounder we ever coached," says then-assistant coach Phil Baccarella, who assisted head coach Arnie Levan. "He had a motor that never stopped. Excellent offensively from 15 feet and in. Led by example and held teammates accountable. Overall one of the top five players Arnie (head coach for over two decades) ever coached. He dominated physically every opponent he went up against." Arnold played briefly for a junior college in Maryland.

Jerome Bash, Ferris, 1987 Although he stood only 6'2", Bash was probably one of, if not the best, offensive rebounders for his size in Hudson County history. He used his quickness and amazing leaping ability to sometimes capture two or three offensive rebounds in one trip down the floor. After making All-County Honorable Mention in 1985, he made the jump to consecutive All-County First Team honors in 1986 and 1987. He led Ferris to back-to-back county championships in 1985 and 1986. In addition to his rebounding prowess, Bash was also a fine defensive player, who held many opponents under 40 points per game during his three varsity seasons.

Terry Dehere, St. Anthony, 1989 After a stellar career at St. Anthony HS, Terry Dehere led Seton Hall in scoring all four of his years with 2,494 points and, to this day, continues to be the program's leading scorer. He led the team to three NCAA Tournament appearances and two Big East Tournament championships. The All-American player had a big year in 1993, earning Big East Player of the Year, Big East Tournament Most Outstanding Player and the Haggerty Award winner. Dehere, the 13th pick in the Draft by the Clippers, played six seasons in the NBA with the three teams as well as two seasons in Germany.

Shelton Gibbs, Snyder, 1981 Not only one of Snyder High School's all-time greats, Shelton helped lead his Jersey City school to "one of the most consistently successful public school programs of the decade." His career at St. Peter's was equally successful. In 111 games with the Peacocks, Gibbs averaged 15.2 points, 3.9 rebounds, and 1.6 assists, shooting 52.4% from the field. He scored a total of 1,688 points. He was a 1991 inductee into the St. Peter's College Hall of Fame. As the basketball coach at his alma mater, Snyder has consistently been the most successful Jersey City public school team over the past 25 years.

Bobby Hurley, St. Anthony, 1989 Bobby Hurley led the Friars to four consecutive Parochial B state titles and in his senior year helped earn the team a national No. 1 ranking. At Duke, he was a First Team All-America and helped lead the Blue Devils to back-to-back national championships, earning Final Four Outstanding Player honors in 1992. Hurley set the NCAA record in assists – a mark that currently still stands (1,076). He was the seventh pick of the first round by the Sacramento Kings, but an automobile accident cut short his NBA career. Currently, he is the head coach at Arizona State, which recorded two wins in the 2023 NCAA Tournament.

Mandy Johnson, St. Anthony, 1981 Known for his outstanding work ethic, Mandy Johnson was one in a long string of outstanding point guards at St. Anthony and a first of four-year starters in the Hurley tenure. He was a two-time First Team All-State player, scoring 1,875 points in his career and leading the team to two NJSIAA Parochial B State championships. At Marquette, Johnson scored a total of 1,126 points while leading the team to two NCAA tournament appearances.

Rafael Addison

Terry Dehere

Shelton Gibbs

Pat Laguerre, St. Mary's, 1985   A star in both baseball and basketball at St. Mary's High School, Pat Laguerre, after leading St. Mary's to a Hudson County Tournament basketball championship, played four years at Division 1 Jacksonville University. He has become one of the most successful high school baseball coaches in New Jersey, winning more than 400 games at St. Peter's Prep.

Ed Lawson, St. Peter's, 1983   A First Team All-County selection as a junior in 1982 and a Second Team pick in 1983, Ed Lawson became St. Peter's Prep's fifth 1,000-point scorer (1,098) when he finished his career. The 6'2" guard still ranks seventh all-time in scoring at Prep and is one of only twelve 1,000-point scorers at the school. At Manhattan College, he accumulated 1,049 career points and still remains the school's assist leader (447) and second all-time for steals. He is the only player in program history with over 1,000 points, 400 assists and 200 steals.

Ed Nierstedt, Hudson Catholic, 1981   A smart, outstanding point guard, Nierstedt enjoyed an outstanding career at Hudson Catholic as he scored 1,000+ points on his way to being selected Second Team All-County in 1980 and First Team as a senior in 1981. Nierstedt then took his all-around basketball skills to the College of Charleston, which he helped lead to the NAIA Championship in 1983. College of Charleston, which now plays as an NCAA Division 1 school, also won District 6 championships in 1985 and 1986, and Nierstedt was named MVP at the 1986 tournament. He finished his career at Charleston ninth all-time in assists (389).

David Rivers, St. Anthony, 1984   Another great point guard from St. Anthony, David Rivers had a standout career at Notre Dame, where he averaged 17.4 points, 3.3 rebounds, and 5 assists a game, shooting 44.2% from the field and 81.3% from the line. A two-time All-American, Rivers scored a total of 2,058 points as he led Notre Dame to four NCAA tournament appearances. In the 1988 NBA Draft, he was selected in the first round by the Los Angeles Lakers. He played in the league for several years before taking his game to Europe, where he played with multiple teams headlined by his time with the Greek League's Olympiacos. In the 1996–97 season, he was named EuroLeague Final Four MVP averaging 27 points per game in the two games.

Clarence Richardson, Snyder, 1981   Competing for one of the most dominant boys basketball programs in Hudson County in the 70's and 80's, Clarence Richardson played alongside two of the county's best players during his era in Rafael Addison and Shelton Gibbs. "Boo-Bee" earned First Team All-County honors as a senior in 1981 by virtue of the team's overwhelming 68-47 victory over North Bergen in the county championship. He was famously known for his backboard-shattering dunk against Paterson Eastside in the state tournament at Snyder High School. The game was halted because of a lack of a replacement backboard and resumed the next day with Snyder winning the game at Dickinson.

Jerry Walker   *Ed Lawson*

Jerry Walker, St. Anthony, 1989 Jerry Walker was one of the greatest big men to come out of St. Anthony High School and started every game in his four seasons there, helping the team to four consecutive state titles and a 115-5 record. At Seton Hall, he scored more than 1,000 points and was Big East Defensive Player of the Year in 1993 and a two-time All-Big East honoree. He currently serves as a Hudson County commissioner and founded "Team Walker," which provides academic and recreational activities to inner-city kids in Jersey City.

Kenny Wilson, St. Anthony, 1985 Teamed with David Rivers to form one of Hudson's most formidable guard duos, Kenny Wilson is another of the great St. Anthony point guards and a two-time First Team All-County player. In the absence of Rivers in the 1983-84 season, Wilson led St. Anthony in the state championship game. He continues to be Villanova's all-time leader in assists with 627 and also scored 1,390 career points. He helped lead the Wildcats to 80 wins over his four years, and he earned All-Southeast Regional honors in 1988, when Villanova made it to the Elite Eight in the NCAA tournament.

Derrick Alston, Hoboken, 1990 After a stellar career at Hoboken High School, Derrick Alston, a 6-10 power forward/center went to Duquesne where he scored 1,903 points and pulled down 879 rebounds. He was inducted into the Duquesne University Sports Hall of Fame. He played in the NBA for three seasons and overseas in Turkey, Spain, France, Russia, New Zealand and Argentina from 1994-2012. Later, Alston kicked-off a coaching career as an assistant with the Houston Rockets followed by the Westchester Knicks (G League). Recently, he was named the head coach of Montreal Alliance in the Canadian Elite Basketball League.

Rick Apodaca, North Bergen, 1999 One of North Bergen High School's all-time greats, Apodaca was a 2,000-point scorer, surpassing Bill Raftery's long-time record in 1999. He currently holds the county record for Hudson boys scoring. At Hofstra under Hall of Fame coach Jay Wright, he scored 1,422 points in his collegiate career. He played pro basketball internationally for 15 seasons and was a member of the Puerto Rican National Team from 2002 to 2008.

Delvon Arrington, St. Anthony, 1996 Another great St. Anthony point guard, Delvon Arrington led the Friars to an 81-1 record and three consecutive Tournament of Champions titles, and he was named MVP of that tournament in his senior year and a starter on the team that earned the USA Today National Championship. After a great career at Florida State from 1998-2002, where he continues to be the all-time assist leader (688), he played pro ball in Europe and the Dominican Republic.

Rashon Burno, St. Anthony, 1996 Rashon Burno was part of two national championship teams during his time at St. Anthony, and he was named MVP of the Tournament of Champions in 1996 after setting a tournament record of 10 steals. In college, he was a member of DePaul University's 2000 NCAA Tournament squad, and later, he moved up the ranks from a high school coach to an assistant college coach before being named to his first head coaching job at Northern Illinois University, where he currently is beginning his third season.

Antwan Dasher, Marist, 1991 An outstanding scorer for Marist, the 6'3" guard was a member of three consecutive county teams that qualified for the county titles (1989-1991), winning two in 1989 and 1991. Taking his talents to Fairleigh Dickinson, Dasher was an immediate star during the 1992-93 season, averaging 15 points per game (eighth in the Northeast Conference), and followed up that season by averaging 16.9 as a junior (seventh in the NEC) and 17.6 (sixth in the NEC) during his senior seasons. He was also fourth in the NEC in assists (4.7 a game) in 1993-94 and made first-team all-NEC. Dasher finished with a career total of 1,299 points, making 48 percent of his two-point attempts.

John Giraldo, Marist, 1992 One of the greatest players to attend Marist High School, John Giraldo led his

his school to their only Parochial State B Championship in 1992. He was named to Monmouth University's Hall of Fame, where he was a two-time First-Team All-Northeast Conference selection and graduated tied for the all-time scoring leader with 1,749 points, as well as holding several other team records. He led Monmouth to its first ever NEC Tournament Championship and NCAA Tournament appearance in 1996. After college, he played overseas from 1996 to 2005. The guard played in Venezuela, Portugal, Germany, Argentina and Colombia, where he was a three-time MVP.

Jack Gordon, St. Peter's Prep, 1992 At the time of his graduation, Jack Gordon was the leading scorer in Prep history with 1,603 points. Gordon earned First Team All-County honors in his junior and senior years and was named the Hudson Dispatch Player of the Year in 1992 as he led the Marauders to their first South Hudson championship since 1979. He continued his career at Monmouth University where he played on the first team in school history to reach the NCAA Tournament. By the time he graduated Monmouth, he had climbed into Monmouth's top-10 in career points (1,096), rebounds (437), assists (709) and steals (150). Currently residing in Miami, he serves as a managing member of Next Level Aviation.

Roy Hairston, Snyder, 1991 Roy Hairston won championships at every level, starting with one at Snyder High School in 1990, a 1993-94 junior college championship at Hutchinson Community College in Kansas and back-to-back Big Ten titles at Purdue University. He was National Junior College Player of the Year in 1994 at Hutchinson and was named to the NJCAA Hall of Fame. Upon leaving Purdue, he enjoyed a career playing overseas, and then forged a career in coaching. He has been an assistant with Iowa Energy in the NBA D-League as well as Marion University, University of Indianapolis and Division I IUPUI.

Roscoe Harris, Marist, 1992 Marist High School's Roscoe Harris was one of five Hudson County players to amass 2,000 points during his career at the Bayonne school and graduated as the school's all-time leading scorer with a total of 2,051 points. He led his team to win multiple HCIAA titles and the 1992 NJSIAA Parochial B state crown. Harris went on to play three years at Villanova University before transferring to Rowan University in 1996, where he led the team to the NCAA Division III national championship.

Danny Hurley, St. Anthony, 1991 Danny Hurley's career at St. Anthony was highlighted by leading the team to a 31-1 record and No. 2 national ranking as a senior. Out with an injury for his entire sophomore season, he scored 1,000 points in slightly more than two seasons and also earned the MSG Tri-State Player of the Year Award. A standout point guard at Seton Hall, he scored 1,000 points as he teamed with Terry Dehere and Jerry Walker in capturing the 1993 Big East Tournament and regular season championships. His coaching career has skyrocketed from Wagner to URI to UConn, where he most notably led the Huskies to their fifth national championship last April.

Rick Apodaca

Rashon Burno

Ray Lucas, Harrison, 1991 The finest all-around athlete in the history of Harrison High School, Ray Lucas was a football and basketball star, who led the Blue Tide to an NJSIAA North Jersey Section I, Group I Championship in football, while scoring 2,191 points in his basketball career – one of six Hudson male players to do so. Lucas passed on NCAA Division I basketball scholarship offers and instead opted for football. He had a distinguished career at Rutgers and in the NFL (Patriots, Dolphins and Jets). Later, he became a broadcaster and studio analyst on the Jets for SNY as well as a color analyst for Rutgers Football Radio Network. In 2021, he returned to his former high school as a football coach.

Roshown McLeod, St. Anthony, 1993 Roshown McLeod led St. Anthony to two state titles. After attending St. John's he transferred to Duke his sophomore season and averaged 15.3 points and 5.6 rebounds per game. He was named First Team All-ACC and honorable mention All-America in his senior year. He was drafted in the first round by the Atlanta Hawks, but his career ended after four seasons because of an injury.

Anthony Perry, St. Anthony, 1997 One of very few players in Hudson County history to be named All-County in all four seasons and another St. Anthony great, Anthony Perry was a McDonald's All-American and one of the most highly recruited players in the country. The all-time leading scorer (1,925 points) in St. Anthony's illustrious basketball history, Perry played on three-straight St. Anthony Tournament of Champions teams. He led Georgetown in scoring his freshman year, but injuries slowed him down after that. The 6-3 guard recorded a total of 950 points in his collegiate career.

Rodrick Rhodes, St. Anthony, 1992 Rodrick Rhodes led St. Anthony to three state titles in 1989, 1990 and 1991 and was a McDonald's All-American. He scored 1,209 points at Kentucky, leading the Wildcats to the 1992 Holiday Festival Championship at MSG, where he was selected MVP as a freshman. After transferring to USC, Rhodes was selected in the first round by the Houston Rockets. He played three seasons in the NBA and later enjoyed a successful career overseas.

Jalil Roberts, St. Anthony, 1993 Another St. Anthony great, Jalil Roberts was named First Team All-County in 1992 and 1993 as well as First Team All-State. He scored a tournament record of 44 points in the Torrey Pines Invitational championship based in California, which earned him tournament MVP honors. The 6'4" guard played at both Wisconsin and Seton Hall in a total of 39 collegiate games.

Jason Roberts, St. Mary's, 1994 Jason Roberts was one of the best players to come out of St. Mary's High School. He was First Team All-County two years in a row in 1993 and 1994. He went on to Wagner University, where he was a four-year starter. In 106 games, he averaged 8.7 points, 3.3 rebounds, and 1.1 assists, shooting 37.8% from the field, 31% from three, and 71.4% from the line, scoring a total of 923 points.

Wilmer Torres, Union Hill, 1997 Wilmer Torres graduated as Union Hill's all-time leading scorer with a career total of 1,931 points. After making Honorable Mention All-County as a freshman, he made First Team All-County his remaining three seasons, led the county in scoring his sophomore and junior years and was All-State his senior year. An ankle injury cut short his college career at Rutgers-Newark.

Donnell Williams, Marist, 1993 Based on his proficiency as one of the best deep shooting big men in county history, Donnell Williams was named to the First Team All-County squad in back-to-back years in 1992 and 1993 and was a member of the Parade Magazine All-America Team in 1993. In 111 games with Seton Hall, the 6'7" forward averaged 11.6 points, 4.7 rebounds, and 1.3 assists. Williams scored a total of 1,289 points in his collegiate career.

David Bullock, St. Anthony, 2006 Bullock was proof of how looks could be deceiving as the 6-foot-0 guard set the tone with his physicality. The Star-Ledger's Hudson County Player of the Year in 2006, Bullock averaged 11.5 points, 6.9 rebounds and 2.9 steals per game for a young Friars squad that won 25 games. As a junior, he led the team in rebounds (seven per game), steals (four) and blocks (three) in addition to averaging nine points per game for a 21-6 St. Anthony team.

Eddie Castellanos, Hoboken, 2006 The definition of a floor general, Castellanos' arrival produced arguably the best era in the history of Hoboken basketball. In 2005, he was the Star-Ledger's Hudson County Player of the Year his junior season, capped off by a brilliant 25 points, seven assists and seven steals in HCIAA Seglio final. A year later, the Redwings again were Seglio champs with Castellanos scoring his 1,000th point in the win. Castellanos had 1,029 points and 610 assists in three seasons before a solid career at Stony Brook University.

Dominic Cheek, St. Anthony, 2009 A gifted athlete, this 6-foot-6 swingman made difficult plays look effortless. As a junior, Cheek averaged 12.3 points and seven rebounds per game on the Friars' 32-0 Tournament of Champions team. As a senior, despite a nagging knee injury, averaged 14.1 points per game. Both seasons saw Cheek selected as an All-State, First Team selection by The Star-Ledger and a McDonald's All-American. Cheek went on to play at Villanova.

Donald Copeland, St. Anthony, 2002 Copeland was the defensive stopper of the Friars' famed three-headed monster at guard alongside Elijah Ingram and Dwayne Lee. The 5-foot-10 guard hit the winning basket – a baseline jumper with 3:30 left in St. Anthony's 2001 Tournament of Champions finals win over Shabazz. Copeland had 10 points that game and 16 the following year in the TOC final against Neptune. An All-State, First Team selection by The Star-Ledger as a senior, he averaged 14.3 points, five assists and four steals per game. Copeland played at Seton Hall and, after a nine-year international pro career, returned to the area to coaching. In 2022, he was hired as the head coach at Wagner.

Jiovanny Fontan, St. Anthony, 2008 On a Friars team that had perhaps the greatest and deepest collection of ball-handling guards in Hudson County history, it was Fontan who served as the primary point guard and floor general. The 5-foot-10 guard earned All-State, Third Team honors by both The Star-Ledger and Associated Press for his steady hand with an electrifying St. Anthony team that finished No. 1 in the country. In college, Fontan showed he was more than a distributor, averaging 15.3 points per game to earn Atlantic 10 Freshman of the Year honors at Fordham. Fontan transferred to USC after his sophomore season and started 56 games for the Trojans.

Elijah Ingram, St. Anthony, 2002 One of just seven players to ever be a four-year starter at St. Anthony, this 5-foot-11 guard is on the short-list of top point guards in the storied program's history. Ingram led the Friar to back-to-back Tournament of Champions titles in 2001 and 2002, both seasons saw Ingram named All-State, First Team by both The Star-Ledger and Associated Press. A McDonald's All-American and the 2002 Gatorade State Player of the Year, Ingram scored 1,333 points over his college career at St. John's and New Mexico State.

Tymel Jackson, Lincoln, 2008 A 6-foot-0 guard, this sharp-shooter keyed Lincoln's incredible 2008 state championship run, averaging 20 points per game in the state tournament, including a game-high 23 in the Group 2 final against Collingswood for the Lions' first state title. Jackson made 69 3-pointers that season as he averaged 16.7 points, 5.2 rebounds and 3.8 steals per game. A key cog in the Lincoln's 2007 Coviello championship team as well averaging 12.4 points, 7.4 rebounds and 4.9 steals per game. A three-year starter, Jackson scored 1,203 points with 490 rebounds and 390 steals.

Dwyane Lee, St. Anthony, 2002 A part of the three-head monster at guard that led the Friars to back-to-back Tournament of Champions titles, Lee had one of the biggest defensive plays in program history when, with 0.7 seconds left, knocked away Devonne Giles' potential game-winning shot out of bounds as St. Anthony held on for a 48-47 win over Shabazz in the TOC final in 2001. A year later Lee earned All-State, Third Team honors when he averaged 12.6 points, five rebounds and four assists per game. Lee, a member of St. Joseph's 2004 Elite Eight team, is currently an assistant at George Washington.

Linoll Mercedes, Bayonne, 2006 This 6-foot-5 center was one of the state's top rim protectors and a defensive anchor for the Bees. Despite playing just two seasons for Bayonne, Mercedes graduated as the program's career blocks leader with 229, highlighted by 10 against Plainfield in the North 2, Group 4 semifinals. A two-time All-Hudson, First Team selection by The Jersey Journal, he averaged 13 points, 10 rebounds and five blocks per game for the 23-4 Bees. As a junior, his 13 points, 10 rebounds and three blocks per game helped lead Bayonne to HCIAA Coviello Tournament title.

Derrick Mercer, St. Anthony, 2005 Of all the tough point guards to come through the doors of St. Anthony, this 5-foot-7 Jersey City product might have been the toughest. A three-year starter, Mercer successfully ran the Friars' offense, while also being one of the state' top defenders. Mercer was an All-State, Second Team selection as a senior, averaging 11 points and five assists per game. He was the defensive specialist on the undefeated 2004 TOC champion team immortalized in the book "The Miracle of St. Anthony" and averaged nine points per game. Mercer went to American University where he led the Eagles to back-to-back Patriot League titles. In 2009 he was named Patriot League Player of the Year and an All-American, Honorable Mention by the AP.

Daquan Pettiford, Lincoln, 2009 The interior complement to Tymel Jackson, this tandem powered Lincoln to a Group 2 championship in 2008. Pettiford, a 6-foot-3 slasher, who played above the round, averaged 21.3 points and 8.5 rebounds per game during that state tournament run, highlighted by a 34 point, 10 rebound outburst against Englewood in the Group 2 semifinals. Pettiford averaged 19.2 points and 9.9 rebounds that season. The next year, as a senior, he led the county in scoring at 20.4 points per game, while also averaging 12.8 rebounds and 3.6 steals per game. Pettiford finished his career with 1,325 points.

Steve Richardson, Dickinson, 2000 This hard-nosed point guard set the tone on both ends of the floor for arguably the greatest team in Rams history. In addition to being a stellar defender, Richardson, The Star-Ledger's 2000 Hudson County Player of the Year, averaged 14 points, six rebounds and four assists per game for the 25-4 Rams. In the North 1, Group 4 final, the guard scored six of his 10 points in the fourth quarter and added six assists and five steals to defeat Memorial just days after scoring 20 points to lead Dickinson to its first HCIAA title in 25 years.

Brian Robinson

Donald Copeland

Terrence Roberts

Terrence Roberts, St. Anthony, 2003 Roberts showed uncommon quickness for a 6-foot-9 forward/center. That frame also was key in him shouldering the load for a young Friars squad in 2003 when he averaged 18 points, 11.5 rebounds, three steals and three blocks per game, earning him All-State, First Team by The Associated Press and a spot on Parade Magazine's All-American, Fourth Team. A year earlier, Roberts aeraged 10.1 points and eight rebounds per game as the interior presence of St. Anthony's Tournament of Champions title team. Roberts had 963 points and 717 rebounds at Syracuse.

Brian Robinson, St. Peter's Prep, 2001 This skilled big man made his presence felt in the paint, but according to his head coach Joe Macchi his passing was what helped set him apart. The 6-foot-7 center averaged 15 points, 12 rebounds and three blocks per game his senior season to lead the Marauders to the Coviello title, the program's first HCIAA championship since 1963. As a junior, Robinson averaged 15 points, 10 rebounds and two blocks per game as St. Peter's Prep made the Non-Public, North A final.

Farod Robinson, Lincoln, 2007 Nicknamed "Mr. Triple-Double" Robinson was named The Star-Ledger's Hudson County Player of the Year his senior season when he averaged 13.8 points, 10.4 rebounds 7.1 assists and 5.5 steals per game for the 23-5 Lions. Termed a "power guard" by head coach Troy Smith, the 6-foot-1, 195-pound Robinson had 12 points and 13 rebounds in the HCIAA Coviello final to give Lincoln's its first title since 1980. A 1,000-point scorer, two-time All-Hudson County selection by The Jersey Journal, Robinson led the county in steals his junior season.

Mike Rosario, St. Anthony, 2008 Blessed with a deadeye outside shot matched only by his non-stop work ethic and efficiency in transition, Rosario was the engine of a Friars offense that was one of the best in the program's storied history. As a senior, he averaged a team-best 18 points per game, leading St. Anthony to its 10th Tournament of Champions title in 2008 and earned Rosario Star-Ledger State Player of the Year and McDonald's All-American honors. After starting his college career at Rutgers, Rosario transferred to Florida and started 36 games for the Gators' 2013 Final Four team.

Manny Suriel, Emerson/Memorial, 2002 A feared outside shooter, Suriel won sectional titles at two different schools in a stellar career. In his one season at Memorial, the 6-foot-2 guard averaged 18 points per game to lead the Tigers to a North 1,Group 4 title, its first section title in 28 years, and earn Third Team, All-State honors by the Associated Press. A three-time All-Hudson First Team selection by The Jersey Journal, Suriel burst onto the scene his sophomore year when he averaged 12.4 points to help lead Emerson to the North 1, Group 3 title and the HCIAA final. He averaged 15.1 points per game as a junior, making 50-percent of his 3-point attempts.

Tyshawn Taylor, St. Anthony, 2008 Taylor's above the rim athleticism and 6-foot-6 wingspan allowed him to thrive on both ends of the court for St. Anthony. A key cog on a Friars team which went 32-0 and ranked No. 1 in the country, Taylor averaged 10 points and five assists per game while also serving as St. Anthony's defensive stopper to earn First Team, All-State honors by the Associated Press. Taylor had 1,580 points and 575 assists as a four-year starter at Kansas, leading the Jayhawks to the NCAA Tournament final his senior year and played two seasons with the Brooklyn Nets.

David Vega, Memorial, 2001 A 6-foot-6 wing who could light up the scoreboard from all areas of the court, Vega was a Second Team, All-State selection for the Tigers in 2001, averaging 19 points, six rebounds and four assists per game, while being capable of playing any position on the floor. As a junior Vega averaged 12 points, eight rebounds and five assists per game to help lead Memorial to the North 1, Group 4 final and its best record since 1974. Vega later played at Felician University and professionally in Venezuela and Puerto Rico.

Marcus Williams, St. Anthony, 2004 As documented in Adrian Wojnarowski's famed book "The Miracle of St. Anthony" the 2004 Friars team lacked the marquee go-to player of past versions, but what they did have was a 6-foot-2 swingman, whose versatility, toughness and leadership proved paramount. Whether it was playing inside against much larger foes or chasing down guards on the perimeter, Williams was equally comfortable in both roles.

A member of three TOC teams, Williams was a First Team, All-State selection and Hudson County Player of the Year as a senior after averaging 13 points and 11 rebounds per game while playing all five positions for the 30-0 Friars. After a stint in junior college, Williams was a two-year starter at St. Francis (NY).

Travon Woodall, St. Anthony, 2008 The 2008 Friars would not have gone undefeated if not for Woodall's maturity and selflessness by coming off the bench after starting the previous two years. The overqualified sixth man did a bit of everything, capable of playing the point, scoring and playing big defense that season, earning All-State, Third Team honors by The Associated Press. A rare four-year varsity player at St. Anthony, Woodall went on to play at Pittsburgh, where he scored 1,108 points with 580 assists.

Noel Allen, North Bergen, 2010 This 6-foot-5 power forward terrorized opponents in the paint, scoring 30+ points in six-straight games in 2010. Named the Tri-County Division A Player of the Year, his senior year, Allen averaged 24 points and 15 rebounds per game to lead the Bruins to a 21-5 record and a trip to the Hudson County Tournament final. A two-time All-Hudson, First Team selection by The Star-Ledger, Allen averaged 18 points and 13 rebounds per game as a junior.

Kyle Anderson, St. Anthony, 2012 On the shortlist of greatest players to ever wear a Friars uniform, this 6-foot-8 point-forward's do-everything game propelled St. Anthony to a 65-0 record in his time at the school. Anderson was a two-time All-State, First Team selection by The Star-Ledger and in 2013 was named New Jersey Player of the Year as well as a Parade All-American. That season he led St. Anthony in points (14.7 per game), rebounds (6.5), assists (3.9) and blocks (2.0) to lead the Friars to a second-straight Tournament of Champions title. Nicknamed "Slow Mo" for his methodical pace on the floor, Anderson starred at UCLA and is set to begin his 10th NBA season, a career that has included stops at San Antonio, Memphis and Minnesota.

Nassir Barrino, Hudson Catholic, 2015 Barrino's relentless effort on the defensive end allowed him to make an instant impact for the Hawks. A skill slasher and distributor, this 6-foot-0 combo guard scored 1,089 points with 283 rebounds, 280 assists and 211 steals. Barrino won four Hudson County titles during his time at Hudson Catholic and was the leading scorer on the 2014 and 2015 title teams, averaging 14.2 points per game during those two years. He started 14 games in one season at the University of San Diego before his career was cut short due to a knee injury.

Tyrek Battle-Holley, Dickinson, 2018 One of best offensive talents to ever come out of Dickinson, this 6-foot-2 guard graduated as the program's career scoring leader with 1,608 points. A skilled slasher, Battle-Holley averaged 21.2 points, 9.2 rebounds, 3.9 assists and 3.0 steals per game his senior season. As a junior, he averaged 21.1 points, 8.4 rebounds and 5.0 assists per game. After two years of junior college, Battle-Holley became the first Ram to sign a scholarship in two decades when he finished his career at Bloomfield College.

Josh Brown, St. Anthony, 2013 For decades, St. Anthony was defined by its suffocating defense and few guards were better on that end of the floor than Brown. His 6-foot-3, 180-pound frame and physicality allowed him to match up with the opposing team's top player regardless of position. A key role player on the Fariars' 2011 and 2012 Tournament of Champions teams, this defensive stopper took on a lead role his senior year, averaging 15.0 points, six rebounds, four assists, three steals and two blocks a game to earn All-State, First Team honors by The Star-Ledger and lead St. Anthony to a North Jersey, Non-Public B title. Brown went on to play at Temple, posting 927 points and 389 assists.

Reggie Cameron, Hudson Catholic, 2013 Hudson Catholic's fortunes immediately changed with the arrival of Cameron and Kavon Stewart following the closure of Paterson Catholic in 2010. Cameron, a 6-foot-8 sharpshooter, made 245 3-pointers in three seasons and graduated as the program's second leading career scorer with 1,792 points. A two-time All-State selection, Cameron averaged 20.1 points and 10 rebounds per game in 2012 to lead the Hawks to their first county title in 37 years. The next year, Cameron was a First Team, All-State honoree after averaging 22.4 points and 7.7 rebounds per game before going on to play at Georgetown.

R.J. Cole, St. Anthony, 2017   The last of a long line of All-State, First Team guards, Cole led a young Friars squad to a Non-Public, North B final in 2017, averaging 21.4 points in what turned out to be St. Anthony's last year. This crafty, lefty, was a Third-Team, All-State selection as a junior when he averaged 10 points per game as the Friars went 32-0 and won the Tournament of Champions.The 6-foot-1 Cole averaged 22.5 points per game at Howard before transferring to UConn. Playing for fellow St. Anthony great Dan Hurley, Cole was a First Team, All-Big East selection in 2022.

Isiah Dasher, Ferris, 2017   At Ferris, this 6-foot-4 guard was one of the state's best kept secrets. Over his junior and senior seasons, Dasher scored 1,064 points in just 46 games (23.1 points per game), averaging 6.6 rebounds and 3.8 steals per game for the Bulldogs. Five years later, Dasher returned home to play for Saint Peter's University and thanks to the Peacocks' legendary NCAA Tournament run finally found himself in the spotlight, averaging 17.3 minutes per game during the run. One of the few who stayed afterwards, Dasher averaged 13 points in his final year for the Peacocks.

Myles Davis, St. Peter's Prep, 2011   A dynamic shotmaker, Davis put St. Peter's Prep on the national stage when he scored 33 points with eight 3-pointers when the Marauders defeated legendary Oak Hill at the PrimeTime Shootout in 2010. Davis earned First Team, All-State honors by The Star-Ledger that season, averaging 20.1 points and 3.6 3-pointers per game as St. Peter's Prep went 25-4 and won its first Non-Public, North A title in 26 years. Davis, who averaged 18.1 points per game as a sophomore, finished his HS career at Notre Dame Prep and went on to play at Xavier.

Jerome Frink, St. Anthony, 2012   This 6-foot-6 enforcer delivered one of the best Tournament of Champions performances in the history of the event when he had 26 points and 13 rebounds when the Friars downed Plainfield in the 2012 final. The performance capped off a First Team, All-State season for Frink. As a junior he averaged 10.3 points and 5.4 rebounds for a St. Anthony team that went 33-0 and finished ranked No. 1 in the country. Frink went on to play at Florida International and then at LIU-Brooklyn where he was named Northeast Conference Player of the Year in 2017.

Gabe Johnson, Union City, 2019   In a time where non-public powers have reigned supreme in Hudson County, this 6-foot-0 attacking guard scored one for the public schools in 2019. The 6-foot-0 guard struck for 16 points to lead the Soaring Eagles to a win over seven-time defending Hudson County champion Hudson Catholic in the semifinals. Less than 24 hours later, Johnson scored 18 of his game-high 22 points in the second half to lead Union City past Marist for its first ever county title. Johnson averaged 16.7 points per game that season, earning HCIAL Player of the Year by NJ.com as he led the Soaring Eagles to a North 1, Group 4 title.

Jahvon Quinerly

Kyle Anderson

Louis King, Hudson Catholic, 2018 A 6-foot-9 small forward capable of scoring at all three levels, King was instrumental in the Hawks winning their first sectional title in 41 years when he had 20 points and six rebounds in the North Jersey, Non-Public B final against St. Anthony as a junior. A McDonald's All-American, he was averaging 15.4 points per game before having his senior year cut short due to a knee injury. In one season at Oregon, King averaged 17 points per game during the Ducks' Pac-12 Tournament title run, then 16.3 points per game in the NCAA Tournament. King has played parts of four seasons in the NBA, suiting up for Detroit, Sacramento and Philadelphia.

Keith Lumpkin, St. Peter's Prep, 2011 Lumpkin's greatest success came in football, where he was a three-year starter at Rutgers, but on the court, this 6-foot-8 center was a force in the paint. As a freshman, Lumpkin led the Marauders to a stunning HCIAA Coviello title run as the No. 8 seed, getting 13 points and 12 rebounds in the final against Union Hill. A four-year starter in the middle, Lumpkin scored 1,057 points, which was seventh most in program history at the time of his graduation.

Myles Mack, St. Anthony, 2011 Two years at delivering a crushing upset at St. Anthony's expense, Mack came to the Friars after Paterson Catholic and delivered one of the best single seasons by a St. Anthony point guard. The 5-foot-10 speedster averaged 15.1 points, 3.6 assists and 2.9 steals per game, earning him Second Team, All-American honors by USA Today and First Team, All-State by The Star-Ledger. In arguably the biggest high school game in state history, Mack scored a team-high 19 points to lead St. Anthony past St. Patrick, 62-45, in a matchup of the nation's top two ranked teams. Mack went on to score 1,658 points at Rutgers.

Jagan Mosely, St. Anthony, 2016 The rare four-year starter at St. Anthony, Moseley's explosiveness and physicality allowed him to thrive in any role. When injuries struck the Friars' front court the 6-foot-3, 205-pound guard moved to forward and thrived there, scoring a game-high 16 points in the 2016 Non-Public B final against Roselle Catholic. Moseley earned NJ.com State Player of the Year, averaging 14.2 points per game and St. Anthony went 32-0 and won its 13th Tournament of Champions title. Moseley, who was a Second Team, All-State selection after averaging 13 points per game as a junior, scored more than 1,000 points before playing at Georgetown.

Luther Muhammad, Hudson Catholic, 2018 This 6-foot-4 guard was a tone setter with his downhill style on offense and physicality on defense. A starter on four Hudson County championship teams, Muhammad scored 30 points in the 2016 final, a season that saw him average 21.7 points and 5.6 rebounds per game to earn Second Team, All-State honors by The Star-Ledger. A year later in the Non-Public, North B final he had 15 points and six steals when the Hawks beat St. Anthony for their first section title in 41 years. Muhammad, who finished with 1,605 points, went on to play at Ohio State and Arizona State.

Jahvon Quinerly, Hudson Catholic, 2018 A showman with the ball in his hands, this point guard twice was named Gatorade's New Jersey Player of the Year. Quinerly scored a game-high 25 points when the Hawks won their first sectional title in 41 years, defeating St. Anthony in the Non-Public, North B final in 2017. That season, Quinerly averaged 20.5 points and 5.4 assists per game as a junior, then followed it up as a senior by averaging 18.5 points and 5.9 assists per game, earning First Team, All-State honors both years. A McDonald's All-American and four-time county champion, Quinerly finished with 1,789 points. After one year at Villanova, Quinerly went to Alabama and was named SEC Tournament Most Outstanding Player in 2022.

Ronald Roberts, St. Peter's Prep, 2010 Few Hudson County forwards have played with the elevation of Roberts. The 6-foot-8 forward's arrival as a junior immediately vaulted the Marauders into one the top teams in the state as he averaged 16 points and 12.8 rebounds per game in 2009. A year later, Roberts was named All-State, Third Team after averaging 19.0 points and 12.7 rebounds to lead Prep to its first Non-Public, North A title in 26 years. Roberts starred at St. Joseph's University and later signed with the Philadelphia 76ers.

Isaiah Small, Snyder, 2017 A late bloomer, Small grew from a relatively unknown guard to one of college basketball's better forwards. After growing from 6-foot-3 to 6-foot-6, Small had a breakthrough senior season for the Tigers, averaging 20.0 points, 9.2 rebounds and 3.5 blocks per game. Small, who grew to 6-foot-8 and 200 pounds while starring at Seward County Community College for two seasons, before starting 83 games over three seasons at Texas State where he averaged 9.8 points and 6.5 rebounds per game. The small forward currently plays professionally in Germany.

Kevin Walker, St. Peter's Prep, 2011   Walker's teammates might have provided the flash, but this four-year starter always provided a steady hand at the point for the Marauders. A four-time county champion, Walker averaged 17 points, 7.2 assists and 4.0 rebounds per game in a senior season highlighted by his 16 points, 12 rebounds and eight assists in the 2011 county final. The 5-foot-10 Walker was fourth on the St. Peter's Prep scoring list with 1,145 points at the time of his graduation and went on to start 105 games at Caldwell University.

Austin White, St. Peter's Prep, 2014   This 6-foot-0 combo guard with a distinctive headband could score from virtually anywhere on the court. A smooth shooter, White sank 74 3-pointers his senior season, averaging 18.2 points per game to lead the Marauders to a second-straight Non-Public, North A title and earn Third Team, All-State honors. He averaged 15.9 points per game as a junior when the Marauders won Non-Public, North A. White's 1,412 points in three seasons are third most in St. Peter's Prep history. White went on to play at High Point University.

Marvin Williams, Marist, 2011   This 6-foot-0 guard not only embraced the role of being a lead scorer, he thrived in it. As a senior, the Royal Knights made a surprising trip to the Hudson County Tournament final with Williams averaging 22.5 points in four games. Marist went 18-7 that season with Williams averaging 21 points, five rebounds and three assists per game. A two-time Conference Player of the Year selection at Marist, Williams went on to Bloomfield College and scored 1,648 points for the Bears.

Mark Armstrong, St. Peter's Prep, 2022   One of the most explosive guards ever to play in Hudson County, Armstrong rewrote the record books at St. Peter's Prep. Despite playing just 92 games due to a Covid-shortened junior season, Armstrong is the Marauders' career scoring leader with 1,776 points (19.3 per game) and was a three-time All-State selection by NJ.com. Armstrong averaged 24 points per game his senior season, earning First Team, All-State honors. As a sophomore, he averaged 20 points per game, to lead St. Peter's Prep to its first county title in nine years and the Non-Public, North A final. Armstrong, now at Villanova, represented Team USA in the FIBA U-19 World Cup in the summer of 2023.

DeAvion Ellis, North Bergen 2021   This 6-foot-2 guard seemingly glided to the basket and proved near impossible to stop at that point. As a junior in 2020, Ellis averaged 18.1 points per game, while also notching countless assists from kickouts to a host of skilled shooters, to lead the Bruins to an 18-7 record and trip to the Hudson County semifinals. A three-year starter at North Bergen, Ellis moved on to Bloomfield College and has averaged 8.1 points per game in his first two seasons at the Division 2 program.

Rayshawn Ford, St. Peter's Prep, 2021   Ford's physicality allowed him to play bigger than his 6-foot-3 height. In 2020, he averaged 19.5 points per game in the postseason as the Marauders won the Hudson County title and reached the Non-Public, North A final. Ford averaged 14.3 points and four rebounds that season and also averaged 14.3 points and four rebounds per game as a senior in the Covid-shortened 2021 season. Ford went on to play at Fairleigh Dickinson University.

Elijah Gertrude, Hudson Catholic, 2023   The name Gertrude elicits memories of some of the best scorers in Hudson County history, but this 6-foot-4 wing made his mark as one of the country's top defenders in his class. An absolute terror in transition, Gertrude averaged 14.3 points per game as a junior to help lead the Hawks to the Hudson County title in 2022. In the final against St. Peter's Prep, he and Tahaad Pettiford combined to score 15 consecutive points to give Hudson Catholic a lead it never relinquished. Gertrude, who signed to play at the University of Virginia, missed his senior season due to a torn ACL.

Shy'Heed Jenkins-Floyd, Snyder/Union City, 2022   One of the county's best on-ball defenders, Jenkins-Floyd averaged 4.1 steals per game over his varsity career and often turned those turnovers into a transition basket for himself or a teammate. A pass-first guard for most of his career, Jenkins-Floyd showed he can be a lead scorer, averaging 17.3 points his senior year to lead a young Union City team to a Hudson County semifinal. After scoring 1,025 points in high school, Jenkins-Floyd went on to play at Rutgers-Newark.

Mike Jackson, Marist/Union City, 2021 This sharpshooter's arrival from Christ the King in Newark helped elevate the Royal Knights to a higher level. Jackson was the leading scorer in both 2019 (12.0 points per game) and 2020 (15.3 per game) on Marist teams that reached the Hudson County Tournament final. After Marist's closure, the 6-foot-3 guard went to Union City, where he scored 102 points in a season shortened to just five games due to Covid. For his career, Jackson scored 1,316 points with 239 3-pointers before going to play at Montclair State.

Corey Manning-Floyd, Snyder, 2020 This 6-foot-5 wing immediately made a name for himself scoring 18 points in his first varsity game, then scoring 21 points, including a game-winning 3-pointer when the Tigers stunned Hudson Catholic five weeks later. One of the most prolific scorers to ever play for Snyder, Manning-Floyd averaged 20.3 points and 9.3 rebounds per game as a junior, then 15.7 points and 10.3 rebounds per game his senior year. For his career, Manning-Floyd had 1,462 points and 753 rebounds in 99 career game.

Keith Mency, Marist/Hudson Catholic, 2021 Mency's physicality and rugged on-ball defense would have allowed him to thrive in any era. A key component of Marist's back-to-back Hudson County finalist squads, Mency averaged 11.4 points, 3.7 assists and 2.2 steals per game his junior year. After Marist closed down, he averaged 11.9 points per game for Hudson Catholic in the Covid-shortened 2021 season. Mency took his defense and point guard skills to Division II Millersville.

Toriano Munford, Hoboken/Lincoln, 2021 At 6-foot-4, Munford could punish opponents inside, while also putting up points as a mid-range shooter. As a senior, Munford averaged 23.6 points and 8.2 rebounds per game in the Covid-shortened season, finishing with exactly 1,000 career points. Munford averaged a team-high 15.3 points per game to lead the Lions to a 20-win season with back-to-back 22-point efforts in the state tournament as a junior. He also averaged 13.2 points per game as a sophomore for Lincoln's Central, Group 2 finalist team.

Maurice Odum, Union City, 2022 An explosive offensive talent, Odum led the state in scoring in 2020, averaging 27.3 points and 5.2 assists per game. As a freshman, the 6-foot-2 guard gave a glimpse of what was to come when he averaged 13.5 points over eight playoff games when the Soaring Eagles won both the Hudson County and North 1, Group 4 tournaments. Covid limited Union City to just five games his junior year and he transferred to West Oaks Academy for his senior years. Even so, Odum, who plays at Division 1 Pacific, scored 1,127 points in just 58 games at Union City.

Tahaad Pettiford, Hudson Catholic, 2024 This left-handed guard is in complete control whenever he's running the point with the ball in his hands. Pettiford erased all doubt that he was the latest great point guard to come out of Jersey City in the 2021-22 season, when he averaged 18.4 points per game to lead Hudson Catholic to a Hudson County title. A Third Team, All-State selection by NJ.com, Pettiford stole the show in the HCT final with a 25-point effort. A knee injury limited him to just two games as a junior, but the 5-star Auburn University commit is healthy and ready for a huge senior year.

Jackson Tindall, St. Peter's Prep, 2023 This 6-foot-7 forward proved more than comfortable in the starring role, averaging 13.4 points and 7.0 rebounds per game to earn HCIAL Player of the Year his senior year and lead the Marauders to Hudson County and Non-Public, North A championships. He averaged 14 points and 10.3 rebounds in the state tournament with three double-doubles. Big state tournament performances were nothing new for Tindall, the most prominent a 16-point, 11-rebound, eight-assist outburst in a 2022 win at arch-rival Hudson Catholic.

Alice Schmidt, St. Anthony, 1975   A catalyst with the ball for St. Anthony and Montclair State's NCAA tournament semifinalist team, Schmidt was enshrined in the Halls of Fame for Hudson County and Montclair State (inducted in 1994). She went on to coach successfully at St. Dominic and St. Anthony high schools as well as New Jersey City University. In her senior year at St. Anthony, Schmidt averaged 17 points, six steals and five rebounds a game and showed a knack for passing the ball to open players for high percentage shots throughout her career.

Pat Colasurdo, Holy Family Academy, 1975   A member of the first All-County team, Colasurdo was able to dominate a game in her final three seasons of her high school career. Colasurdo finished with 1,200 career points, more than 1,000 rebounds, 500 steals and 400 blocks. In her senior year, she led Holy Family to a 24-1 season, a Section 1 state title and a North Jersey Catholic Conference championship. She was one of four Hudson County players to go on to play for Montclair State's women's basketball team in the NCAA tournament when all colleges were combined into one pool before divisions 1, 2 and 3 were established. Montclair lost in the semifinals to UCLA before winning the third-place game.

Elaine Carroll, Bayonne, 1976   A dynamic player with the ball, Carroll was Bayonne's first of many multi-year All-County selections -- a two-time pick. Carroll showed explosive speed on defense as well as on offense where she could pull up to reliably drop in short jumpers.

Jean Cutillo, Hoboken, 1976   At a time when versatility was becoming a vital part of the game, Cutillo measured up in many respects. The Hoboken High star was one of the early players from a public school to earn a reputation for her many skills in the wake of an era when parochial schools commanded most of the attention.

Cathy Meyers, St. Anthony, 1976   A force inside the lane as well as outside with her tough, aggressive style that made her one of the best rebounding guards in the county during her era in the mid-1970s. Despite her physical play, Meyers also showed quickness and agility as one of the most athletic players in her time, which made her asset when she continued her basketball career on Montclair State's Final Four team.

Pat Quilty, St. Dominic Academy, 1976   A household name in Hudson County basketball circles, Quilty was a steadying force and reliable scorer for St. Dominic Academy. She went on to be another member of Montclair State's national semifinalist team.

Lisa Gomez, Holy Family Academy, 1977   Gomez thrived in Holy Family's disciplined, system style with and without the ball as an All-County repeat choice.

Pat Lillis, St. Dominic, 1978   One of the first big scorers over the years at St. Dominic, Lillis took her high percentage shooting on to St. Peter's College where she finished with 1,202 points from 1974-1978, currently 13th on the all-time scoring list.

Sandy Smith, Holy Family Academy, 1978   The two-time All-County selection continued the legacy established by Colasurdo with Holy Family with all the tools: scoring, rebounding, assists and steals.

Robyn Venner, St. Dominic, 1978 When fans talked about St. Dominic Academy basketball, Venner was the first player's name that came up with her sound fundamentals and poise under pressure.

Diane Casella, St. Anthony, 1979 A reliably steady player for taking care of the ball, she rarely had it stolen or turned over with a bad pass while coming through consistently with scoring when it was most needed.

Carolyn Gadsden, Lincoln, 1979 Lincoln High School developed many gifted players over the years, starting with Gadsden. She used her speed to her best advantage on both ends of the floor as girls basketball was evolving in the mid-1970s from six players on a side -- two strictly on offense and two on defense and two who could cross half-court -- into a 5-on-5 full-court game. Gadsden took her skills to St. Peter's College where she currently is second on the all-time list for career scoring average at 15.5 ppg over 56 games and first in field goal percentage at 63.0.

Linda Odenwalder, Holy Family Academy, 1979 Always reliable to get results with the ball in crucial situations, Odenwalder was a proven go-to player who kept Holy Family in contention in the Hudson County league.

Sharon Ross, Bayonne, 1979 The first three-time All-County selection from Bayonne, Ross showed creativity dribbling the ball and also was selfless with her teammates despite her prolific scoring. Defensively, Ross usually guarded the best opposing player.

Diane Ashe, St. Anthony, 1980 Ashe played three different positions in four years while consistently leading St. Anthony in points, assists and steals per game. Standing at 5 feet, 7 inches in her senior season, Ashe also got her share of rebounds.

Linda Mitchell, Academy of St. Aloysius, 1980 One of the most highly regarded frontcourt players of her era, the 6 feet, 1 inch Mitchell routinely converted entry passes for points and, when she missed, often followed up on offensive rebounds. Mitchell also was a defensive presence in the paint as a shot-blocking threat.

Sharon Taylor, Snyder, 1980 Although she stood at 6 feet, 3 inches, Taylor got many of her 26 ppg on outside shots as her career blossomed in her senior year while becoming Snyder's first player to score 1,000 career points. She also was a catalyst to the start of many winning seasons for the Lady Tigers. Taylor committed to St. Peter's College.

Blanche Jones, Lincoln, 1981 One of the most feared scorers in the county in the early 1980s, Jones reached 1,000 career points by her junior season when she tallied a county record 56 points against Dickinson High School and also scored 51 against Bayonne, many coming off her raw speed and elusive moves driving to the basket. A smooth guard who averaged nearly 30 points a game and dictated tempo for the Lions, Jones also was regarded as the county leader in steals. Jones went on to a stellar career at St. Peter's College where she currently is ranked No. 3 on the school's all-time list with 1,610 points, third in scoring average at 14.7 ppg and 15th in field goal percentage at 46.8 percent.

Margaret Grierson, North Bergen, 1983 An All-County player at North Bergen High School who would finish her career as a standout on St. Anthony's high powered teams, Grierson committed to a college career at Boston College from there. Grierson was at her best running St. Anthony's up-tempo style for layups or alertly passing the ball on the break to teammates for better scoring opportunities.

Mercedes Porro, Memorial, 1983 Widely regarded as the heart and soul of Memorial teams in the early 1980s, Mercedes Porro continued the trend of some of the most memorable seasons for the Tigers in the aftermath of fellow All-Decade player Maribel Ewens's legacy. A two-time All-County selection, Porro had a knack of often spotting open teammates with sharp passes for high percentage shots. An undaunted floor general on both ends of the court, "Mercy" was merciless on defense, keeping resilient pressure on ball handlers as one of the top defenders in the county at that time while making the most of her opportunities for timely baskets on the other end to keep the Tigers in the thick of contention in the county.

Adrienne Goodson, Bayonne, 1984 Another three-time All-County player from Bayonne, Goodson was Hudson County's premiere 2,000-point scorer while becoming a consensus high school All-American who went on to become the first player from the county to play on a college women's basketball championship team. At Bayonne, the quintessentially versatile player showed deft moves dribbling the ball like a guard and seemed nearly unstoppable on the open floor while using her height and athleticism to strongly rebound on both ends like a power forward. A Hudson County Sports Hall of Fame inductee in 2012, Goodson in recent years served as assistant coach and then as director of women's basketball operations at ODU. Goodson played on ODU's 1985 NCAA National Championship team, scoring 323 points as a freshman, the seventh most by a first-year player in school history. She was a two-time All-Sun Belt performer and was named the Sun Belt Conference Player of the Year as a senior after being named Sun Belt Tournament MVP as a junior. "Goodie" ranks 11th all-time in scoring at Old Dominion (1,574 points) and had 863 rebounds. After ODU, she was the captain of the 1993 USA National Basketball team and played professionally in Brazil and the American Basketball League (ABL). In 1999, Goodson was selected by the Utah Starzz in the WNBA draft, which launched her nine-year career on four teams, highlighted by a 2002 All-Star season with the Starzz. She became only the third woman in WNBA history to score 4,000 points and grab 1,500 rebounds.

Diane Rodriguez, St. Anthony, 1984 One of the more compelling stories in Hudson County, Rodriguez excelled as a forward with a soft touch and steady ballhandling despite being diagnosed with an enlarged heart condition that was controlled with medication. Rodriguez helped St. Anthony's score often off its vaunted fast-break style.

Sheila Wall, St. Anthony, 1985 Teams would "gimmick" their defense, solely to deny Wall getting the ball at point guard where she expertly commanded St. Anthony's offense. She had a knack for turning a breakdown into a scoring opportunity and her ballhawking on defense forced many turnovers. Wall went on to LaSalle College where she currently is ranked in the top 10 in the school's all-time lists in assists (ninth with 359), steals (seventh with 188) and field goal percentage (eighth).

Alice Burgos, Harrison, 1986 The guard who could shoot with 1,815 career points, pass and rebound with the best of guards in the county, Burgos established Harrison High School not just in the Bergen County Scholastic League where it became a perennial contender with many championships while playng alongside Kutt but raised its profile around Hudson County winning tight games against a few larger enrollment, winning programs. Burgos typified Harrison's high speed approach to rate as one of the first three-time All-County selections.

Krissy Kutt, Harrison, 1986   Characterized by many basketball fans as a no-frills, blue-collar style scorer with 1,496 career points, Kutt also was a hard-nosed defender who triggered Harrison High School's quick transition game. A two-time All-County selection in the mid-1980s, Kutt also rebounded well as Harrison emerged as a perennial Group II, Section 1 contender.

Monica O'Halloran, Holy Family Academy, 1986   The disciplined player in the mold of Holy Family stars who stayed within her solid skill level to minimize mistakes. O'Halloran thrived in the "system" style of Holy Family, which rarely squandered leads when O'Halloran was on the court.

Linda Riley, Ferris, 1986   A force on the floor who was a threat with or without the ball, Riley at times carried Ferris High School's team on her back as it emerged as a perennial contender in the HCIAA into the 1990s.

Peg Ryan, Bayonne, 1988   Hudson County's prototype post player entered the Hudson County Sports Hall of Fame in 2010 as the only female inductee in that class. The three-time All-County player kept defenses on their toes while playing with her back to the basket for post-up moves off entry passes en route to 1,864 career points. The towering center also followed up many missed shots for points and pulled down defensive rebounds as the best in the county during her playing career. Ryan also was able to occasionally step out for a short jumper later in her high school career before embarking on a college career at St. Peter's where she played on two conference championship winners.

Millicent Gertrude, Dickinson, 1989   Opponents would double-team and sometimes triple-team Dickinson's first big-name player in the county whose quickness around the basket made her a constant threat when the Lady Rams had the ball. Gertrude's good shot selection and high percentage shots led to her 1,561 career points and two All-County selections at Dickinson before she played at St. Peter's College where she ranks 17th all-time in shooting percentage (46.8).

Millicent Gertrude   *Adrienne Goodson*

Robyn Algeria, Holy Family, 1990 If there was one word to describe the rock-steady Algeria, it's opportunist as she not only smoothly ran Holy Family's offense but made opponents usually regret making any mistakes that often resulted in points on the other end.

Jody Hill, Harrison, 1990 Another 2,000-point scorer at Harrison (2,098 points), Hill also recorded over 1,000 assists as she had a knack to to make her teammates raise their game, a mantra of her coach, Jack Rodgers. Hill was deadly from all over the floor and regularly hit three-point shots to rattle opposing defenses into changing coverages. After concluding her career in the 1989-90 season, Hill went on to Pace University where she was an All-Conference player with more than 1,000 career points and set a school assists record. She later was named to the Hudson County and Pace University Sports Halls of Fame.

Kim Lee, St. Anthony, 1990 Reminiscent of the flamboyant style of former NBA star Earl Monroe, St. Anthony High School's electrifying playmaker always seemed to be playing in "fast forward" as she awed fans throughout her career with her unpredictable, explosive sprints to the basket. When she missed, Lee was expert at getting to the ball for second, and even third, shot opportunities. Lee's quickness on defense forced turnovers that resulted in many of her own breakaway layups.

Consuela Davis, Snyder, 1991 A lethal inside scorer, the speedy Davis occasionally stepped out for a three-point shot while ringing up 20 points a game while leading Snyder to its greatest season ever at 21-4 and a berth in the Hudson County Interscholastic Athletic Association championship game in 1991.

Michelle Ferriero, Harrison, 1991 Very few players performed bigger than their actual height like the 5 feet, 9 inch center who was touted by coach Jack Rodgers as "the best post player in the state." She not only held down taller opposing players from scoring but outrebounded them while finishing with more than 1,000 career points (1,827) and rebounds (1,064). She led Harrison to a 25-win season, its first Group II state title in her senior year in 1991 as well as its eighth straight 20-win season and sixth straight BCSL National title.

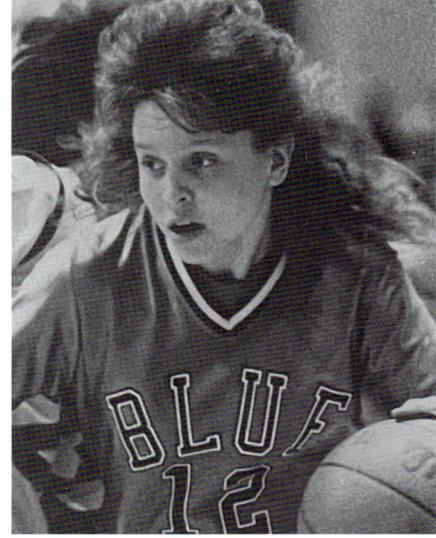

Jody Hill

Angela Zampella

Kerry Szemple, Bayonne, 1991 Another versatile athlete in the mold of Zampella, Szemple had the rare distinction of earning All-County selection in three sports: basketball (twice), softball and tennis. The tenacious, resilient player finished her career at Bayonne in the 1990-91 season on a sixth straight HCIAA championship team and a 123-game win streak in the league.

Jill Finnerty, Bayonne, 1992 Finnerty's textbook style in the pivot helped her take command in the low post but she also stepped away to drop in a number of short jumpers as Bayonne continued its dominance of the HCIAA. As a junior, she helped lead the Lady Bees to the keenly competitive NJSIAA Group IV, Section 1 championship game with Szemple and was named to the All-County team her final two years. Finnerty also played in the midfield on Bayonne's No. 2 nationally-ranked girls soccer team.

Tara Mitchell, Hoboken, 1992 The Hoboken point guard, like Lee, were both regarded as the flashiest players of their era in Hudson County along with Mitchell's fiery, demonstrative passion for the game. Mitchell's quick first step usually left defenders behind and her athletic moves often produced uncontested layups. Defensively, Mitchell not only got her share of steals but drew many charging fouls of opponents handling the ball or driving the lane. A two-time All-County selection, Mitchell jumped into the spotlight from third team All-County as a sophomore to the top five the following year and followed through with a solid senior season, averaging just under 20 ppg her last two seasons.

Tonya Gertrude, Dickinson, 1993 An emerging star who made dramatic strides each year to become a two-time All-County selection after being named to the second team as a sophomore. Gertrude continued her resurgence at St. Peter's College in the mid-1990s where her 1,186 points ranks her 14th on the all-time scoring list.

Iris Garcia, Ferris, 1995 The guard reliably responded as Ferris High School's go-to player and performed best under pressure as a three-time All-County selection. Few opponents had secure leads as Garcia would rally her team in taking the momentum -- and the heart -- out of opponents with her hustle on both ends.

Maritza Rodriguez, Ferris, 1995 When Ferris broke open a close game or was looking to rally from behind, the shifty guard was one of the best at scoring points in a hurry with her quick hands for steals or deflecting the ball from opponents into turnovers that created quick transition opportunities on the other end, many of them finished off by Rodriguez.

Candace Lloyd, St. Anthony, 1996 Lloyd's athleticism and jumping ability outperformed taller opponents and forced them to alter their shots while her sped fit ideally into St. Anthony's quick transition style.

Angela Zampella, St. Dominic Academy, 1996 Arguably the most athletically endowed player of the 1970s-1990s era, Zampella ran the show for St. Dominic Academy as a three-time All-County selection. She also played baseball for youth programs in her Hoboken hometown. At St. Dominic, Zampella not only scored and passed the ball better than anyone in her time, Zampella also was a superb defender and free throw shooter. She was nationally ranked in assists and free throw percentage when she continued her basketball career at St. Joseph's University where she was an honorable mention All-American. Zampella was only the second player at St. Joseph's to earn All-Atlantic 10 honors for all four years and ended her career as the school's all-time leader in assists.

Denene Halsey, Marist, 1997 While teammate Tara Walker sank big baskets, Halsey's consistent scoring as a complementary player kept Marist in position to win many games against top notch competition while earning two-time All-County selection.

Kim McDonough, Harrison, 1998 The first All-County player to be elected in all four of her high school seasons and an All-State selection as well as honorable mention All-American, McDonough scored a school record (for girls and boys basketball) as well as what is believed to be a county record 2,760 points. It led the state in scoring in her career that ended in the 1997-98 season. She also was a four-time all-BCSL selection before committing to a college career at St. Peter's.

Makeda Gleaton, Marist, 2001 As a 5-foot-6 center it would have been easy to overlook Gleaton, at least until the opening tip. Gleaton's toughness and explosive leaping ability allowed her to dominate much taller competition, posting 1,670 points and 955 rebounds as she and Tara Walker formed one of the greatest one-two combinations in Hudson County history. A four-time All-County selection by The Jersey Journal, Gleaton had 20 points and nine rebounds in the 2001 NJSIAA Non-Public B final to give the Royal Knights their only state title.

Ginger Quinonez, Harrison, 2001 Soccer was Quinonez's first sport initially, she didn't even play organized basketball before high school, but she left Harrison as one the greatest scorers in County history, finishing with 2,187 points and 1,108 rebounds. A 5-foot-8 guard, who relentlessly attacked the basket, Quinonez averaged 31.7 points, 12.5 rebounds and 5.0 assists per game her senior year, a season capped off by consecutive 44 point outbursts in state playoff games against Rutherford and Newton. Quinonez, an All-State, Third Team selection twice and a three-time All-County First Team honoree, played at Saint Peter's and Rutgers-Newark.

Tara Walker, Marist, 2001 A dominant force from the moment she arrived at Marist, Walker was a powerful wing, who seemingly could attack the basket whenever she wanted to. A three-time All-State selection, Walker earned All-State First Team honors as a senior when she averaged 23.1 points, 13.4 rebounds and 6.5 assists per game. That season, the Royal Knights won their only state title with Walker averaging 31.5 points, 15.8 rebounds and 5.8 assists in four games leading up to the championship. Walker, who finished with 2,376 points (third most in County history) and 1,391 rebounds, went on to play at St. John's.

Christy Altamirano

Cassandra Callaway

Lauren Jiminez

Danielle Dugan, Bayonne, 2002 A versatile 5-foot-10 wing, Dugan graduated with 1,350 points, 999 rebounds and 312 assists, but her greatest impact may have come on the defensive end. As a senior she averaged 16.8 points and 13.3 rebounds while recording 79 assists, 66 blocks a single-season school record 180 steals to earn Hudson County Player of the Year honors by The Jersey Journal in 2002. A four-time All-County selection by The Jersey Journal, Dugan helped lead the Bees to a sectional title as a freshman and a HCIAA Coviello championship her senior year.

Vanessa Vargas, Emerson, 2002 Stopping this 5-foot-7 guard proved to be an exercise in futility. As a senior, Vargas earned Third Team, All-State honors by the Associated Press after averaging 27 points per game to carry a young Bulldogs team to a winning record. She became Emerson's career scoring leader with a 46-point outburst against rival Union Hill. More than a scorer, Vargas averaged five assists, six rebounds, 4.4 steals and 18.3 points per game as a junior. She was also a star on the volleyball court, leading Emerson to an HCIAA title. Vargas went to Ramapo and remains the program's career steals leader.

Sophia Vucetaj, St. Dominic, 2002 Opposing players had to attack the basket with caution whenever this 6-foot-3 center was patrolling the paint. Vucetaj, who didn't start playing until the age of 12, burst onto the scene as a sophomore, averaging 17.3 points, 16.1 rebounds and 4.8 blocks per game in 1999. As a junior, she was named MVP of the HCIAA final after posting 18 points and 12 rebounds in the Blue Devils domination of Bayonne. Vucetaj, who tragically passed away in 2007 at the age of 24, finished her high school career with more than 1,000 points and 1,000 rebounds before playing one year at Kutztown.

Annie Cossolini, St. Dominic, 2003 From the moment she arrived at St. Dominic, this diminutive point guard was in complete control of the Blue Devils offense. As a freshman, Cossolini's eight points and seven assists helped lead SDA to its first ever county title, a 61-30 dismantling of Bayonne. A three-time All-County selection by The Jersey Journal, Cossolini had 1,273 points and 566 assists. Then, after a fine career at Mount St. Mary's, she coached McNair to a HCIAA Seglio title in 2008.

Danielle Dugan

Betty Mendieta

Corey Roesing

Beth Mayo, Bayonne, 2003 Mayo's versatility and competitiveness allowed her to thrive in any and all roles the Bees asked of her. She was an All-County First Team selection by The Jersey Journal at two different positions during her career. As a junior, she averaged 14.8 points and 11 rebounds, while setting a school record with 66 at forward. As a senior, Mayo shifted to guard and averaged 11.8 points, 6.0 rebounds and 4.2 assists per game and was named MVP of the HCIAA Coviello final as Bayonne repeated as champs .

Betty Mendieta, North Bergen, 2003 The 5-foot-6 guard made a name for herself on the defensive end of the floor, often being matched up against the other team's top scorer. The four-year starter proved to be much more than that, scoring 1,252 points. As a senior, Mendieta averaged 16.9 points, 5.7 rebounds, 5.1 assists and 4.4 steals per game to help lead the Bruins to the North 1, Group 4 final for the first time as well as the HCIAA Coviello final. Mendieta started four years at Adelphi before a long coaching career in high school and college.

Angela Fitzgerald, Marist, 2004 This 5-foot-9 forward was near impossible to defend when she drove in the lane, scoring 1,617 career points, fourth most in program history. That combination of power and quickness allowed Fitzgerald, a four-time All-County selection by The Jersey Journal, to pull down 1,047 rebounds. A starter on the Royal Knights' 2001 Non-Public B state title team, Fitzgerald was The Star-Ledger's Hudson County Player of the Year in 2004, averaging 16.2 points and 10 rebounds per game.

Jen Mayo, Bayonne, 2005 Mayo graduated from Bayonne as the school's career record holder in 3-pointers with 162. That shooting touch carried over to the foul line where she also set a school record with 213 made free throws, 10 of them coming in the fourth quarter of the Bees' North 2, Group 4 final against Irvington in 2005. A four-year starter, Mayo scored 1,165 points for her career, which saw her make The Jersey Journal's All-County First Team twice.

Naeemah Ricketts, St. Anthony, 2005 Nicknamed "Rocket" this four-year starter used her speed to excel in all facets of the game. Ricketts, a two-time All-Hudson County First Team selection by The Jersey Journal, averaged 13.9 points, eight rebounds, seven assists and six steals per game for a young Friars squad her senior season. The 5-foot-6 guard graduated as the third leading scorer in St. Anthony history with 1,237 points and went on to play at Iona.

Christy Altamirano, Bayonne, 2006 A walking double-double, this 5-foot-11 forward was the driving force behind the Bees' back-to-back North 2, Group 4 championship teams. Always a presence in the paint, Altamirano (16.2 points, 14.8 rebounds per game) unleashed a potent mid-range game late in her senior season to lead Bayonne to its first ever state final in 2006 and earn All-State Second Team honors. Altamirano finished her HS career with 1,373 points and 1,032 rebounds before a fine career at Fairleigh Dickinson.

Janelle Biamonte, Marist, 2006 A feared outside shooter, Biamonte knocked down 173 3-pointers to score 1,632 points in her career. A four-time All-County selection by The Jersey Journal, she took her game to a new level her junior and senior seasons after adding the ability to take the ball to the basket. Biamonte, who initially signed to play at Army-West Point, went on to score 1,134 points in three seasons at Felician.

Selena Galloway, Ferris, 2006 A cerebral player, who played multiple positions for the Bulldogs during her career. A three-time All-County selection by the Jersey Journal, Galloway scored 1,412 points in her career and as a senior averaged 16.5 points, 7.1 rebounds, 4.3 assists and 3.0 steals per game. Galloway went on to play four years at Delaware State and averaged 7.4 points per game on the Hornets' MEAC championship winning team in 2007.

Lauren Jimenez, North Bergen, 2007 Jimenez, both literally and figuratively, stood above the rest from the moment she arrived as a freshman. The 6-foot-4 center led the Bruins to three HCIAA Coviello championships and four finals appearances in which she averaged 22.5 points and 13.0 rebounds in those title games. A three-time All-State selection by The Star-Ledger and a four-time All-County First Team selection by The Jersey Journal, Jimenez had 1,818 points, 1,278 rebounds and 410 blocks in a career that's arguably the best of any center in Hudson County history. Jimenez went to James Madison where she had 986 points and 582 rebounds.

Cory Roesing, Secaucus, 2007 One of the best female multi-sport athletes in Hudson County history, the 5-foot-9 Roesing was a three-time All-County First Team selection in basketball by The Jersey Journal. Roesing graduated as the school's all-time leader in points with 1,791 and rebounds with 1,103. As impressive as her basketball resume was, it paled in comparison to her play in volleyball where she twice was an All-State, First Team selection and the school's career leader in kills (905). For good measure, she was a four-time All-County selection in softball and the program's career home runs leader with 25.

Martyna Ruminska, Kearny, 2007 Few Kardinals have been able to stretch the floor the way Ruminska did in a high school career which saw her score 1,475 points. Initially a forward, the 5-foot-8 Ruminska shifted towards guard later in her career. As a junior, she carried Kearny to the North 1, Group 4 semifinals by scoring a career-high 33 points vs West Orange in the quarterfinals, followed by 29 in the semis at North Bergen. Ruminska, who averaged 19-plus points per game her junior and senior seasons, went on to play at Rutgers-Newark.

Cassandra Callaway, Bayonne, 2008 Callaway's all-around offensive game and ability to score from anywhere on the court were unmatched. As a senior in 2008, the dynamic point guard averaged 20.3 points per game for the Bees, shooting 43-percent from 3-point range and 89.7-percent from the foul line, earning Hudson County Player of the Year and All-State Third Team honors by The Star-Ledger. A three-year starter at Bayonne, Callaway, who later led Albany to an American East title, is currently an assistant coach at Seton Hall.

Cristina Centeno, Marist, 2008 A four-year starter, Centeno was the definition of a do-everything guard. As a senior, the 5-foot-9 Centeno averaged 14 points, nine rebounds and six assists per game while often guarding the opposing team's best player to lead the Royal Knights to a 26-4 record and Hudson County and Non-Public North B championships. Centeno, who scored 1,236 points at Marist, was a four-year starting point guard at Siena, played for the Puerto Rican National Team and is currently an assistant coach at Bryant.

Kristal Edwards, Create Charter/Lincoln, 2009 An offensive threat from virtually anywhere on the court, this 5-foot-11 wing led the Lions to its first county final in 28 years, when she averaged 19.1 points, 8.8 rebounds and 4.1 assists per game her senior season. Edwards, who was especially dangerous in transition, scored more than 1,000 points in three seasons at Lincoln after starting her career at CREATE Charter and was a Jersey Journal All-County selection twice. After a stint at Monroe Community College, Edwards started 47 games at Saint Peter's University.

Janitza Aquino, Kearny, 2011 Aquino found herself equally comfortable as a scorer and distributor for the Kardinals. A four-year starter at point guard, Aquino graduated Kearny as the school's all-time leading scorer with 1,732 points. Aquino took her all-around game to Montclair State, where she was named a Division III All-American and led the Red Hawks to the Final Four her senior season. Aquino also played soccer and softball at Kearny.

Andrea Innis, Secaucus, 2011 This point forward rewrote the record books at Secaucus. Innis graduated as the Patriots' career leader in points (1,903), while also being among the top five in rebounds, assists and steals. In 2011, Innis led Secaucus to its first Hudson County Tournament semifinal, averaging 21.4 points, 11.8 rebounds, 4.7 steals and 4.6 assists per game.

Tara Flynn, Bayonne, 2012 A true two-way guard, Flynn's blend of defense, shooting and passing made her one of the state's most complete point guards. Flynn was a key part of three Hudson County championships, scoring a game-high 15 points with five steals as a sophomore in the 2010 final. A 1,000+ point scorer, Flynn made 70 3-pointers her senior year and went on to play at Adelphi.

Lisa Rovatsos, Bayonne, 2012 One of Hudson County's greatest female multi-sport athletes, Rovatsos was the Bees' leading scorer all four years of her career, a span that saw Bayonne win three Hudson County championships and make four title games. A two-time Hudson County Player of the Year selection by The Star-Ledger, the 5-foot-9 wing dominated in the paint and in transition. Rovatsos, who graduated as the Bees career scoring leader in soccer (112 goals) and totaled more than 1,500 points on the hardwood, played both sports at Caldwell University.

Breana Bey, St. Anthony/Lincoln, 2013 A natural guard with a stellar mid-range game, Bey's strength made her an unstoppable offensive force in the paint and a matchup nightmare. A two-time Hudson County Player of the Year, Bey scored 1,148 points over her junior and senior seasons, leading Lincoln to back-to-back County titles, snapping a 30-plus year drought, and consecutive trips to the North 2, Group 2 final. Bey went on to star at Stetson University before embarking on a professional career in Europe.

Janitza Aquino

Andrea Innis

Andie Lennon

She'Kinah Suber, Lincoln, 2014 This 5-foot-7 wing thrived in the biggest moments for the Lions, scoring 43 points in three Hudson County finals, all won by Lincoln. In the 2013 final, she finished with 17 points and nine rebounds in a double-overtime win over Secaucus. The next year, she scored 12 of her 14 points in the fourth quarter and added 11 rebounds in a 46-45 win over Bayonne. Suber, who was comfortable in the mid-range and in the post, finished her career with 1,038 points

Icies Hammer, North Bergen, 2015 An old-school center Hammer made an immediate impact as an interior scorer with her back to the basket, who added to her game as her career continued. Hammer, who was named HCIAL Co-Player of the Year in 2015 after averaging 22 points and 10 rebounds per game, led the Bruins to three-straight trips to the Hudson County semifinals and graduated as the program's No. 2 scoring leader with 1,582 career points.

Andie Lennon, Secaucus, 2015 Despite often being the smallest player on the court, this point guard was fearless attacking the paint and a deadeye shooter from the perimeter. Lennon, who scored 1,631 points, was Secaucus' career leader in 3-pointers (176) and assists (453) at the time of her graduation before a fine career at Caldwell College. Her finest performance came in the 2015 Hudson County finals when she scored a game-high 23 points, leading the Patriots to their first county title.

Hannah Johnson, St. Dominic Academy, 2015 Johnson's speed and athleticism allowed her to do a little bit of everything for the Blue Devils. The 5-foot-7 Johnson scored 1,482 career points and led St. Dominic in points, rebounds, assists, steals and blocks in both her junior and senior seasons.

Kiante Johnson, Lincoln, 2015 A dominant interior presence, Johnson co-starred with fellow forward Breana Bey for two Hudson County titles. Then, following Bey's graduation, Johnson led Lincoln to a third Hudson title as a junior, followed by a trip to the final in 2015. Johnson was selected as Hudson County Player of the Year by The Star-Ledger in 2014 and 2015, averaging 19.8 points and 10 rebounds per game over the two seasons. A 6-0 forward, who could also put the ball on the floor, Johnson scored 1,680 points in her stellar career.

Julia McClure

Lisa Rovatsos

Julia McClure, Secaucus, 2015 McClure's combination of strength, quickness and toughness allowed her to play all five positions on the court. Despite standing 5-foot-8, she did her best work inside where she often got the best of far bigger forwards. McClure, who went on to play at Wagner and was a State Player of the Year in volleyball, had 56 double-doubles in her basketball career, graduating as the school's career leader in rebounds (1,160) and steals (425) while also posting 1,492 points and 451 assists.

Madison McGlone, Bayonne, 2016 McGlone scored 1,149 points in her career, but it was her ability to do the little things when points were hard to come by that loomed large. The 5-foot-7 guard led the Bees in points (354), assists (81) and steals (81) in 2016 when Bayonne won the Hudson County Tournament. In the final, a 34-27 win over Lincoln, McGlone scored a game-high nine points to go with six steals. A two-sport star, McGlone scored 68 goals on the soccer field to help lead the Bees to three county finals

Zhan'e Williams, Lincoln, 2016 This 5-foot-5 point guard was a steady hand in the backcourt throughout her four years at Lincoln. A three-time All-League selection, Williams was named HCIAL Player of the Year her senior season after averaging 17.5 points and 4.9 assists per game to help lead the Lions to their fifth-straight Hudson County final. A 1,000-point scorer, Williams went on to play at Iowa Western Community College before finishing her career at Long Island University.

Emely Rosario, Marist, 2017 This two-way point guard usually focused on setting up her teammates, recording more than 400 career assists, but when forced into a more prominent scoring role, Rosario proved up to the task. Rosario was named NJ.com's HCIAL Player of the Year as a senior, averaging 18.0 points, 5.6 rebounds, 4.7 assists and 3.6 steals per game to lead Marist to the Hudson County final. A four-year starter at Marist, Rosario's college career included stops at Eastern Kentucky, Kilgore College, Troy and Prairie View.

Lindsey Mack, Secaucus, 2018 A deadeye shooter, the 5-foot-10 Mack made 39-percent of her career 3-pointers and 251 in four seasons at Secaucus. Mack made four 3-pointers to finish with a game-high 22 points and 10 rebounds in the Patriots' 2017 Hudson County title game win over previously undefeated Marist. Mack, who went on to play at Fairleigh Dickinson and Youngstown State, scored 1,685 points at Secaucus.

Meagan McClelland, Kearny, 2018 Better known for her play on the soccer field, the future Rutgers star goalie was also one of the finest guards to ever wear a Kearny uniform. Despite playing just 91 games due to soccer commitments with Team USA, McClelland scored 1,348 points for her career. As a senior, McClelland averaged 20.2 points, 5.9 rebounds, 5.9 assists and 4.4 steals per game to help lead the Kardinals to a 22-6 record.

Daniya Darby, Lincoln, 2019 A walking double-double, Darby's work inside and on the glass was often the difference late in games for the Lions. Darby scored more than 1,200 points and averaged 10+ rebounds per game each of her last three seasons. Darby's teams made three Hudson County finals, winning one, and in 2019, her "and-one" with 7.7 seconds left in overtime gave Lincoln its first sectional title in 38 years.

Breyanna Frazier, Marist, 2019 The 5-foot-9 Frazier was a dynamic wing from the moment she first arrived as a freshman at Marist. A skilled slasher and dangerous player in transition, Frazier, the HCIAL's Player of the Year as a sophomore, led Marist to the Hudson County final and a 23-2 record that season. Frazier, who had 1,339 career points and 496 rebounds in just 81 games due a torn ACL that cut short her senior year and prevented her from playing at Central Florida. She will be resuming her career as a graduate transfer at Jacksonville University.

Haylee Ramirez, Hudson Catholic, 2019 Ramirez played bigger than her 5-foot-4 height, especially on the defensive end. She recorded 371 steals in her career, averaging an eye-popping 5.4 per game her sophomore season. Offensively, Ramirez scored 1,177 points, second most in school history, with 114 3-pointers. While Ramirez sacrificed part of her offensive role her senior year, in the Hudson County final, she scored a game-high 14 points to give the Hawks their first ever county title. Ramirez later played at Felician University.

Jesse Semeniak, Bayonne, 2019 This 6-foot-0 wing could and did play every role during her four years as a starter. As a stretch forward and secondary ball-handler her senior year, Semeniak averaged 14.1 points and 5.2 rebounds with 49 3-pointers on a Bayonne team that went 24-5. As a freshman, the Bees won a county title with Semeniak averaging 7.3 rebounds as an interior presence. In between, Semeniak averaged 17.5 points, 8.5 rebounds and 5.2 assists per game as a point guard as a junior.

Amanda Ulrich, Secaucus, 2019 A true scorer, Ulrich is fifth all-time amongst girls in career scoring with 2,224 points. Ulrich had 19 points, nine rebounds and seven assists in the 2017 Hudson County Tournament final against Marist. The 5-foot-7 guard also led the Patriots to four straight sectional finals and was more than just a scorer, finishing with 712 rebounds, 405 steals, 384 assists and countless charges taken. Ulrich went on to play at Saint Leo's and became the Division II program's career-scoring record there as well.

Amanda Ulrich

Tara Flynn

Makoye Diawara, Bayonne, 2020 Perhaps no player improved more during her high school career than this 6-0 forward. Limited to just layups as a sophomore, Diawara made 24 3-pointers in a senior season that ended with a Hudson County championship for the Bees and an All-State, Third Team selection for her. Diawara averaged 17.5 points and 14.7 rebounds per game as a senior, including an 18-point, 17-rebound performance in the HCT final. The mobile center started on Norfolk State's MEAC Championship team in 2023.

Damaris Rodriguez, Secaucus, 2020 A normally fast-paced Secaucus team found a higher gear or two with the dynamic Rodriguez at point guard. As a freshman, Rodriguez scored 19 points in the Hudson County final against Marist. Rodriguez shattered the school career assists record with 834 and is the all-time leader in steals with 474. For her career, she scored 1,735 points, highlighted by a school record 44 in the 2020 Hudson County Tournament at Marist. Rodriguez went on to play at NJCU where she became a D3 All-American and arguably the greatest women's player in Gothic Knights history.

Jakira Coar, Lincoln, 2021 A lights out shooter, this 5-foot-7 guard could, and often did, change a game with just one shot. A valued role player in the Lions' 2019 Group 2 state finalist team, Coar took a starring role the season after, sinking 24 3-pointers and 86 points total over five state tournament games, leading Lincoln to a second sectional title before COVID canceled the Group 2 final. In a COVID-shortened senior season, Coar averaged 22.6 points per game. For her career, Coar scored 1,002 points and sank 197 3-pointers in 78 career games.

Zanai Jones, Hudson Catholic, 2021 Jones' steady presence at the point gave the Hawks a sense of calm even in the most chaotic of game situations. Despite standing 5-foot-6, the Jersey City native was equally confident inside the paint as she was from the perimeter as she led Hudson Catholic to its first ever county title in 2019. Jones, an All-State, Third Team selection her senior year, graduated as the Hawks' career scoring (1,388) and assists (622) leader and No. 2 all time in steals and 3-pointers before going to Villanova.

Erika Mercedes, Union City, 2022 It's not a coincidence that Union City's rise from irrelevance to state sectional champs coincided with the arrival of this slashing guard.In 2020, Mercedes had 31 points and 15 rebounds against Livingston to give the Soaring Eagles their first state tournament win in more than a decade. Two years later, she had 17 points as Union City downed Morristown in the North 1, Group 4 final. Mercedes, the first 1,000 point scorer in program history, scored 1,456 points in just 90 games.

Kyra Rose, Snyder, 2022 Rose had the speed and ball-handling to be listed as a guard, but it was her length and play in the paint that made her nearly unstoppable. In her lone season at Snyder, Rose averaged 18.2 points and 9.9 rebounds per game to be named HCIAL Player of the Year and lead the Tigers to a 20-6 record. The 5-foot-10 wing started her career at Marist, scoring 235 points as a sophomore before the school closed, then went to Paramus Catholic before finishing at Snyder.

Eniya Scott, Bayonne, 2022 Few players have ever made the immediate impact this point guard made. Scott averaged 17.3 points, 4.9 assists and 4.0 steals per game as a freshman as Bayonne won 15 more games than the previous season and reached the North 2, Group 4 final. A cornerstone player on the Bees' 2020 and 2022 Hudson County championship teams, Scott finished her career with 1,301 points and 529 assists despite only playing seven games in a COVID-shortened junior season. Scott went on to play at Division 1 Fairleigh Dickinson.

Alyssa Craigwell, Secaucus, 2024 This do-everything wing did it all for the Patriots, leading the team in points (20.0 per game), rebounds (9.0), steals (3.8 per), blocks (33) and 3-pointers (51) in 2023, to lead Secaucus to its first ever state final. Craigwell scored 639 points on the season, the second most in Secaucus school history. Sheky had 20 points, 16 rebounds and four steals in the North 2, Group 2 final vs. Madison for its first sectional title.

Jaylyn Orefice, Union City, 2024 Pinpointing one strength in Orefice's game can be difficult because she makes an impact in so many ways. Comfortable in the paint and on the perimeter, this 5-foot-8 forward averaged 15.2 points and 7.9 rebounds per game as a junior to help lead the Soaring Eagles to their second consecutive North 1, Group 4 title. She was the leading scorer in each of Union City's sectional finals, posting 19 points in 2022 vs. Morristown and 22 in 2023 vs. Paterson Eastside.

Janaya Meyers, Bayonne, 2025 A true "power" guard, Meyers was HCIAL American Division Co-Player of the Year in her first season with the Bees. She had 14 points, seven rebounds and five assists in the Group 4 final as Bayonne won its first ever state title. The 5-foot-9 Meyers had double-doubles in the Hudson County and North 2, Group 4 Tournaments finals. As a freshman at Hudson Catholic, she averaged 14.2 points and 9.2 rebounds per game.

McKenzie Neal, Bayonne, 2025 Neal's combination of skill and footwork at 6-foot-3 has rarely been seen in Hudson County. The rapidly improving center had 12 points and 10 rebounds in the Hudson County final against Secaucus. Neal averaged 13.8 points, 9.8 rebounds and 3.5 blocks per game with three double-doubles in six state tournament games.

Jaida Guerra, Union City, 2025 Nicknamed "The Waterbug" for her incredible quickness, Guerra had a breakout sophomore season for the Soaring Eagles, averaging 17.8 points per game to earn HCIAL American Division Co-Player of the Year. A member of two North 1, Group 4 title teams, Guerra was selected to the Puerto Rican U16 National Team in 2023.

Alyssa Craigwell

Damaris Rodriguez

Eniya Scott

THE GILLIGAN FAMILY
ANTONIA, MAUREEN, TIM & TOM
CONGRATULATE

FRANK NICOLETTI

AND HIS FELLOW 'HOOPS HOTBED ON THE HUDSON' HONOREES

STEVE ROTH, FRANK ROTHMAN
AND TOM SINNICKSON
CONGRATULATE

FRANK NICOLETTI

AND HIS FELLOW 'HOOPS HOTBED ON THE HUDSON' HONOREES

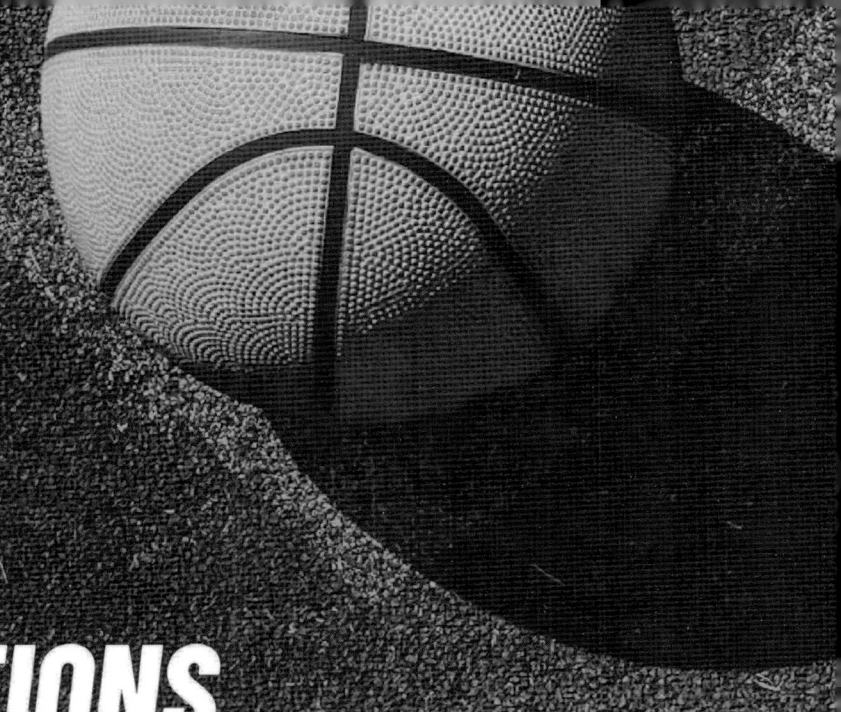

CONGRATULATIONS
TO MY GREAT
BASKETBALL FRIENDS
IN HUDSON COUNTY,
THE GREATEST
BASKETBALL LOCATION
IN THE WORLD.

- TOM MAC MAHON

VI

HUDSON COUNTY
COLORFUL
CHARACTERS

Hudson hoops has its
very own assortment of
Crayolas, figures whose
basketball backstories
transcend the court.

Some are fact, some
are folklore, some are
somewhere in between.

All are colorful characters.

LEM BANKER

"He was approachable. He was a gentleman."

That's the Reader's Digest assessment of prolific professional gambler Lem Banker by Vinny Magliulo. Magliulo is a Las Vegas sportsbook mover and shaker in his own right over quite a number of decades.

Banker died in November of 2020 at the age of 93. Born Lester Banker in the Bronx, but reared in Union City (father was a "candy-store bookie"), he did enjoy a stellar high-school hoops career. Banker was second-team All-County (1945) during his Union Hill days, inducted (2004) into that institution's Hall of Fame.

Banker was a long-time fixture in Sin City. His obituary in the Las Vegas Review-Journal stated that "he never drew a regular paycheck in his life."

He did, however, help bring gambling into the mainstream by penning handicapping columns which appeared in Las Vegas and in other markets.

He was dubbed a "solid contender for the World's Greatest Living Gambler" by the Wall Street Journal and "America's Greatest Living Gambler" by the New York Times. He was profiled by "People" in print and "Lifestyles of the Rich and Famous" on the small screen.

His obit included the glory that came with picking the spread winners (in print) in 20 of the first 23 Super Bowls (including 13 in a row [1973-85]).

That was a Banker baker's dozen, or in this instance, a "Banker's Dozen."

Banker, not unlike JImmy "the Greek" Snyder, developed a cross-country cadre of "associates" in the pre-information overload era.

"He put together a national network of people, especially back East, who would scour local papers in search of anything worthwhile about players and teams," Magliulo said.

Continuing the "family business" is Banker's grandson, Jonathan Ribaste, whose mantra is "do not bet with your heart and stay within your bankroll."

Authoring the eponymous "Lem Banker's Book of Sports Betting" in 1986, he was once described by the renowned Larry Merchant as "an orchid growing wild in a garbage dump."

It wouldn't be a stretch to suggest Banker, having arrived in Nevada as a 30-year-old in 1957, knew nearly everyone. Some were celebrities (Elvis and the "Rat Pack") and some (Lefty Rosenthal comes to mind) couldn't pass a background check. This was Vegas, after all.

It's the goal of any professional gambler to find the "off" line (stating the obvious here), and "once (Lem) made his selection, some of the lines did move," Magliulo said. "Lem didn't bet teams, rather he bet numbers." Statistics don't lie. Since the bettor is often laying 11-10 odds, he/she needs to win more than 52 percent of the time.

Banker's obit also mentioned how "(he} had money down going way back to when you could bet in different parts of the country, getting a line in Seattle you couldn't get in New York.

"He was a wiseguy before they invented the term."

"There wasn't a bookmaker dead or alive I didn't beat," he said.

"Even with his success, money never changed him," Ribaste said. "He was meat and potatoes, but he enjoyed the Italian restaurants in Las Vegas, and you know every time he came back to New York, there was Sparks Steak House (East 46th Street)."

With the wins (and the losses) came the stories. One of Banker's favorites was the 1964 football game between then-No. 1 and undefeated Notre Dame and USC at the Coliseum.

"I was down to my last $10,000, so I bet the Trojans, bought tickets and took my friends to the game in a limo," he said.

USC, down 17-0 at halftime, scored 20 unanswered points after intermission to win, 20-17.

How would Banker react to today's seismic explosion of gambling?

"He'd relish it," Magliulo said. "It's come a long way,"

(Author's aside...appreciation to Vinny Magliulo, the Las Vegas Review-Journal [Todd Dewey] and Jonathan Ribaste, all of whom directly and/or indirectly greatly assisted with this story).

–

By, Frank Drucker

VINCE DOHERTY

Once the name Jimmy Breslin is invoked, it automatically (and exponentially) increases the street cred of any story.

We're shamelessly piggybacking on a December, 1959, Breslin article out of the long-gone New York Journal-American entitled "You Can't Have a Heart."

It was an interesting piece about Vince ("Doc") Doherty.

Doherty, out of Jersey City, had a game-high 26 points as St. Peter's Prep won its first county championship in 1949.

(A quick note about the St. Peter's Prep 55-46 win over Union Hill in '49...the game also featured John Clune (12 points) and Earle Markey (10) of St. Peter's Prep, while Pete Innis and Fred Shabel (15 points each) and Togo Palazzi (10) led Union Hill, so some pretty fair Hudson County representation on both sides)

Doherty then joined coach Elmer Ripley at John Carroll (Class of '53) in suburban Cleveland. There was a 28-point effort with the Blue Streaks at Seton Hall as a senior (Ripley departed two seasons prior), earning Doherty a place on the Pirates' all-opponent team.

Gaining a reputation as an impeccable advance man (offense and defense) of the collegiate hardwood, Doherty told Breslin, "I work for everybody, with the only allegiance "to the coach who was paying for (today's) report."

This particular story was a preview of LaSalle-Manhattan at a previous incarnation of Madison Square Garden, and Doherty providing a six-page summary to LaSalle coach Dudey Moore.

Harkening back to the title of the Breslin tome, "This is a business where you can't have a heart," Doherty said. "Take on any job they offer. Forget the personalities. The only job is to give a good, clear report to a coach. That's your whole value."

Try this as a pull quote..."Tonto was America's number 1 scout until Vince Doherty got into the business."

Whether that was actually written by Breslin or (more probably) interjected by Doherty, that was Vince.

Be it Tonto, Pat Riley, Fr. Earle Markey (his earlier-in-story St. Peter's Prep teammate), Eddie Arcaro, Bill Raftery, former San Francisco 49ers' owner Ed DeBartolo, Rollie Massimino, long-time NBA public relations director (creator of league's All-Star Game) Haskell Cohen, Senator Dianne Feinstein or anyone in the military short of the Chairman of the Joint Chiefs of Staff, he wasn't above naming names. Whether any of those "names" knew Doherty's name was not relevant.

What was known was Doherty eventually found his way to Northern California. What wasn't known was Doherty's vocation.

He claimed to have been employed by a congressman, an old business card had him as president of San Francisco-based VIP International, while another "theory" had him working in sales. According to Fr. Markey, Doherty, "did not want a job. He just wanted a paycheck."

He was living at the ritzy Olympic Club in San Francisco, site of five U.S. Opens. Whether Billy Casper was given as a reference is not clear, though wouldn't surprise.

Among the definitions of "chutzpah" is nerve or audacity. "That was Vince."

This is Dan Kuhnert, whose wife, Sharon, is Doherty's niece.

Kuhnert offered a late 1990's story involving Doherty and the USS Kitty Hawk, a naval supercarrier docked at Coronado Island outside San Diego.

"Vince somehow managed to get an invitation, and I joined him," Kuhnert said. "He introduced himself as 'Retired Captain Vince Doherty,' and there we were, seated in the front row (perhaps next to Bob Uecker).

"People somehow accepted what he was saying as fact."

More about the intersection of Doherty and chutzpah.

It was the early 1960's, when Japanese automobiles were first finding their way into America. Attempting to familiarize potential customers with such vehicles, dealerships offered loaner cars to be taken on a few-day's test drive. Well, Doherty redefined the term 'test drive' by taking one such autos clear across the country. This didn't go over well, either with the dealer or the next prospective customer awaiting the vehicle. There's no record of exactly how many chutzpah miles Doherty registered per gallon, but the best guess was substantial.

Oh, and he had alligator arms, which is a polite way of saying a dinner check never found its way his way.

We now welcome Joe McVeigh to the discourse.

"I met Vince first in Jersey City," McVeigh said. "We both eventually worked at a hotel down on the Jersey shore. "There wasn't anyone else quite like him. Nice guy, but whatever he said had to be taken with a grain of salt.

"I'd describe him as 'incomparable' ".

Doherty died at age 68 in 1999. He stopped claiming he was a friend of so-and-so around 2012.

–

By, Frank Drucker

HOWIE FINK

It's highly doubtful any high school anywhere had a more loyal fan. Howie Fink was known as "Mr. Dickinson," because he loved anything to do with Dickinson High School.

He graduated from the school on the hilltop in the mid-1930s, and his loyalty to the school lasted until his death in 2004.

It didn't matter whether it was basketball, football or baseball, if it was Dickinson, it was almost a sure thing he would be there rooting, but his devotion went much further than that. He founded the Dickinson High School Hall of Fame and was also the president of the Dickinson Athletic Booster Club, starting in 1961.

He was a familiar figure in front of the Stanley Theater on Saturday nights, selling the Daily News Night Owl edition. He also served under a staggering total of 18 Jersey City mayors as an employee of Jersey City.

In baseball, he was a manager in the Hudson County Build Better Boys Baseball League was the president of the Hudson County Semi-Pro Baseball League, and was a member of the Hudson County Umpires Association for more than 40 years.

His generosity to youth sports teams was well known, donating thousands of dollars to baseball and basketball teams, through his Howie Fink Association. Recipients of his donations would often be surprised when Fink would give them a stack of $50 bills which looked and felt a little bit strange. A closer looked revealed they were from Series 1950, which led to legends about money being stored in a mattress or in the walls of his home in the Heights.

In Jim Hague's stirring obituary column to Fink, he quoted legendary basketball coach Bob Hurley.

"He truly cared about the kids," said Hurley of Fiink. "He had an affinity for sports and dedicated his whole life to it, discussing sports, organizing games, sponsoring teams. He was a great natural resource. He's gone and won't be replaced. You don't find many like him. They're a dying breed. You don't know where they came from."

HANK FINKEL

Gospel According to Hank Finkel

–

It's difficult to fathom how someone who grew to be seven feet tall needed to be "found." Such was the case with Henry ("Hank" to his friends) Finkel. Raised in Union City, the now–81-year-old Finkel sheepishly remembers "as a delivery boy, chickening out before I could get Togo Palazzi's autograph," but at the same time fondly recalling "ringing five doorbells and getting five kids to play."

"School was over at 1:30 in those days. There was plenty of time."

...but his initiation into team sports was sort of by happenstance.

"I was a sophomore at (now-defunct) Holy Family High School, walking down the corridor. I'm then about 6-foot-5. Matty Sabello, the basketball coach, was also a chemistry teacher. My sister was in his class. He then asks her about me, and that's how it started."

Finkel went on to star at Holy Family, but as a self-described "work in progress," he didn't didn't get many collegiate offers. One was local – St. Peter's in Jersey City.

"It wasn't working," so Finkel left the Peacock program and went to work, at a shipyard also in Jersey City. Then, a la the wannabe Hollywood actor discovered at a drugstore, Finkel was spotted by a University of Dayton "scout," whisking him away to southwestern Ohio.

Winning the 1962 NIT had put the Flyers on the map, as did Finkel. He averaged 23.7 points and 13.3 points in his three seasons, all the while (because he began his collegiate playing career at the age of 21) getting drafted three different times.

Thus, after the Los Angeles Lakers chose him a second time (1964 and '66, in between the Philadelphia 76ers selecting him in '65), he finally signed.

"Here's a quick story," Finkel said. "With the Lakers in practice, Leroy Ellis rejected my first two shots. Jerry West pulls me aside and tells me I don't have to shoot all the time. He then teaches me the correct way to set a pick. I didn't forget that lesson. The pick and roll was what I did throughout my career."

That...

"...and never turn my back to the ball. Once, at an all-star game in New York, it was the great Vinnie Ernst (Jersey City's St. Aloysius) leading the fast break. He threw it to me, and it bounced off my head."

Finkel, who lists Sabello as his biggest influence in the game, has nothing but good things to say about his tenure in the NBA. "I was fortunate to play nine seasons (1966-67 thru 1974-75, the last six with the Boston Celtics) on the same teams as Hall of Famers such as (John) Havlicek, (JoJo) White, (Don) Nelson, (Dave) Cowens, not to mention (Jerry) West. That's my best memory in basketball."

That's not bad, considering way back when, "I had no desire to play organized basketball." Now, about that common misconception that Finkel was the world's tallest Jewish basketball player...

"I was traded (actually sold by the San Diego Rockets) to the Celtics (August of '69), and the team priest, Father John Creed, meets me at the airport to go to the Celtics' camp in the summer."

"Well, Red (Auerbach), of course is Jewish, and was excited to have a Jewish player on the team. So, he arranged to have a lot of (lantzmen) as his guests at a preseason game." (Author's aside...a fellow Jew is known as a lantzman.)

"I'm fouled, and on the free-throw line, before shooting I make the sign of the cross."

He later learned from Red that all of his guests exited the Boston Garden shortly thereafter.

Turns out the "World's Tallest Jewish Basketball Player" is German-Catholic.

—

By, *Frank Drucker*

ED 'THE FAA' FORD

It's almost impossible to adequately describe Ed "The Faa" Ford to someone who has never met him. Maybe the best way is to use his own words about himself: A larger-than-life "Damon Runyan-esque" character who "looks like Captain Kangaroo."

A Jersey City tavern owner, influential sports columnist and regional scouting director for the Chicago Cubs, The Faa (pronounced as in ah) as he preferred to be called, was rarely in public without a huge wad of tobacco in his mouth. He loved to amaze young athletes by rolling a wad of tobacco into a baseball-sized ball and stuffing it into his mouth.

His column, Faa's Corner, was read by thousands every week first in The Hudson Dispatch and later in The Jersey Journal. His Faa's Dream Teams in basketball, football and baseball rivaled the all-county teams in popularity and included a greater number of players. Although his primary sport was baseball, Ford was also a basketball referee, and few who saw him will forget the animated way he made his calls. He once threw a cheerleader out of the game for stepping onto the court one too many times.

He became close friends with North Carolina coaching legend Dean Smith and made at least one trip a year down there. Hudson Catholic High School great, Mike O'Koren, recalls when The Faa and Smith first became friends.

"Well, one of my favorite stories is when I was at Carolina. I just got to Carolina and Coach Smith, during (the) recruiting phase, got to know Eddie Ford," said O'Koren. "And Coach Smith, he didn't realize the Faa was an official because you remember the Faa didn't look like an official. You know what I mean? So, he said, 'Faa, you could ref the blue-white game.' Now, the blue-white game at North Carolina is the teams are split up. The Carmichael Auditorium where we played would have 10,000 people literally to watch our blue and white games. The Faa reffed it. And the people just didn't understand. You have a Southern crowd, obviously in Chapel Hill, North Carolina, and the Faa's calling a travel by running halfway down the court. 'Nah, that's traveling. No good, go the other way,' with his big belly. And when he called an offensive foul, he knelt down."

Prior to that game, Smith said: "Oh my God. I survived the Olympics but I don't know if I'll be able to survive the Faa and Gibby Lewis," who was also refereeing the game. Jim Boylan, former St. Mary's High School and Marquette University star, recalled one game refereed by Ford when Boylan was playing for St. Paul of the Cross in the CYO grammar school league: "So we're sitting there watching the game ahead of us and someone drove down the lane and someone stepped in and took a charge,

"And Eddie Ford was on the baseline under the basket, blew his whistle and did a skipping, hopping, sliding dance all the way to half court with his right hand behind his head and his left hand facing forward. "And he skipped, hopped, jumped and then he just led out a charging scream and pointed the other way."

The Faa was also legendary for the number of young athletes he helped get into college. One phone call to one of his many coaching friends in various sports was all it took. Never a man of means, Ford never turned down a friend or youth in need. "It was a unique experience working with Eddie," David Willcomes said. "I was just starting to work varsity games in Hudson County, and he was very helpful with his advice and guidance. I guess the one memory I really had working with him was that he always knew everyone. I guess the one memory was that during timeouts he was always talking to people in the stands. I usually had to go get him to continue the game. He was somewhat unorthodox but always was tough and very fair. Always talking to players and encouraging them. Eddie, as you well know, was a character, but I don't think anyone had a greater love of Hudson County sports. (He) was always a guy who went out of his way for the kids."

There are several stories out there about how he became known as The Faa, and if you asked him, he would just give you that Irish smile of his. The most prevalent legend, and probably the most plausible, involved his fondness for Chinese food. On one of his trips to NYC's Chinatown, he was greeted by a head waiter who knew him, but who had trouble pronouncing "Ford." Or so the legend goes.

Ford was also known for both his fierce loyalty to his friends and his unpredictable hair trigger mood swings. His good friend Ed Finn remembers when he and Ford were partners in the tavern Dohoney's on West Side Avenue in Jersey City. He said the three years they were partners were "the longest 10 years of my life."

Members of the Jersey City Stars of Tomorrow baseball team remember waiting with the other coaches for Ford to show up with the equipment for their first practice at Pershing Field. When he got out of his car with the equipment bag all the way down the right field line, he immediately started screaming and throwing each bat and piece of equipment over the chain link fence one at a time, and then stormed away, still screaming. To this day, no one there knows what he was upset about. A close friend described him this way: "You never knew what was going to set him off. You'd be buddies one day and fighting with him the next. He would always say 'feuding with the Faa is part of life.' But as soon as you needed a friend, the feud was over. He was always there for you and he seemingly knew almost everyone, and I'm talking about all over the country. One phone call from him and your problem was solved." He also would often say, "I hate the name Ed Ford," and claimed he wanted to legally change his name to The Faa, but never followed through.

When the New Jersey Devils won one of their Stanley Cups, the trophy was entrusted overnight to one of the team's public relations men. Early the next morning, a Jersey City sports writer was awakened by the doorman downstairs. "Lord Stanley is here to visit you," the doorman told him. "Huh? What?" the writer answered. "Lord Stanley is downstairs and would like you to come down." When the reporter got downstairs, the employee and Ford were there with the Stanley Cup. After letting the reporter pose for pictures with the cup, Ford, who had his usual wad of tobacco in his mouth, playfully spit several times into the Stanley Cup. That night, David Letterman drank coffee out of the cup on his TV show, unaware of what had been in it just a few hours earlier. The reporter said he never laughed so hard that night.

GIBBY LEWIS

When you said the name Gibby for several decades in Hudson County basketball circles, everyone knew who you meant.

Gibby Lewis was one of the most impactful basketball referees in the history of Hudson County basketball.

He was unorthodox, to say the least, and a well-known character throughout the county.

Mike O'Koren, arguably one of the greatest scholastic basketball players in Hudson County history, remembers Gibby officiating a highly anticipated high school showcase game in Trenton that featured future NBA legends LeBron James and Carmelo Anthony.

"Carmelo complained to Gibby that LeBron fouled him and Gibby didn't call it," remembers O'Koren. "Gibby told Carmelo to 'hit him back.' He said, "if I didn't call the first foul, I won't call that."

Joe Macchi, who was Gibby's boss as the assistant director of Jersey City Recreation for many years, recalls Gibby officiating games when he was the head coach at St. Peter's Prep. "Gibby was always entertaining. He was one of the better referees."

As a young teenager in the early 1970s, I was waiting at St. Joseph's Schoolyard for a game to end and possibly be picked to play in the next game. Gibby lost both the game and his temper and he fired the basketball through the first-floor bathroom window of the grammar school. With the shattered glass laying on the ground, Gibby began to trot out of the schoolyard. When somebody yelled to ask, "where are you going?" Gibby's answer was "the rectory to report what I did."

Gibby's legend extended to Chapel Hill, North Carolina, starting with O'Koren's freshman season in 1976-77 that concluded with a trip to the NCAA Championship game. Gibby and a large continent of Jersey City fans would travel down to Tobacco Road, via car (with some high-speed rides) or plane for many games.

O'Koren recalls one game in Carmichael Auditorium that ended with a much-celebrated victory over arch-rival Duke from nearby Durham.

"We played Duke in an afternoon game at Carmichael," recalls O'Koren. "I'm with a group of about 10-12 guys from Jersey City after the game and Gibby said he had a shortcut. I was thinking 'what shortcut?' Gibby took us by the Duke bus and he was calling out (assistant) coach Bob Wenzel, who had recruited me. He was calling for him to get off the bus. Wenzel was being held back. Gibby yells to him 'if you come off the bus, you'll have two losses today.'"

Gibby didn't care who he was messing with, including legendary North Carolina Coach Dean Smith.

O'Koren had two signings for his National Letter of Intent to go to the University of North Carolina. O'Koren will never forget the one held in Jersey City at the home of Alan Cancro Sr., a longtime mentor whose son played at St. Joseph's with O'Koren.

"Mr. Cancro asked Coach Smith what he would like to drink and he said he'd have a little milk," recalls O'Koren of that 1976 party. "Coach Smith had the white whisker from the milk on his lip. Gibby said 'I'll drink what Coach Smith had.' Gibby then took Coach Smith's tie and wiped off the milk."

Gibby would always be there to help a youngster in Jersey City or a friend, longtime or recent acquaintance.

The Jersey City native worked at the Department of Recreation and later the Department of Public Works for over 30 years. Gibby was the Coordinator of the Youth Football Operations from 1992-2000, re-building what had once been a flourishing program back to its heyday.

"Remember we used to have a Recreation League with teams like the Greenville Tigers, West Side Bears, Downtown Bulldogs, Journal Square Rams, etc.," says Macchi. "But it was different by the early 90s and the football numbers had declined. Through his networking and selling the program to different people, Gibby kept it going."

Hudson County lost Gibby at the age of 70 in 2020, but for many years our county and its kids benefitted from "craziest dude" many people have ever experienced.

–

By, Michael Hogan

JIM HAGUE

There have been scores of scribes who have written about Hudson County basketball and sports over the past century.

But none have been more prolific that Jersey City native Jim Hague, who easily wrote thousands of stories on basketball and other sports for the defunct Hudson Dispatch, followed by the Hudson Reporter for over two decades after the demise of The Dispatch in 1991 and The Observer in West Hudson for a combined period of over four decades.

After playing football and wrestling for St. Peter's Prep, where he graduated from in 1979, Jim headed to Marquette University in Milwaukee, Wisconsin, as a journalism major.

Jim started working for the now-defunct Hudson Dispatch in the mid-1980s and worked there until it closed on one day's notice in April, 1991.

"Jim was the most talkative person I've ever known," says Stan Eason, who was a sportswriter at The Hudson Dispatch with Jim until the paper closed. "He never had a shortage for words. He was unparalleled and seemed to know everybody. We covered the sports scene like hawks. I grew up in Passaic County. Jim was better familiar with everybody in Hudson County. We had aggressive coverage."

"I credit Jim with me getting my first writing award," says Eason. "Jim cracked the story about St. Peter's College dropping football, but Mike Spina and I wrote the story. Jim knew the players, the coaches, and he was probably best friends with the parents of the players. He was an institutional reference. He had a great wealth of knowledge about all sports in Hudson. County, especially the big three (baseball, basketball and football)."

Eason stressed that Jim's legacy was how he treated Hudson County athletes in his stories.

"His legacy is undoubtedly helping so many kids and treating them like they were major-leaguers or big-time players and worthy of being interviewed, says Eason. "He interviewed players like they were professionals to get their insights into the game. That was foreign to me before I worked at The Dispatch."

I was from Passaic County. Sports ruled in Hudson County. We covered soup to nuts. They knew me by name from The Dispatch, but people knew Jim personally. Sportswriting like that doesn't exist anymore. We treated sportswriting like news reporting. Jim gave so many people their due. If we didn't make them celebrities, we'd make them feel like they were celebrities."

Longtime St. Peter's Prep football coach and athletic director Rich Hansen first met Jim when Rich was playing at St. Joseph's High School and his football team scrimmaged Jim and St. Peter's Prep in 1976. "We used to sneak into the Prep gym with a group of my Jersey City friends to play basketball and Jim with his friends."

Hansen also recalls a humorous story about Jim, who along with being a big fan of Marquette and the New York Mets, absolutely adored the Rams, whether they were the Los Angeles or St. Louis version. Knowing how Jim loved the Rams, Hansen called Jim because the Rams were playing at the Meadowlands about seven years ago, and the team was using the Prep football facility, off Grand Street, for a Saturday practice before the game.

"I'll get you on the field, but you can't tell anyone about it," says Hansen. "Be there at 9 o'clock. Jim showed up wearing a Rams' jersey, Rams' hat, Rams' sneakers, Rams everything with a pad in his hand. I introduced him to Coach McVay. I stood there watching him (Jim) for about 10 minutes. He looked like an eight-year-old watching practice. He looked like a Rams' billboard."

Growing up in Jersey City and living there for many years before relocating to Kearny after his marriage in 1995 to Hudson County Superior Court Judge Mary Costello, Jim cared greatly about athletics in Hudson County.

"Jim wrote with his heart," says Hansen. "He was a Hudson County protectionist, but never let it come out in his writing. He loved what he did (sportswriting) and he was always supportive of Hudson County athletes and coaches. I always appreciated that. That was his thing."

Kevin Canessa, who is editor of The Observer and has worked for the weekly newspaper since 2006, is still amazed at Jim's dedication to writing about the athletes in the western parts of Hudson County (Kearny and Harrison) in addition to covering the towns of North Arlington, Lyndhurst, Belleville, Nutley and Bloomfield.

"Jim never took a week off (from producing stories) for vacation," says Canessa, also a St. Peter's Prep graduate. "He did three stories a week for those 20 years. He did at least 3,000 stories and probably much more in those 20 years. He didn't like doing stuff on the phone. He would cover games sitting in his lawn chair and people would gather around him.

"Jim never stopped working," says Judge Costello. "If we went to the Final Four (an annual trip), or our honeymoon, he was always writing. He was not on salary for a lot of his jobs, but he loved it."

"When we went on vacation before laptop computers and iPads, Jim would be putting the CPU, the monitor and everything he needed in the trunk for the drive to Cape Cod or wherever we were going," added Costello. "He'd be writing every single day. Jim would get up in the middle of the night to go to the bathroom and the Muse would hit him. He'd continue out to the living room and write. I could hear the keys clicking. He wasn't a 9-to-5er."

After the closing of The Dispatch and in addition to writing for the Hudson Reporter and The Observer, Jim stayed plenty busy covering Seton Hall University basketball games and New Jersey Devils' games at the Prudential Center along with practices for the Giants and Jets for the Associated Press, under New Jersey Sports Editor Tom Canavan. Jim also was the PA announcer for the Newark Bears' minor league team in a job that included being the official scorer for home games and doing all kinds of odds-and-ends jobs around the stadium. In the winter, he continued his PA jobs for New Jersey Institute of Technology and later Rutgers-Newark before he retired from the PA gigs in 2021.

And if that didn't keep Jim busy enough, he started doing a sports blog about 10 years ago and then a podcast when COVID hit the country in 2020. He produced dozens of podcasts that included legendary St. Anthony's basketball coach Bob Hurley, former Harrison High and Rutgers University standout Ray Lucas (a 2,000-point scorer for the Blue Tide), Olympian Gail Marquis, heavyweight boxing legend Chuck Wepner, and Hudson County basketball legend Mike Rooney, who took a two-part podcast to tell all his stories. It was also the most-listened to of Jim's podcasts."

Thousands of Hudson County athletes can thank Jim Hague for making sure that "the light" shined on them for decades.

–

By, Michael Hogan

**ANY TICKET.
ANYTIME.
ANYWHERE.**

GreatSeats ltd
Any ticket, Anytime, Anywhere

**GREAT SEATS LTD
333 W.39th ST.
New York, NY 10018**

212/302-1642

ROBERT McLAUGHLIN

Try some word association to describe Robert McLaughlin.

First, let's eliminate "Boy Scout." Read between the lines however you wish.

Described as having as much skill as any player to come out of Hudson County, McLaughlin's end, in 1989 at the age of 49, was a direct result of loving the fast lane more than the fast break...and no one who knew him was surprised.

Used as target practice at or near the old Madison Square Garden (having failed to, ahem, square his account with the creditors), the list of those he crossed paths with, or just plain crossed, includes one Jack Roland Murphy. "Murph the Surf" in social circles was a convicted murderer and jewel thief (it was back in October of 1964 when the Star of India and other gems walked out of the American Museum of Natural History), perhaps not necessarily in that order.

McLaughlin was a human change-of-address form. There were several high Hudson high schools (Lincoln and St. Joseph's among them), working on his game, if not his grades.

Colleges, shockingly, looked past his transgressions. There was first a JUCO stop in North Carolina (at the behest of UNC). That didn't last long, supposedly something about our subject and the daughter of a dean.

Then, after returning home to Jersey City, there was LaSalle in Philly. A short, inattentive stay there, apparently expedited by a professor uttering the phrase, "Why are you here?"

(He was an Explorer sufficiently long to room with one Bill Raftery, and score 37 or 38 points [roomie wasn't exactly sure] in the school's freshman-varsity game.)

When Thomas Wolfe wrote "You Can't Go Home Again," he wasn't referring to McLaughlin, who went back to Jersey City. Next stop, Baton Rouge, where he found success (albeit briefly) at LSU. McLaughlin had played so well, he was selected for the Sugar Bowl's all-tournament basketball team.

How about Pete Maravich before Pete Maravich...but not long.

NYU and Coach Lou Rossini took their shot with McLaughlin. Shots at McLaughlin were later.

Then, finally, in the fall of '63, it was "Hudson County West," aka St. Mary of the Plains in beautiful, downtown Dodge City, Kansas.

Why was Robert McLaughlin so nomadic?

Gambling (fixing card games?), drinking, skipping classes and fighting with opponents may not be among the seven deadly sins, but in his case, they weren't exactly enhancers of the resume.

Here's a not-too-hard-to-believe aside, courtesy of former Snyder (Jersey City) standout Mike Rooney. According to Rooney, the two often played against each other – full court, by themselves – at Jersey City's renowned Audubon Park. Seems that one day, around the time of the 1964-65 New York World's Fair, McLaughlin asked Rooney to do him a favor. Providing the subway fare (then 15 cents, now $2.90, kid you not), McLaughlin – who was working as a bartender – wanted Rooney to pay him a visit.

Once at Flushing Meadows, Rooney was to lay down a dollar and order a libation. Rooney was perplexed when he received change for a hundred, but shortly after, that was cleared up when he received a message to meet McLaughlin in the men's room, where Rooney handed him the full amount of change for a hundred.

Hey, even at Robert Moses' place, sh–t happened.

The last word belongs to another fine Hudson player in his own right, Richie Donnelley.

"Anytime something mischievous happened, connect the dots to McLaughlin," Donnelley said. "He was a confident individual who thought he was better than anyone else."

"He was an asshole." ...or a colorful character. PO–TAY–TO, PO–TAH–TO.

–

By, Frank Drucker

JERRY MOLLOY

New Jersey's 'Toastmaster General'

–

They used to say that if you wanted to play college baseball for St. Peter's back in the '60s, expect to ride the bench until your sense of humor improves. Such was a southpaw compliment to the Peacocks' coach, Jerry Molloy, who kept audiences in stitches for decades as New Jersey's humorous "Toastmaster General."

The rotund Irishman from Hoboken went on to become known, first and foremost, for his after-dinner skills at some 300 banquets and dinners each year. His stories, talks and lines were often inspirational, always hilarious. And memorable, let's not forget memorable. Jerry Molloy stories abound – stories he told and stories told about him.

If he saw you in the audience, you could bet the farm he'd use you as a foil.

"Pete was the James Bond of our team. He hit .007. Remember when you got the hit, Pete? Only time I ever saw you on first base without your glove."

And you wore his jibes as a badge of honor and found yourself in great company.

"I was there when you played your first high school football game, Kevin. I was there for your last game, too. Same game. Kevin was the quarterback. He threw four interceptions before the coach sent in a replacement. Kevin stormed to the sideline, took off his helmet and flung it to the ground. It was intercepted."

His son, Jimmy, recalls being in the audience at some of those dinners. "Had to have been about 25, 50 times," he says, "each one remarkable. Of course, I was the butt of his jokes those nights."

"My kid is an honor student. He's always saying, 'Yes, Your Honor. No, Your Honor.'"

But Jerry Molloy was more than an after-dinner raconteur. To most who got to know him, he was simply "Coach."

He was my baseball coach at St. Peter's, where he worked from the 1950s until 1970 – that was the year I graduated, so if he were still here, for sure he'd say that I and my teammates drove him out of the game.

We'll get back to his dugout domain shortly. First, though, there was Jerry's formidable career in basketball, first as a college referee in the 1950s where he'd occasionally treat crowds – including those in the old

Madison Square Garden on Eighth Avenue – to the sight of the rotund ref sliding on his knees across the hardwood, blowing his whistle and making a call.

Somewhere along the way, though, Jerry discovered coaching. Nothing was ever the same again.

It started when Jerry was 22. The late Msgr. James J. Carberry asked Jerry if he would coach boys basketball at St. Mary's High School in Paterson. Jerry said he'd give it a try. Some try it was – Jerry won 508 games in 38 seasons there.

One of those games, against Stevens Academy, was memorable, not just for Coach Molloy but also for Prep Coach Sal "Yorkie" Calabro. Jerry and Yorkie not only were lifelong Hoboken friends, they were best friends, and as Yorkie Jr. tells it, "That was the greatest day of my dad's life because his team beat Jerry's!"

The best friends had other games to remember as rival coaches, including the time Jerry was so worked up over a ref's call that, mid-argument, Jerry's denture flew out of his mouth and seemed destined to find a resting place under the bleachers. Yorkie made a kick save, scooped it up and handed it back to Jerry – who popped it back in without ever pausing his heated discussion.

And he always knew a good referee when he saw one.

"There are good refs and there are great refs. Bobby here was the best referee money could buy."

But his time at St. Mary's was only about half the story. While still working the sideline in Paterson, he also coached at two schools in Elizabeth: St. Patrick's (200 victories) and St. Mary's (100). That's three teams, simultaneously. He would later add 92 victories at St. Michael's in Newark.

For those of you keeping score, by the time he retired his whistle, Jerry had won 900 games, a then-record for a New Jersey high school coach. His total has since been eclipsed only by Naismith Hall of Famer Bob Hurley's 1,185 victories at St. Anthony in Jersey City and Paul Rodio's 1,000 at St. Augustine Prep in Richland.

"Remember those billboards that said 'Drink Canada Dry'? By God, my uncle sure tried. But he died a natural death. He got run over by a beer truck."

As his high school basketball career was winding down, Jerry devoted his attention to his other favorite sport: Baseball. As St. Peter's College skipper, usually the most memorable thing about Peacocks games in those days was the presence alongside him in the dugout of a fellow Hobokenite named Marty Sinatra. Marty's son never played for Jerry, but you probably heard of him anyway.

At St. Peter's, baseball might best have been regarded as the red-haired stepchild. The Peacocks had no home field or practice facility, so they scouted about for places to practice, often in sections of city or county parks strewn with broken bottles or a huge tree in the middle of right field. But Jerry and his Peacocks made do. It was, after all, still baseball.

And Jerry added his comic touches often enough to keep players on both teams – and umpires – on their toes.

"For cryin' out loud! You ought to go on "What's My Line?" Nobody's ever guess you're an umpire!"

Jimmy recalls a game against Seton Hall that ran into the gathering dusk with the Peacocks nursing a one-run lead.

"My dad kept yelling to the umps that it was getting too dark to continue, that somebody was going to get hurt out there," Jimmy said. "So he walked out to the mound, lighting matches along the way so he could see where he was going."

Yorkie Jr. remembers another time Jerry ambled to the mound to rescue his pitcher from constant shelling.

"The pitcher said, 'Coach, I'm not tired.' Jerry replied, 'No, but the outfielders are.'"

"I was one of several ushers at my church who collected offerings at every Mass. They'd give us a collection basket for one hand and, for the other, gave each of us a live housefly. This was Hoboken, remember, so our job was to bring back the fly alive."

But Jerry was much more than just a dugout jokester. He made his share of shrewd managerial moves, such as the time he had a runner steal home to break a tie in the bottom of the ninth. Or the day at Roosevelt Stadium when his Peacocks were up by a run with two outs in the top of the ninth and a runner on second. Jerry called time, ambled out to the mound and had the left fielder swap positions with the second baseman, who happened to have a stronger throwing arm.

The next batter lined a clean single to left but -- wouldn't you know it? – the runner got thrown out at the plate. Game over. As Casey Stengel liked to say, you could look it up.

All the while, Jerry held the job of Hoboken's superintendent of recreation. So beloved was he in that role, the city renamed its youth center after him. That's in addition to the Jerry Molloy Youth Center, which had been the gym he prowled at St. Mary's in Paterson. And the Jerry Molloy Good Guy Award presented annually by the N.J. Sportswriters Association. And the Hoboken Hall of Fame's Jerry Molloy Award.

And did I mention that Jerry was a member of the charter class of the Hudson County Sports Hall of Fame in 1991 along with Tom Heinsohn, Bill Raftery, Alex Webster and James J. Braddock?

"My wife came home from a doctor appointment, so I asked her what he said. 'He said, for a woman my age, I have a wonderful figure.' Really? What'd he say about your big, fat Irish ass? 'He didn't mention YOU at all.'"

But my favorite Jerry Molloy memory has nothing to do with basketball, baseball or even humor. I was working the night shift in Sports at the Los Angeles Herald Examiner in 1985, and I received a phone call. From Jerry. We hadn't seen or spoken with each other for about six years. Out of the blue, Jerry calls.

"I had to have the Hoboken cops call the L.A. cops to track you down because I didn't have your number," he said. "Just wanted to see how you were doing and to say hello."

He didn't stay on the line long and let me get back to work. A few weeks later, Jerry was dead, succumbing to maladies of age. That's when it hit me: He wasn't saying hello, he was saying goodbye.

That next spring, during a college reunion, I sat at a table with baseball teammates and told them that story. As I'm talking, I see stares of astonishment and dropping jaws, and I'm thinking, "Man, I must be mesmerizing the guys with this story."

But, when I stopped, I heard every other guy at the table mutter in various degrees of awe, "Same here." Or "I also got one of those." Or "He called me, too."

That's the best Jerry Molloy story I've got. Top that.

—

By, Pete Wevurski

NICK PIANTANIDA

Nick Piantanida was a basketball player, but that's only part of the story, one with many chapters in a life that lasted just 34 years.

However, since this is a book about basketball, that's where we're going to begin.

Born in Union City in August of 1932, Piantanida had a hardcourt rivalry with none other than Tommy Heinsohn. There were stories about the two battling in the Jersey City summer league, with Pintanida's team winning the title and he earning MVP honors.

There was a tournament where Piantanida and his team traveled to North Carolina, opposing a Philadelphia squad with some guy named Chamberlain. While the Philly team won this title, both Piantanida and Chamberlain (whatever happened to him?) made the all-tourney team.

There was Jersey City's famous Mt. Carmel tourney, which Piantanida turned into his personal playground with a 67-point performance in one game.

There was a college sojourn (at least temporarily) to now-defunct St. Mary's of the Plains, part of a Hudson County caravan that somehow surfaced in beautiful, downtown Dodge City, Kansas.

(Among the Hudson 'plainsmen,' though not concurrently, were two Piantanidas [Nick and younger brother Vern], Gerald Govan (he of a fine career in the ABA), the 'peripatetic' Bob McLoughlin [more about him in another 'Hotbed' story], Rich Donnelly, Ed Hudson, Tom Glatt, Jack Nies [long-respected NBA referee], Lou Perino, Charles Branda, Bob Tagalieri and Jack Szegis.)

There was a (refused) contract with the New York Knickerbockers, because Piantanida could make more playing in a variety of non- NBA leagues.

There was also Nick Piantanida the adventurer/daredevil, his downfall trying to complete a downfall (ironic).

At the ripe old age of 10, he was making parachutes, using some unsuspecting neighborhood cats as test pilots.

Parachuting turned into climbing, with Piantanida becoming the first (or among the first person(s) to scale several summits (see Angel Falls, Venezuela). Climbing then became skydiving, with Piantanida insatiably ingesting knowledge on the subject, aiming to become the world-record-holder. That, and aiding the US military with it came to bailing out at altitudes. Attempting free-falls at staggering heights. Piantanida had his first try in October of 1965. "Aboard" Strato Jump I, he was victimized by wind shear, tearing his balloon at 16,000 feet. It ended in a meet-and-greet with a Twin Cities garbage dump.

Next was February of 1966, with Strato Jump II in Sioux Falls, SD. In what would have been a record, there were instead "technical difficulties," a failure to disconnect the oxygen line and thus an (gondola-only) aborted jump.

Piantanida's third time was not a charm. It was May of '66, returning to Sioux Falls, trying (again) to successfully descend at more than 120,000 feet (approximately 23 miles). Strato Jump III climbed to more than 57,000 feet when something went amiss. Piantanida's "emergency" call was accompanied by a hissing sound. It was some 26 minutes before he landed, nearly 60 miles off course near Worthington, MN. Alive but unconscious, he had apparently (accidentally) depressurized his helmet, perhaps while trying to clear his visor.

Piantanida died of hypoxia (an insufficient oxygen level) Aug. 29th, more than four months after the attempt, leaving behind a wife, three daughters and one helluva legacy.

Author's aside...appreciation to Vernal [Vern] Piantanida, Nick's brother, who assisted with this story.)

—

By, Frank Drucker

JOE 'ROCKY' POPE

It's possible – not likely, mind you, but possible – that a visitor to Joe "Rocky" Pope Gymnasium at Hudson Catholic Regional High School in Jersey City might know nothing about the man whose name – and spirit – graces the Hawks' facility.

Joe Pope was ... (it gets difficult here because folks who did know him understand there's no singular description for Rocky).

Let's start with this: Rocky was the Hawks' basketball and baseball coach in the 1970s.Rocky was big. Rocky was burly. Rocky was loud. Above all, Rocky was imposing.

"When I first met Rocky, the first impression was something," says Jim Boylan, who played freshman and junior varsity ball for Pope at St. Mary's H.S., also in Jersey City. "Just the visual: crewcut, black glasses, big cigar, rough talking, 6-foot-4, pretty intimidating!"

"I remember Rocky always packin' a cigar, sometimes even at games," confirms Mike O'Koren, who starred for Rocky along with Jim Spanarkel at Hudson before both moved on to the Atlantic Coast Conference. "But, obviously, he was a very, very good coach."

"Hudson Catholic was a doormat in basketball and baseball but, boy, did he change that," says Jack Cullen, who played basketball and baseball for Pope at Hudson. "He took us to the county championship in 1975. Even better, we beat St. Anthony in that game."

The Hawks would go on to win eight other Hudson County titles, along with two runner-up finishes, but Rocky's team broke a long drought by capturing that first one. It was Rocky's only county crown – his team won a Group A state championship the next year – but 4,000 fans packed the Jersey City Armory for that landmark game against St. Anthony and most of them spilled out incredulously onto Montgomery Street and onto the Hudson campus a block away when the final buzzer sounded on the Hawks' 63-53 victory.

"He was good," offers O'Koren, who went on to a great ACC career at North Carolina and the NBA. "He sure knew what he was doing."

"But he never did get credit for the Xs and Os," Cullen says. "He did things a little different. Take Jim Spanarkel. Jim was something like 6-foot-7. Any other coach would have put him in the post. But Rocky had him playing point guard, bringing the ball up. You just didn't see that anywhere else."

"He sure helped each of us improve," relates Spanarkel. "He was particularly instrumental to me my freshman year and sophomore year. I was 6-4, almost 6-5 at the time, and he'd have me bringing the ball upcourt.

If they had a kid that tall, most high school coaches generally would put him under the basket. Not Rocky. He saw right away that I could do more, so he gave me the opportunity and the responsibility."

Pope did things differently on the diamond, too.

"I rode the bench as a backup catcher at Hudson so I got to watch how he did things," relates Cullen. "He was a little bit ahead of his time. Most coaches would leave his starter, if he was pitching well, in the game until about the seventh inning. Not Rocky. He'd go through 4-5 pitchers a game – but that was his game plan. He'd tell the starter, 'You're going four, then Billy will pitch the fifth and sixth, Ken will take seventh & eighth and Mike will wrap up the ninth.' "

"Another Xs & Os thing," Cullen continues. "Jimmy Spanarkel was a power hitter, so teams sometimes sent their third baseman out to become a fourth outfielder. So what does Rocky do? He has Jimmy bunt down third for a hit.

"But that points up another huge thing about Rocky: He was all about unselfishness, and his players bought into it. Spanarkel and O'Koren would score 14-15 points a game at Hudson. Everyone knew they were each capable of 40 points or more but they'd score their 14 or 15 and be happy because we won."
Rocky could keep his players on their toes, too.

"He was also very smart. He knew more than he let on. Certainly, he knew more about us than we thought he knew," O'Koren relates. "One game we played was a big one at St. Mary's. Their gym held maybe 200 people but, I swear, there must've been about 500 crammed into the place."

That game was nearly postponed because the perspiration of all those bodies made the gym so humid that the floor was slippery. But the game was played and Hudson Catholic won.

"After the game," O'Koren continues, "we were feeling so good about ourselves that most of us snuck off for a few beers at Joey Starr's tavern on Newark Avenue. We're feeling pretty good, I'm telling you, when all of a sudden, in walks Rocky. How in the world did he know? Anyway, I had to climb out the men's room window to escape!

"Anyway, Rocky was a very colorful guy. He had this carting business as a main job -- he collected garbage – you don't get more colorful than that."

"To me, he was always a big, strong, husky, intimidating guy," contends Spanarkel, the lone Hudson Catholic athlete to play four years of basketball and four years of baseball for Rocky and whose post-Pope career continued at Duke and in the NBA. "He was an early proponent of tough love with all his players but he had a real gentle heart. I wish I had a nickel for every hamburger he'd buy us. He was a really serious guy who loved his players off the floor or field.

"Actually, he was kind of like another parent. He'd drive down your street at 11 o'clock or 11:30 and, if you were out – we usually were out – he'd roll down his window and tell us it was time to go home. I didn't appreciate it back then but, looking back, it was a wonderful thing he did for us."

"He was a very caring man. He had a business picking up garbage with his own trucks. He'd take care of business in the morning, leaving the afternoons and evenings to coaching – and looking out for his players," agrees Cullen. "Yeah, he was like a third parent and a lot of kids needed that. I had excellent parents but a lot of kids weren't as fortunate, so Rocky became very much a strong parental figure for them. And he kept them and the rest of us out of trouble.

"That's what I remember most about Rocky. Oh, and that he never got any names right! Not ours, not our opponents. My favorite was when he was talking about a pitcher on the Mets. Kept talking about this Ryan Doylan guy. We eventually figured out that he was referring to Nolan Ryan."

OK, so maybe Rocky didn't know names. But he sure knew talent when he saw it.

"I played for Rocky as a freshman/sophomore at St. Mary's -- he was the JV coach," says Boylan, who later played at Assumption College before transferring and helping Marquette beat O'Koren and the UNC Tarheels for the 1977 NCAA championship. "Bill Kuchar, the head coach, brought me in on scholarship but there were 20 guys under scholarship my freshman year and I was feeling a bit lost on my first day in school.

"We had an open gym session, scrimmaging against varsity and JV players. On one play, I caught the ball at half court and was immediately covered by the varsity starting center. He was 6-6, 6-7 and here I was, maybe 6-1, 140 pounds … but I dribbled around and past him and drove toward the hoop. But I could feel him coming up behind me to block the shot so I went under the basket and made it a reverse layup.
"Rocky blew his whistle. 'THAT's how you play basketball,' he told everybody. 'You've got to use your head!'"

Right from that auspicious start, Rocky took Boylan under his wing.

"The very first day of official practice with all the freshmen, we worked about an hour and a half. When it was over, Rocky said, 'I want you to stay for the JV practice that starts in 15 minutes.'

"Well, JV practice lasted just as long and when it was over, Rocky said I should stick around and practice with the varsity. I told Rocky I was starved. He ran out and bought me two cheeseburgers and a milkshake about 5 minutes before varsity practice started. So I went from 9 a.m. straight through to about 1:30 in the afternoon. I sure was tired but I'm forever grateful to Rocky for that support."

After college, Boylan was a player coach in Europe and then an assistant at Michigan State under Judd Heathcoate – Tom Izzo was another assistant -- before embarking on a 25-year career as an assistant with six different NBA teams.

"I just remember Rocky Pope as being the first person who significantly acknowledged, to me, that I had something – a skill and talent that could be nurtured," Boylan confides. "Without that, I don't know if I could have put myself on that path."

Getting back to Rocky's Xs and Os – and Ws and Ls – in 1971, he became head basketball coach at Hudson, a position he held for 13 seasons. He led the Hawks to the North Jersey Parochial A Championship in 1973, to the aforementioned county championship in '75 and state Parochial A title in '76. In state tourney play, his '73, '74 and '75 Hawks lost each time to the eventual champion.

Rocky became Hudson's baseball coach in '72 and, by the time he hung up his spikes in '90, his Hawks had captured six Hudson County Division championships and the 1984 county championship. Two of his baseball players went on to pro careers – John Furch with the White Sox organization and Jose Colon with the Padres'.

He was inducted into the Hudson County Sports Hall of Fame in 1994 along with, appropriately enough, two guys named Spanarkel & O'Koren.

–

By, Pete Wevurski

MIKE ROONEY/ DANNY WADDLETON

During the 1950s and '60s, the inner-city game of basketball emerged into the sporting spotlight in Hudson County, particularly in Jersey City.

Quite naturally, you'd expect that the game's leading players would come from the projects, where a growing boy's non-school choices were pretty much limited to: You either played sports or you got into trouble.

And, in the Jersey City housing projects, there wasn't always a baseball or football field next door and there wasn't a golf course in the entire county. So it almost always came down to the one sport you could play right outside your door and almost year round: basketball.

From Holland Gardens and Curry Woods, two projects on opposite ends of Jersey City, came two youngsters who played basketball – lots and lots and lots of basketball – and became trailblazers for the dozens of hoop stars the city and county have produced since.

They say sports builds character, but it probably helps if you're a character to begin with.

Read and learn:

Dan Waddleton lived with eight siblings in three rooms at Holland Gardens, raised by a single mom who lost their father when she was 38. Living day to day was a constant struggle.

"We were so poor," Waddleton recalled, "when burglars broke into our apartment, they left stuff for us instead of taking things.

"But our tremendously strong mom told us, 'Your father died and there's nothing you can do about it except get up every day and outwork people. And that's what we did. I had a brother who was a really, really good athlete, and I just followed in his footsteps.

"I was fortunate to play biddy basketball, like Little League baseball, and played with a guy named Vinny Ernst and we won United States championships two years in a row."

Ernst went on to lead Providence College to the 1961 and '63 National Invitation Tournament championships back when the NIT was considered as important – or even more important – than the NCAAs. Ernst was the NIT MVP as a sophomore.

Waddleton sort of followed in his footsteps, too. He went to St. Michael's High School in Union City, where he played in four Hudson County Championship games, the last in 1964 against his counterpart trailblazer from Curry Woods, Snyder's Mike Rooney.

He was named to the first High School All-America Team in 1960 and later captained St. John's University to the NIT finals in 1962. A Hudson County Sports Hall of Fame inductee, he later coached at Dickinson High.

Although he was recruited by many colleges, Waddleton decided on St. John's because of a promise the Redmen coach made to his mom.

"Lou Carnesecca came to our house and saw the conditions we were living in," Dan said, "and he told my mom, 'We'll guarantee that he gets his degree, even if it takes him five or six years.' And that's the exact reason why I went there."

At the other end of town, Rooney was shooting the lights out at Snyder. He also was shooting at baskets all around Snyder long after lights were out.

Already as a high schooler, Mike was bona fide local legend for two things: Shooting basketballs – 600 of them a day – and, more important, sinking most of them.

"Basketball was everything to me," Rooney said. "I'd be shooting at Bayside Park until 1 in the morning, sometimes later, until somebody would call the police. The cops would come, confiscate and deflate my ball and send me home. But the police station was next to Snyder, so the next day I'd got to the station and tell the sergeant that somebody stole my ball last night. I'd always get the ball back, reinflate it and shoot some more that night. One time the cops told me if I wasn't home by 10 o'clock, still shooting baskets, they'd take a gun and shoot my ball!"

Rooney's reputation as a prolific scorer extended far and wide – he had interest from 80 colleges. One day, walking down a second-floor hall in Snyder, he was approached by a gentleman wearing a suit who asked if he was Mike Rooney.

"A guy in a suit? He had to be a cop, I thought, so I told him no," he said, laughing. "Next thing I know, I'm being paged on the loudspeaker to report to the principal's office. I show up and that same guy is sitting there: the head recruiter for UCLA.

"They invite me out to California," Rooney related. "I didn't have any clothes, so my family got together and I had my cousin's pants on, my uncle's coat, another uncle's hat, and I flew to California.

"When I get off the plane, it's 90 degrees! The guy who greets me is John Wooden and he says, 'What? Did you expect it to snow here!?!' I spent the weekend there – had dinner with Bob Hope, stuff like that. I had a chance to go to UCLA and I would have been on those national championship teams if I went there. But what I didn't like about UCLA was they had a lot of kids there and some of them complained about not playing. It was a really big thing.

"I also had a chance to go to St. Bonaventure and St. Bonaventure was fifth in the country at the time. They flew me and my father up to Buffalo and when we got there, it was a whole 'nother situation. They had only 10 kids on the team and two of them were backcourt kids who were seniors and would be graduating. I would have started right away.

"I wound up going to St. Bonaventure and it was the best thing I did in my life because for two years I really 'went to school.' "

Two years might have become three or four but …

"I got thrown out of St. Bonaventure," Mike acknowledged.

Turns out there was a dress code for team travel that he sometimes would violate. One of those times, the team issued him a suit to wear on a bus trip but the suit was incredibly wrinkled.

"I told the coach there was no way I was going to wear such a wrinkled suit," Mike said. "So the bus pulled away without me. I hitch-hiked two hours to get to the game and I watched it from the stands. The coach saw me and, after the game, said: 'That sure is a nice suit, Mike.' The relationship went downhill from there."

Eventually out of school, "I'm back at Audubon Park shooting baskets and there's a guy there, Alfred T. Eschbach the Third, from Fulton and Ocean avenues, who's now a legend in radio in Oklahoma. He's the Mike Francesa of Oklahoma."

(He's a little more than that. Eschbach has had a sports talk show in Oklahoma City for the past 47 years, said to be the longest ongoing sports talk program in U.S. history.)

"So I'm shooting baskets there for hours every day and Al is rebounding for me. One day he's wearing a Seton Hall Prep jacket, so I ask him where he's going to college. He says, 'Oklahoma.' I'm only fooling with him and say, 'Maybe you can get me in there?' "

Unbeknownst to Rooney, Eschbach then wrote a letter to Sooners coach Bob Stevens, telling him all about this phenomenal shooting friend he knows in Jersey City.

"He was a pure shooter, he was so smooth and he had a great knack for the game," Eschbach said. "He would dribble a basketball all the time no matter where he was going. His jump shot was unbelievable."

A week later, Al tells Rooney, "They called!"

"Who called?"

"Oklahoma, they want to talk to you."

"I get a call at my house as soon as they read my letter," Eschbach explains, "so we make an appointment for Mike to come to my house and talk to them on the phone."

"My parents didn't have a phone, so I went to his house and talked with them," Mike confirmed.

"Well, things worked out, and I'm going to Oklahoma! They'll have somebody meet me in front of the Holland Tunnel. So I'm standing there, I've got a basketball under one arm and about seven sports magazines under the other and a guy pulls up and asks, 'Are you Mike Rooney?' 'Yeah.' 'Where's your clothes?' 'I got 'em on!' He shakes his head laughing and tells me to get in the car. And we drove all the way out to Oklahoma.

"When we got there, though, they never saw me play and they told me I've got to pay tuition. I didn't have any money. But that night they saw me play and from then on, it was whole different story. They told me that in the morning I was going to have breakfast with somebody. So next morning I go to this little diner and this fella is there and the coach is there. We shake hands, then the coach leaves.

"The fella gave me some money, a lot of money that paid my tuition. And he gives me a job to pay for some clothes. He had a ranch with cattle and horses. I only went to 'work' to pick up my checks but we got to be good friends. They took really good care of me: I drove a Mustang and was one of the best dressed kids in school."

Eschbach remembers watching Mike play for the Sooners.

"Rooney was Maravich before Maravich as far as mannerisms, and the sloppy stuff before Maravich and the kooky stuff before Maravich."

Eschbach remembers something else.

"He walked around campus with a tennis racquet in his hand. Why? He thought it was cool."

Waddleton missed all this about Rooney.

"I never knew Mike growing up," Waddleton said. "I was from Downtown, he was from Greenville. We never played each other, except in that one county championship game, but we had heard of each other. After that, we still weren't close until after college when we started working at the same place, as investigators for the Hudson County Welfare Department in 1966.

"We've been like brothers – not friends, brothers – ever since. Whenever something happens to him, I'm there; whenever something happens to me, he's there."

Brotherhood fit Rooney like glove, always has.

"When I went to Oklahoma, they started to integrate the school and I roomed with a Black fella, Howie Johnson," Rooney said. "We would play all over the place. One time, we were playing in Kansas City and during games, I would fool with people in the stands. They'd be screaming, 'You're a bum, Rooney!' and I'd yell back at them.

"This night when we're leaving, we go outside the auditorium and there's a guy waiting for us. I told Howie, he's the guy we were arguing with in the stands. They guy comes up, introduces himself, says he's a lawyer and he wants to take us to the Playboy Club. I said, 'We got no money!' but he says, 'You're my guests.'

"We go with him and stay there until 3 or 4 in the morning and when we got back to the hotel, an assistant coach was sitting in the lobby with two plane tickets. We had gotten thrown off the team. Howie screams, 'Why'd I get involved with you?'

"But 40 years later, I got a call from Howie. 'The Black guys are having a reunion. How come you're not here?' I said, 'You nut, I'm white, that's why I'm not there!' He started laughing and said, 'You gotta be here, you're one of us."

Waddleton's background was similar. His teammate at St. John's was Donnie Burks, who went on to be an original cast member – with Diane Keaton and Melba Moore – of "Hair" on Broadway in 1968.

"He was my really best friend," Danny said. "When he died a few years ago, I went up to the funeral in Harlem. I was the only white guy in the whole auditorium. Coach Carnesecca got up to speak and said, 'That guy in the back there (me) was his partner. They were like ebony and ivory.' We never looked at colors. Everybody grew up in the same way. We grew up in a special time. It was just a good time to grow up."

And it was a great time to play hoops.

"Growing up in the projects, we had a Project League, 10 in the morning on Saturday: Booker T., Lafayette, Marion, Hudson, Montgomery, Holland. But from the Project League, I'd run down to No. 5 School, we had a CYO grammar school team. From there, I'd run up to the CYO to play in the Biddy League. Every night I was in a gym, if it wasn't School 37, I'd run up the viaduct to No. 6. We were playing basketball all the time. Plus, in the afternoons, we had recreation leagues up at No. 6. Plus, every Sunday we were playing games all over the state.

"I coached later, at Dickinson, and told them you had to have discipline. If you go someplace for 2-3 hours that somebody else isn't, that's discipline. But you have to be there. If you show up, you're going to get something out of it, especially if you work hard."

As a point guard, Waddleton understood the game.

"First, you have to take a leadership role. It all starts at that position. I was a point guard; Mike was a 2 guard. I liked to pass the ball, Mike liked to shoot it. It worked out great. It worked out perfect. One game, he scored 58 and I didn't score a point, in an all-star game in the Eastern League. But we won.

"It's all skills. You have to develop skills at an early age. It has to be taught. I used to work with two balls all the time, dribbling two balls up and down the floor. If I was going out to play somebody, I want to be competitive, so you had to work on your skills. Working with two balls, going this way, going that way, backing up as if they're pressing. As you're working on those strengths, you're also working on your weak hand. Kids don't do that nowadays. You want to be a good ballhandler, you've got to be out there practicing 3 or 4 hours a day; if you want to be good a shooter, you've got to be taking 600 shots. There's no secret to this stuff.

"Another thing, at school in the gym, the coach is teaching everybody the same thing. Then they're going home and we were going to another gym or another playground. That's how you get better. There's no secret to it. It's all work ethic.

"My brother was an all-state player at St. Peter's Prep in 1953 and I was all-state in '60. So I'd hang around with him when I was 13 years old and he was playing with Tommy Heinsohn. If they didn't have enough guys, I'd be the point guard. So playing with older guys like that, when you're playing in high school – guess what? – you're ahead of everybody."

Former McNair Academic basketball coach Mike Reilly remembered Waddleton taking him under his wing as a mentor.

"I was lucky I got indoctrinated by a Damon Runyon character. You can't do better than that,"said Reilly, who found Waddleton's intensity as coach remarkable. "He would start the game wearing a three-piece suit and, by the second half, he was down to a T-shirt and pants."

Rooney didn't coach a high school team but he ran a league at Dickinson H.S. for 45 years.

"Three games a night," he said. "We had 26 teams and no referees. It was on the honor system. If anybody got out of hand, I threw them out!"

Rooney had been drafted by the Lakers but didn't make the team. But team officials told him they had a "farm team" in the Eastern League.

"The Eastern League was heaven to me. I was getting $200 a game – big money in those days. It was a basketball junky world. Remember, there were only 8 NBA teams at the time. I played in the Eastern League with some great players. I would practice at the "Y" three times a day to be in shape for the Eastern League. I'd be there at 9 in the morning to shoot, then at 1 in the afternoon to shoot, then play a game at night. Like I said, I love basketball. I'm 67 years old and I'm at Dickinson still taking 100 shots a night."

Along the way, he teamed up with Waddleton on teams for the Mt. Carmel Tournament and other contests.

Both lament that most players these days don't share their passion for the game. "Today they don't understand the game," Waddleton said. "When I played with Mike, I was the second best shooter on the team, he was the first. If you want to win and he's open and I'm open, he gets the shot. But he understood at the game when he didn't have to score anymore, he'd get me the ball and I'd end it on the foul line."

And that partnership started in '66 when each signed on to be an investigator for the county welfare department.

"It was my first job ever," Rooney said. "I get there 9 in the morning and I'm sitting there, reading the manual. This nut walks in at 11 o'clock and says, 'You're Rooney?' I say, 'You're Waddleton?' He says, 'Let's go have breakfast.' And we never worked since."

But they've been best friends ever since, right up until the day Danny died in 2011 following a massive stroke. Until then, Dan and Mike could be found unfailingly in one of two places every night: On a basketball court somewhere, or sitting in beach chairs talking hoops and whatever on McGinley Square in Jersey City. Often, a crowd would gather just to listen in.

On Friday nights, though, the pair would head off to one of their favorite restaurants in Jersey City or Bayonne for a fine meal, followed by a fine cigar. They likely would still be out there on McGinley Square if Danny hadn't passed away.

"He had the stroke alone at home at night and they didn't find him until 7 the next morning. The news crushed me; I've never gotten over it.

"I left two cigars in his casket with a note: 'Make sure you look up St. Michael the Archangel when you get there. And get a light ready for these cigars, I'll be joining you soon.' "

—

Patric Fharah of "Old School Sports" contributed to this chapter.

ROBERT STEINMETZ

Mike O'Koren undoubtedly ranks as one of the greatest Hudson County basketball players ever, but behind the outstanding career is his former coach, Jersey City native and resident Ronnie "Stymie" Steinmetz. Stymie, who played high school basketball at Dickinson High School for Coach Sam Kaplan, nurtured O'Koren's career as a grammar school player at St. Joseph's that led to All-County honors at Hudson Catholic, All-America accolades at the University of North Carolina and an eight-year career in the National Basketball Association.

O'Koren and Stymie both lived in Hudson Gardens that stands on the corner of Newark and Palisade Avenue, across from Dickinson High School. "Stymie lived in the back (near Washburn Street), and I lived in the front (next to Newark Avenue)," recalls O'Koren. "Back in the day, we played bottle caps in the courtyard in Harden Gardens — 1, 2, 3, 4 poison — and I was on the floor playing and Stymie walked by. I was in the 4th or 5th grade, and he asked if I wanted to play basketball over at the St. Joseph's Schoolyard (that was a block away on Pavonia Avenue)."

That was the beginning of a legendary grammar school career at St. Joseph's, where as a 7th and 8th grader, O'Koren didn't lose a single game. Stymie was the coach of the team and mentor to young Mike, whose father, Frank, died when he was 12-years-old. O'Koren was raised by his mom, Rose, who passed away in 2015 at the age of 94, and his older brother, Ron.

"We lived in Building No. 44 right above the tunnel (leading out to Newark Avenue), and we could look back (north) into the Gardens," O'Koren recalls. "My father would see Stymie coming from his building and say, 'Here comes your manager.' We spent a lot of time together."

Stymie started coaching the St. Joseph's basketball teams in 1968. "I was ineligible to play at Dickinson and St. Joseph's had a coaching opening and I stepped up," remembers Stymie, who played for the Rams as a junior with All-County star Ron Dabney — one of the greatest players in Dickinson history. "The Junior ABA (Biddy) team was undefeated for two years and the Grammar team for three years. It was so enjoyable. No problems with the parents."

Those teams accomplished all those winning streaks practicing outside at St. Joseph's or Hudson Gardens, which had lights on the court.

"We might, on a Tuesday, get into No. 8 from 6–8 p.m. The janitor would open the door for us. We'd walk up Palisades (Avenue) and cut across to No. 8, but most times we practiced outdoors at St. Joseph's. (Occasionally) in high school we would practice under the lights in Hudson Gardens."

Stymie's grammar team had a winning streak that totaled over 80 games, including a tremendous victory over a squad from Holy Spirit (West Orange) that was unbeaten for five years.

"Their best player got a T (technical), and we had (O'Koren) going to the foul line. Two free throws. We pulled off a quick one," Stymie said. St. Joseph's would move on to win the New Jersey CYO Championship.

O'Koren remembers how he misinterpreted Stymie's scouting report for that big game.

"Stymie told us if you blink, they'll leave their feet, so I started blinking and thinking they'll jump," says O'Koren, laughing about his basketball naivety from more than 50 years ago.

"Stymie alled timeout and said, 'What the hell are you doing?'"

O'Koren stressed that Stymie was a coach who was well ahead of time in coaching grammar-school basketball.

"When I got to high school, he got out of it (coaching)," says O'Koren. "He was a great coach. He loved (Hall of Famer) Elgin Baylor and taught me to do reverse lay-ups like Elgin. He'd say, 'When you play bigger players, they'll block your shot. You have to use the rim.' He taught me to do crossover dribble and double crossovers. Everything (he taught me) helped. You have to have some talent, but even if you're a gas attendant, you have to work at it."

And Stymie gave unlimited time to enhance O'Koren's career and help him and his teammates produce some great teams.

"Once I started playing (basketball), I enjoyed it," says O'Koren. "He (Stymie) gave me my foundation. I had a great passion for baseball (that he used to play in pickup games on the grounds in front of Dickinson High School). Who knows what would have happened without Stymie? He was an important piece. He always said fundamentals never let you down. He taught me lessons about basketball and lessons about life. He is more than a friend. My mother did a great job of raising my sister Mary Jane, brother Ron and myself, but Stymie and Mr. (Alan) Cancro were big helps."

Stymie always stressed how you need dedication to become a good player.

"I'll never forget one day we were about to get on the Turnpike extension down by Ferris going to the Cancro house in Point Pleasant," remembers Stymie. "We saw these kids playing basketball in the courts (long gone) under the Turnpike. I said, 'Look how dedicated those guys are and we're going down the Shore.' I think that stuck with Mike."

O'Koren can't forget one game at the St. Joseph's Schoolyard, where brother Ron ran a summer league featuring some of the county's best players on the small court that was well known for its small dimensions, tin backboards and steel chains on the rims. Stymie, O'Koren and St. Peter's Prep standout Kevin Cummings (now a banking millionaire) played for Stym's Five.

"We beat a team from Bayonne something like 177–169," says O'Koren. "Cas Rakowski (a legendary sportswriter) put that in the paper (The Jersey Journal), 'O'Koren and Stymie combined for 72 points. O'Koren had 71 and Stymie 1.'"

When O'Koren moved on to Hudson Catholic, Stymie was a dedicated fan. Ronnie has never had a driver's license, so he rode to games on the bus, hooked up rides with someone else, and walked.

Stymie had been a big fan of high school basketball since his days at Dickinson, when he would ride the bus to Weehawken to watch their great teams featuring Tony Holm, Harry Anderson and Ray Huelbig, travel to watch Harvey Smith at Snyder High School, see Russ Johnson and Phil Baccarella at Bayonne or Ted Martiniuk at Emerson.

"Everyone seemed to have good players," recalls Stymie. "I'd take the 44 bus to watch Jackie Gilloon at Memorial. I'd go to watch great coaches like Jerry Halligan (St. Peter's Prep) or Warren Buehler coach his great teams at Weehawken High School."

A shining moment for Stymie came in 1975, when O'Koren and Hudson Catholic beat St. Anthony's at the Jersey City Armory before a crowd of over 6,000 fans.

"You were a celebrity if you played high school sports," he says. "It's a little different today."

After O'Koren led Hudson Catholic to the school's first and only NJSIAA championship in 1976 (the Hawks lost to Christian Brothers Academy in the 1973 finals when Mike was a freshman), he went on to a great four-year career in Chapel Hill at the University of North Carolina.

O'Koren had two National Intent signings, one in Chapel Hill for the Atlantic Coast Conference, and another at the Cancro house on Alan Terrace in Jersey City – a few blocks from O'Koren and Stymie's house, where he still lives today.

"We sat in Coach Dean Smith's office after the signing, with Coach Smith, (future North Carolina head coach) Bill Guthridge and Coach Eddie Fogler, who was Mike's main recruiter," says Stymie.
"No other school really had a chance."

Then, there were four years of being a rabid North Carolina fan that continues to this day, still without the benefit of a driver's license.

Stymie and friends, including Ed "Faa" Ford and Gibby Lewis, would travel to Chapel Hill to watch O'Koren play for the legendary Smith in Carmichael Arena, where the Tar Heels men's team played in those days. "Dean Smith wanted to know if everyone in Jersey City was crazy like the Faa," remembers Stymie. "(Faa) was one of a kind."

Stymie also created quite a legend in Chapel Hill, a quieter town in the late 70s than it has grown to be now. The Jersey City gang were notorious for having a good time. In those days, Chapel Hill bars and restaurants were only allowed to sell alcohol (beer excluded) if 50 percent of their business was food. So, the Jersey City entourage stayed at the Holiday Inn, just outside the downtown area. Needless to say, the group developed a reputation with the manager, Herbie.

During a January trip to Chapel Hill to watch O'Koren, Stymie, Gibby (Lewis) and Faa were staying at the hotel.

"One year, it was the coldest January in Chapel Hill and the pool was frozen over," says O'Koren. "Faa jumped into the pool and Gibby jumped into the pool to save Faa, who couldn't swim. Faa was disappointed that the hole Gibby put into the ice froze back over because it wasn't that big while Faa's spot didn't freeze back over because it was so big."

Nearly a decade later, St. Anthony's coach Bob Hurley drove his sons, Bobby Jr. and Danny to Chapel Hill for the North Carolina Basketball Camp. Because it had a swimming pool that Bob's wife, Chris, wanted, the Hurleys chose to stay at the same Holiday Inn, still managed by Herbie. When Bob registered the family for the week-long stay, Herbie noticed that Bob was from Jersey City.

Herbie turned a little pale and asked Bob if he knew Stymie, Gibby and the Faa. "You're not crazy like them, right?," Herbie asked Bob.

While acknowledging that, of course, he knew the trio, Bob stressed that he was there with his wife, sons and younger daughter, Melissa, and not to wreak havoc.

The Hurleys were good for the week, but Herbie still remembered the exploits of the Jersey City contingent in the late 1970s. Let's just say they had some unpaid bills at the hotel.

Years later, Jersey City basketball legend Mike Rooney, who has known Stymie for decades, helped his pal get a job with the Jersey City Department of Public Works.

"After I got him the job, his boss called me up and said, 'He doesn't have a license,' and I told him, '(The boss) that he just needs to drive the cars around the pound and doesn't need a license,'" recalls Rooney. "Then, he and a guy named Kelly would argue about North Carolina and Duke. The boss said I need to get rid of them. I had them draw straws. One would work days and one nights. Stymie won and took nights."

–

By, Michael Hogan

WILLIE 'VALENTINO' WILLIS

When names of the best guards in Hudson County high school basketball history get tossed around, his is one you seldom hear. Which is surprising because:

"He was the best one-on-one player of his era in Hudson County," claims George Blaney, who played for St. Peter's Prep, Holy Cross and the New York Knicks, then coached Stonehill, Dartmouth, Holy Cross, Seton Hall and was associate head coach with UConn's 2011 and 2013 national championship teams."

"He was a 'big guard' with the ball-handling ability of a point guard together with the scoring ability of a 2-guard," says Bob Hurley, long-time coach at St. Anthony in Jersey City."

The "He" both Hall of Fame coaches mentioned played for Lincoln High in the early 1960s, was an All-County guard and held the Lions' career scoring record. His name is Valentino Willis, a name they never quite knew. At Lincoln, he was Willie Willis. After graduating Lincoln and playing for the Norfolk (Va.) State Spartans, Willie Willis returned to Jersey and told his friends to call him by his "new" name: Valentino Willis. Most of them shrugged and starting calling him "Val." "He's a legend … all I knew was that he was supposed to be a 'lover,' " Gerald Govan says with a laugh. Govan, himself a county great who played at rival Snyder High, was Willis's longtime rec and Rucker League teammate.

"He was interesting … I never knew where he lived," Govan says and laughs again. "When I'd pick him up to go to the Rucker League in Harlem, he'd just say, 'Pick me up at the Junction.' So I drive through the Junction and out he'd pop, jump in the car and off we'd go."

Be all that as it may, the man could play. You had to, if you were a member of the Harlem Wizards along with Connie Hawkins, Tiny Archibald, Harthorne Wingo and other standouts on the Wizards' three touring squads.

"He was an excellent player, All-County at Lincoln," says Charlie Brown, who achieved the same status toiling for the Lions three or four years earlier. "He was a good athlete with a lot of style to his game."

Willis could do a bit of everything needed but had a specialty. "He was more of a scorer," Brown continues. "OK on defense, OK as a passer but you know he's going to get you 20 points a game. Had a good mid-range jumper but he sure could get to the basket to score, too."

"He was a very good player," Govan agrees. "He could play and had a lot of skills. He was a funny guy, a colorful character and such a showman!"

That showmanship attracted its share of attention, though not always from coaches, fans or opponents. Brown likes to tell of the time the Simonetti Bondsmen, for whom he, Govan and Willis played, were in a tournament in Rockland County. The Bondsmen had a good lead in the third quarter and the coach wanted his younger players to get in some court time against tough competition. Willis was one of them. The coach looks down the bench: No Willis! Where in the world? Turns out, Valentino was leaning against the wall about 15 feet behind the bench, watching the game and chatting up a lady friend of Brown's wife. The coach calls out to him to get in the game. Val hollers back, "You've got this game pretty much in hand. I think I'll just continue talking to my friend here."

Professional basketball came next. "When the ABA came into existence, they were putting together the New Jersey Americans and I think he was there," says Govan. Well, Willis was close. "Mark Binstein took me over to their training camp in Jersey," Val says of the former Dickinson backcourt standout who went on to play at West Point. "But they already had the team picked."

After missing out with the Americans/Nets, Willis played in the Eastern Professional Basketball League, where he averaged a couple of dozen points a game before joining the Wizards. Next, he spent 14 seasons playing with Marques Haynes' Harlem Magicians. During that time, he also appeared in Pepsi and National Car Rental commercials.

He also spent several seasons playing internationally in Germany, Okinawa and the Philippines following two years in the European Pro League.

"Elnardo Webster helped me land with the team in Lugano,
Switzerland, where I scored 30 points a game."

Through his travels with Harlem barnstorming troupes, Willis found a home in Tulsa, Okla. There, he told the Tulsa World newspaper, he finds joy in working with kids, first getting them to laugh, then getting them to think. He talks with youngsters throughout Oklahoma about the value of avoiding drugs, alcohol and
bullying others.

"I love to work with kids", Willis says. "I tell them never to give up and always give it their best, no matter how difficult it may seem sometimes."

Willis emphasizes education and to listen to the people who care about them: parents, teachers, counselors and principals. He says, "It's OK to laugh at yourself sometimes! We all need a little fun!"

Google "Valentino Willis" and you'll see a vast array of photos of "Captain Valentino Willis" working with kids on basketball courts and in classrooms. Always the showman. Govan hadn't realized just how much of a showman Willis could be until the night he and a date strolled through Greenwich Village. "Suddenly there's Willis," Gerald relates. "He says, 'You comin' to my movie?' "

"What movie?"

"The Wiz!"

Yeah, that one, the musical with Diana Ross, Michael Jackson and a cast of dozens, scores, hundreds,
maybe more.

"I'll get you tickets to the premiere,' Willis tells me," Govan continues. "Well, we didn't make the premiere but we saw it when it came to Journal Square. He must have been one of that cast of thousands. I've watched that movie a few times since and I haven't seen him YET!"

CHUCK WEPNER

Photo courtesy of Joe Shine

At the southern tip of Bayonne, at Dennis P. Collins Park, stands a seven-foot-tall statue to the city's most famous citizen.

Chuck Wepner is best known as the inspiration for the "Rocky" films, a heavyweight boxer who suddenly got the chance to face Muhammad Ali in a championship bout and against overwhelming odds, not only knocked Ali down for the first time in his career, but lasted into the 15th round.

But Wepner is also well known in Bayonne for his prowess on the basketball court, where he was just as tough a foe.

Just ask Eugene O'Connell, who played against him.

"After college I played in the Bayonne League," said O'Connell. "One of my opponents was Chuck Wepner. I blocked his first three shots, then he punched me in the chest and said 'don't block my shot again'. I said all you had to do was ask."

Wepner recalled playing against Mike Rooney in a game in which he scored 36 points, but was outdone by the Snyder great, who scored 51.

Rooney entered a team in the Mt. Carmel Tournament and for strength off the boards recruited Wepner to be a strong inside man. Six minutes in the first game, after Rooney took a number of shots, Wepner called a time-out and when the team came to the bench, the coach asked who called it.

Looking straight at Mike Rooney, Wepner said, "I called it as I want to know if anyone else is going to get a chance to try one or two shots before the end of the first half."

Rooney's response: "In all walks of life, we all have roles. I'm a shooter and you're a rebounder so shut the fuck up and get out there and keep rebounding." Wepner then asked Rooney, "Have you ever been knocked out"?

Wepner scored 34 points in one game in the Mt. Carmel tournament and was asked how many of them were on assists from Rooney.

"No way, that guy hasn't had an assist in his entire career," Wepner replied. He gained his reputation for toughness after he grew up poor.
"I used to play at the PAL on 23rd Street and Avenue A, the old building and I got some free memberships to that and the YMCA because we were very poor," he said. "My mother worked in a factory called Solar on Avenue A and 23rd Street and I used to get stuff for free because we didn't have any money."

Wepner played varsity in his senior year at Bayonne High School, but quit midway through the season and went to play in a city recreation league.

"I was busy doing other things, you know, playing, in other leagues and I really wasn't probably good enough. But by my senior year, I was about six three, six three and a half. I was tall I was a better ball player. I got more experience and I was good enough to make the varsity because you had to try it out to make it. And I made it."

Wepner credits basketball with making him a better fighter.

"It was a good sport and kept me shape and it paid off later on in my career because in my boxing career I was never a great or gifted fighter. I was just in great shape to wear guys out. And so I beat them."

. . . Congratulation to "Hoops on the Hudson"
And the honorees that have been recognized

Special shout-outs to my late pals,
Howard Garfinkel and Larry Pearlstein

They were big fans of Hudson basketball who would've joined me
as huge supporters of this project.

All the Best,

Hubie Brown

VII

'HOOPS HOTBED' HISTORY LESSON

Watershed events and marquee moments which placed the national spotlight squarely on Hudson County basketball (players, coaches and teams)

1943

Memorial HS All-America John Mahnken and Weehawen's Danny Gabbianelli lead Georgetown to the 1943 NCAA title game against Wyoming in MSG.

1953

Harry Brooks earns All-State honors in baseball and basketball at Emerson, scoring 1,468 points during his HS career while leading Seton Hall to a 69-15 record, and the Pirates' '53 NIT championship.

1954-1955

Hudson County legends Tommy Heinsohn of St. Michael's and Togo Palazzi of Union Hill power 3rd-ranked Holy Cross to the 1954 NIT title by defeating Duquesne, which featured defensive stalwart Mickey Winograd of Lincoln. Heinsohn was consensus All-America in 1955, the same year Winograd held Dayton's high-scoring Jack Salee to two points in the final for Duquesne's first NIT championship.

1957-1958

Led by St. Peter's Prep's Hank Morano, Snyder's Tom Gaynor and Jay Olmstead, and Dickinson's Bill Prettyman, St. Peter's College earns berths in consecutive National Invitation Tournaments, giving the Peacocks their first national exposure. Previously, the Peacocks earned berths in the NAIA regionals from 1952 through 1955 and had advanced to the NAIA Tournament in Kansas City, where they reached the second round in '53 and the quarterfinals in '54.

1958-1959

Tony Nicodemo led St. Michael's (Vt.) to the NCAA College Division championship game in 1958 and the Elite 8 in 1959. His national prominence surged after a record 49-point outburst in the 1958 tournament, which currently is the 7th highest individual point total for both Division 1 and 2 national tournaments.

1961

Vinnie Ernst, who had led Jersey City to the 1953 & '54 National Youth championships and, as an All-Stater, led St. Aloysius to the '58 & '59 New Jersey Parochial State Championships, earned MVP honors after leading Providence to the 1961 NIT championship.

1963

As a senior, Ernst led the Friars to a second NIT championship in 1963 with a school record 17 assists against Canisius. He was named to the UPI Small Player All-America team, as well as AP and UPI honorable mention All-America.

1968

One year after being ousted by Walt Frazier and Southern Illinois U. in the first round of the NIT, unheralded St. Peter's College, forever known as the "Run, Baby, Run" Peacocks for their blistering fast-break offense – fueled by Lincoln's Elnardo Webster and Harry Laurie – that scored 93 points per game (third best in the NCAA), shocked sellout crowds in the new MSG with a double-overtime upset of Marshall and 100-71 quarterfinal blowout of 10th-ranked and top-seeded Duke in the NIT. Future Hall of Famer Jo Jo White paced Kansas past the Peacocks in the semifinal seen by an overflow crowd of 6,000 on closed-circuit TV in the Stanley Theater on Journal Square. In spite of that loss, their magnificent performance in the 1968 NIT generated 'Hoops Hysteria on the Hudson.'

1969

St. Peter's returned to the NIT, defeating Tulsa in its opener but losing to Temple in a quarterfinal.

1971–1973

Mike Boylan of St. Peter's Prep earned College Division Player of Year and All-America honors after leading Assumption College to three NCAA Small College tournament appearances, along with Prep teammate Serge DeBari and Dickinson's Neal Burgess. Coached by St. Prep alum Joe O'Brien, the Greyhounds compiled a 88-16 record from the 1969-70 through the 1972-73 seasons, finishing twice in the Elite 8 and once a 3rd-place finish in the small college tournament.

1973

Mercer County Community College (34-3) won the 1973 JUCO (NJCAA) national championship with a shocking 80-61 defeat of fifth-ranked Hutchinson CC on its home court. Mercer featured five Hudson County players: MVP Mel Weldon, Mike Leaphart and John Ford of Ferris, Marty Pendergrass of St. Aloysius and Richie Freda of St.Anthony who was the high scorer (23 points) in the final game. Mercer became only the third program to capture back-to-back NJCAA championships, defeating Chipola for the 1974 title.

1975–1976

In back-to-back postseasons, St. Peter's lost opening-round games to Rutgers and St. John's, respectively, in the ECAC Invitational but went on to the NIT in MSG, where the Peacocks lost to Oregon and Holy Cross, respectively.

1977

Jim Boylan of St. Mary's and Mike O'Koren of Hudson Catholic squared off in the NCAA title game, Boylan and Marquette topping North Carolina in an emotional conclusion to Coach Al McGuire's storied career.

1978

After teaming with O'Koren at Hudson Catholic, Jim Spanarkel blazed his own path down Tobacco Road. As a junior he helped Duke advance to the NCAA Final Four before falling to Kentucky in the final. Spanarkel was named All-America, ACC Tournament MVP and to the Final Four All-Tournament team.

1978

In the 1978 AIAW Women's national semifinals, unheralded Montclair State lost to UCLA 85-77 at Pauley Pavilion, ending their season with a No. 4 national ranking in the AP poll. The Red Hawks, who stormed to a 25-7 record without offering athletic scholarships, were led by Hall of Famer Carol "Blaze" Blazejowski, featured Holy Family Academy's Pat Quilty and Colasurdo Mayo, and St. Anthony's Alice Schmidt DeFazio, Cathy Meyers O'Callahan and Pat Quilty, and were coached by Hoboken's Maureen Wendelken, who compiled a 152-62 career record.

1980
After beating Fairfield and Fordham, St. Peter's lost to Iona in the ECAC Division Playoff, then defeated UConn and Duquesne in the first two rounds of the NIT before falling to UNLV in a quarterfinal on the winner's court.

1982, '84, '87, '89
St. Peter's earned NIT berths each season but lost first-round games on the winner's court to Syracuse, Tennessee, St. Louis and Villanova.

1986
Tom Heinsohn, who enjoyed an iconic career as a player with St. Michael's H.S., Holy Cross and the Boston Gardens, who won eight NBA titles during his nine-year playing career, was inducted into the Naismith Basketball Hall of Fame as a player.

1986
Unheralded New Jersey City University, coached by Lincoln's Charlie Brown, made an unforgettable run to the 1986 NCAA Division III semifinals.

1991
St. Peter's earns a spot in the NCAA Tournament for the first time, losing to Texas in the first round.

1991
Bobby Hurley Jr., considered one of the great point guards in college basketball history, was the floor leader of the 1991 Duke team that earned Coach K's his first NCAA title and ignited the Blue Devils dynasty. Young Hurley, whose St. Anthony team won four N.J. parochial state championships with a 115-5 record, teamed with Thomas Hill, Grant Hill and Christian Laettner to stun unbeaten UNLV in the semifinals (after losing to the Running Rebels in the title game a year earlier) before beating Kansas for the championship.

1992
Hurley helps Duke crush Michigan's "Fab Five" to become the first team since UCLA to win back-to-back NCAA championships. Duke finished 34-2. Hurley was selected Most Outstanding Player of the NCAA tournament and named to the All-America team. His 1,076 career assists stand as an NCAA record.

1992
New Jersey City University reaches the NCAA Division III Tournament semifinals and finished fourth in the country behind point guard Danny Waddleton, son of St. Michael's legend Dan Waddleton; Darren Savino of St. Anthony; and Neal King of Ferris. Savino now is associate head coach at UCLA.

1995
St. Peter's returns to the NCAA Tournament but bows out in the opening round to UMass.

1972–2004 Mike Granelli guided St. Peter's women to national prominence, compiling a record of 607-249 (70.9%), while also coaching the Peacocks soccer team and teaching public school in Hoboken. His Peahens won nine Metro Atlantic Athletic Conference titles in his 32-year career and appeared in seven NCAA Division Tournaments. He was four-time MAAC Coach of the Year.

2006 After a stellar playing career at St. Cecilia H.S. and at LaSalle, and coaching FDU-Madison and Seton Hall, Bill Raftery has been a courtside fixture on hundreds of Fox, ESPN and CBS basketball broadcasts since 1983. He receives the Naismith HOF Curt Cowdy Award. His broadcasting career continues.

2010 Bob Hurley, Sr. becomes one of only three prep coaches enshrined in the Naismith Hall of Fame after amassing 1,118 victories in his 39-year career building St. Anthony into a national power. His teams earned five No. 1 national rankings, won 26 state championships and 13 Tournament of Champions titles and enjoyed 8 undefeated seasons while he sent more than 150 players to major college programs. Overall, his career record is 1,185-125.

2011 Following a first-round bye, St. Peter's exits the NCAA Southwest Regional with a loss to Purdue in the Southwest Regional.

2011–2012 Kyle Anderson and Jerome Frink led St. Anthony to two of the most memorable seasons in its storied history. Over the span of two seasons, the Friars were a perfect 65-0, winning two NJ state titles and finishing as the nation's No. 1-ranked team by USA Today. In addition, Anderson was named to the 2012 McDonald's All-America Team.

2015 After guiding the Boston Celtics to a 416-240 record and two NBA championships as coach, Tom Heinsohn became only the fourth member of the Naismith Hall of Fame to be enshrined as both a player and coach joining John Wooden, Bill Sharman and Lenny Wilkens. In 2021, Bill Russell became the fifth.

2017 St. Peter's University, led by St. Peter's Prep's Trevis Wyche, captures the championship of the College Insider Tournament by defeating Texas A&M-Corpus Christi on the Islanders' home court. This followed victories over Albany, Texas State and Furman. The CIT was ranked immediately behind the NCAA & NIT postseason tournaments.

2017 Nick Galis, who played at Union Hill HS and Seton Hall, is inducted into the Naismith Hall of Fame after leading his Aris club to seven straight Greek championships. Nick was the honorary torch bearer in the 2004 Athens Olympics, and is an inaugural member of the FIBA Hall of Fame. He is recognized as Europe's greatest scorer, with 33.5 average and 12,864 career points.

2020

St. Anthony alumnus Juvaris Hayes averages 3.9 steals per game for the third consecutive season and finishes his career at Merrimack as the NCAA's all-time steals leader with 457.

2022

In the "greatest underdog story" in NCAA tournament history, unheralded St. Peter's stuns the college basketball world by knocking off second-seeded Kentucky, No. 7 Murray State and No. 3 Purdue to become the only 15th seed to advance to the Elite 8, where they lost to North Carolina. The Peacocks were led by Daryl Banks, Doug Edert and Lefty Driesell Defensive Player of the Year KC Ndefo among the starting five and Ferris' Isiah Dasher off the bench. Banks and Edert were named to the All-East Regional Team and Shaheen Holloway was named National Coach of the Year.

2023

Jersey City's Dan Hurley, who played for his dad at St. Anthony and later for George Blaney and P.J. Carlesimo at Seton Hall; and coached at St. Anthony and at five other schools for 15 years, completes a five-year transformation in turning University of Connecticut into a national powerhouse by beating San Diego State for the NCAA championship. Hurley's Huskies defeated every tournament opponent by double digits. UConn's staff also featured J.R. Lynch (Hudson Catholic) as a graduate assistant and Matthew Johnson (St. Anthony) as a Video and Scouting Coordinator.

CONGRATULATIONS
TO EVERY PLAYER, COACH, ADMINISTRATOR, REFEREE, PARENT, JOURNALIST, FAN, AND OF COURSE "CHARACTER" WHO MADE
"HOOPS HOTBED ON THE HUDSON"
THE COMPELLING STORY IT IS.

WE ARE HONORED TO SUPPORT THIS PROJECT.

Congratulations

TO ALL HONOREES!

Mike Wilson
ILLUSTRATOR

336 816-5583   jmikewilson52@gmail.com

VIII
—

HUDSON COUNTY PLAYERS OF DISTINCTION

1940-2023
—

BOYS

We made a conscientous effort to obtain as much accurate information as possible. Unfortunately, in some cases, our attempt was hindered by older players, defunct schools and inability to contact appropriate school officials.

PLAYER	YEAR	HIGHEST ALL COUNTY HONOR	NO. OF ALL COUNTY HONORS	COLLEGE	1000 PT SCORERS	2000 PT SCORERS
MURPHY, BUDDY	1940	FIRST TEAM	AC1			
MERCER, WALT	1941	FIRST TEAM	AC1 TWICE			
ISENBERG, MARVIN	1942	FIRST TEAM	AC1			
HUDAK, EMIL	1944	FIRST TEAM	AC1 TWICE + AC2	DARTMOUTH		
JENNINGS, EMMETT	1944	FIRST TEAM	AC1 + HM	EAST STROUDSBURG		
EGGERS, GEORGE	1946	SECOND TEAM	AC2 + HM			
LOTOSKY, MYRON*	1947	FIRST TEAM	AC1			
SZYSKOWSKI, FRANK	1948	FIRST TEAM	AC1 + AC2			
ZYGMUND, GENE**	1949	THIRD TEAM	AC3			
CONNORS, JIM**	1950	SECOND TEAM	AC2	FORDHAM		
CHAKEY, ED**	1951	SECOND TEAM	AC2	MONTCLAIR STATE		
BUEHLER, WARREN**	1952	FIRST TEAM	AC1	GEORGETOWN		
KONTJE, WAYNE**	1952	SECOND TEAM	AC2			
CALLARI, CARMEN	1954	FIRST TEAM	AC1			
PURNELL, JOHN	1956	SECOND TEAM	AC2 + AC3 + HM		🏀	
CAPITANO, PETE	1958	FIRST TEAM	AC1 TWICE	MONTCLAIR STATE	🏀	
STASULAITIS, BILL	1959	FIRST TEAM	AC1	MARYLAND	🏀	
DIVOCK, JERRY	1961	HONORABLE MENTION	HM	ADELPHI		
CAMPBELL, GREG	1964	FIRST TEAM	AC1 + HM	NORTH CAROLINA		
JOHNSON, RUSSELL	1966	FIRST TEAM	AC1 TWICE		🏀	
BACCARELLA, PHIL	1968	FIRST TEAM	AC1 + AC2 + HM	MONTCLAIR STATE	🏀	
THORPE, LARRY	1969	SECOND TEAM	AC2 TWICE	INDIAN RIVER JC	🏀	

---

* BAYONNE TECH
** SWEENEY

BAYONNE

PLAYER	YEAR	HIGHEST ALL COUNTY HONOR	NO. OF ALL COUNTY HONORS	COLLEGE	1000 PT SCORERS	2000 PT SCORERS
VAUGHN, STAN	1970	SECOND TEAM	AC2 + AC3		🏀	
WISE, TOM	1972	FIRST TEAM	AC1 + AC3	ST. PETER'S	🏀	
GREEN, THURMAN LEE	1978	FIRST TEAM	AC1 + AC2	WINSTON–SALEM	🏀	
MCGINNIS, JOHN	1978	SECOND TEAM	AC2 + HM	LOYOLA (MD)	🏀	
RICHE, ED	1978	HONORABLE MENTION	HM	MONTCLAIR STATE		
CHAKEY, JIM	1979	SECOND TEAM	AC2			
WATT, HENCY	1985	FIRST TEAM	AC1 + HM	BRIDGEPORT		
ARNOLD, ROBERT	1986	FIRST TEAM	AC1 TWICE + HM		🏀	
O'SULLIVAN, DAN	1986			FORDHAM		
DIAZ, ALFREDO	1993	HONORABLE MENTION	HM TWICE		🏀	
MASCIALE, DAVE	1993	FIRST TEAM	AC1	LIU		
PORCH, SAM	1995	FIRST TEAM	AC1			
ELAM, GARY	2004	FIRST TEAM	AC1 TWICE		🏀	
ELAM, ARTHUR	2005	FIRST TEAM	AC1 + AC2			
MERCEDES, LINOLL	2006	FIRST TEAM	AC1 TWICE			
CALLAWAY, RASHAD	2007	FIRST TEAM	AC1 + AC2	TAMPA		
MOORE, GREG	2008	FIRST TEAM	AC1			
HOLMES, TARIQUE	2009	FIRST TEAM	AC1 + AC2			
WILSON, RODNEY	2012	FIRST TEAM	AC1			
GASTON, GARRY	2013	FIRST TEAM	AC1 + AC2			
RICHARDSON, DESMEN	2013	FIRST TEAM	AC1			
BALDERAMO, CODY	2014	FIRST TEAM	AC1			
CALLAWAY, QADRY	2014	FIRST TEAM	AC1 + HM TWICE		🏀	
SMALLS, DAMON	2015	SECOND TEAM	AC2 + HM			

DICKINSON

PLAYER	YEAR	HIGHEST ALL COUNTY HONOR	NO. OF ALL COUNTY HONORS	COLLEGE	1000 PT SCORERS	2000 PT SCORERS
CROTTY, VIN	1946	SECOND TEAM	AC2 TWICE			
BUDD, BOB	1949	FIRST TEAM	AC1 + AC2			
BURNS, CHARLES	1950	FIRST TEAM	AC1			
BINSTEIN, MARK	1952	SECOND TEAM	AC2	WEST POINT		
FLORA, DOM	1952	THIRD TEAM	AC3 + HM	WASHINGTON & LEE		
ADER, SANDY	1955	SECOND TEAM	AC2	YESHIVA UNIVERSITY		
KUCHAR, BOB	1955	THIRD TEAM	AC3	VERMONT		
SNIDER, JIM	1957	SECOND TEAM	AC2 + HM			
BAUER, ROGER	1961	FIRST TEAM	AC1 + AC3	ST. BONAVENTURE		
PERROTTA, JOE	1961	HONORABLE MENTION	HM TWICE			
BOLTIN, ALAN	1963	SECOND TEAM	AC2 + HM	MIAMI (OH)		
BURGESS, BILL	1964	HONORABLE MENTION	HM	NJCU		
DABNEY, RON	1967	FIRST TEAM	AC1 TWICE + HM TWICE	ST. LOUIS UNIVERSITY		
BURGESS, NEAL	1968	SECOND TEAM	AC2			
COPELAND, DON	1969	SECOND TEAM	AC2 + HM	HARTWICK COLLEGE		
DABNEY, STEVE	1970	HONORABLE MENTION	HM	BOSTON UNIVERSITY		
WALKER, KERRY	1970	FIRST TEAM	AC1 + HM	BOSTON UNIVERSITY		
MOORE, GORDON	1971	FIRST TEAM	AC1	LIU		
ALLEN, BEN	1972	FIRST TEAM	AC1	ST. PETER'S	🏀	
EMANUEL, DAVE	1972	SECOND TEAM	AC2			
WINSTON, JERRY	1975	SECOND TEAM	AC2 + AC3	UNC CHARLOTTE		
VILLANUEVA, EDWIN	1981	FIRST TEAM	AC1 + HM TWICE	LIU		
KUPREL, JOE	1984	SECOND TEAM	AC2 + AC3 + HM	RAMAPO		
FUENTES, MARIO	1990	FIRST TEAM	AC1			

PLAYER	YEAR	HIGHEST ALL COUNTY HONOR	NO. OF ALL COUNTY HONORS	COLLEGE	1000 PT SCORERS	2000 PT SCORERS
WATSON, KASSAN	1992	FIRST TEAM	AC1			
RANSOM, CHARLES	1998	FIRST TEAM	AC1 TWICE	RAMAPO		
RICHARDSON, STEVE	2000	FIRST TEAM	AC1 + HM	RAMAPO		
WILSON, RASHAWN	2000	FIRST TEAM	AC1 TWICE	RAMAPO		
HARRIS, LEONARD	2002	FIRST TEAM	AC1	FDU MADISON		
MIRABEL, ALEX	2002	HONORABLE MENTION	HM			
HAIRSTON, BRANDEN	2005	FIRST TEAM	AC1	BERGEN COUNTY CC		
CUMMINGS, TRAVIS	2009	FIRST TEAM	AC1			
BURGESS, BRENT	2011	FIRST TEAM	AC1 + HR	NJCU	🏀	
BURNO, TYQUAN	2012	FIRST TEAM	AC1	NJCU		
JAMES, DUANE	2013	FIRST TEAM	AC1 TWICE	NJCU		
LOPEZ, TROY	2016	FIRST TEAM	AC1 + HM TWICE	RUTGERS NEWARK	🏀	
BATTLE-HOLLEY, TYREK	2017	FIRST TEAM	AC1 TWICE + HM	BLOOMFIELD	🏀	
GERTRUDE, JACQUAL	2019	FIRST TEAM	AC1	ALBERTUS MAGNUS		
JONES, TYMAIR	2020	FIRST TEAM	AC1	BROOKDALE CC		
DAVIS, ISAIAH	2021	SECOND TEAM	AC2 + HM			

PLAYER	YEAR	HIGHEST ALL COUNTY HONOR	NO. OF ALL COUNTY HONORS	COLLEGE	1000 PT SCORERS	2000 PT SCORERS
FITZPATRICK, KENNY	1943	FIRST TEAM	AC1 + AC2			
MORTON, RAY	1945	THIRD TEAM	AC3 + HM			
DEL PURGATORIO, PERRY	1946	THIRD TEAM	AC3 + HM	VILLANOVA		
PIA, DARIO	1946	FIRST TEAM	AC1 TWICE			
STEINMETZ, FRED	1946	FIRST TEAM	AC1 + AC2			
TOMASINI, NICK	1946	FIRST TEAM	AC1 + AC2 + HM			

PLAYER	YEAR	HIGHEST ALL COUNTY HONOR	NO. OF ALL COUNTY HONORS	COLLEGE	1000 PT SCORERS	2000 PT SCORERS
FLORIO, MATT	1949	FIRST TEAM	AC1 + AC2 + HM			
BREDE, HOWARD	1949	THIRD TEAM	AC3			
BROOKS, HARRY	1950	FIRST TEAM	AC1 THREE TIMES	SETON HALL		
NEVILLE, JERRY	1951	FIRST TEAM	AC1			
MADSEN, ED	1952	FIRST TEAM	AC1			
ALOI, NICK	1954	SECOND TEAM	AC2			
GRAMLICH, BILL	1956	SECOND TEAM	AC2 + HM			
BARAKAT, FRED	1957	SECOND TEAM	AC2 + HM	ASSUMPTION		
ORLANDO, RAY	1959	THIRD TEAM	AC3 + HM TWICE			
ZACCAGNA, RICHIE	1959	THIRD TEAM	AC3 + HM			
KICKEY, AL	1964	FIRST TEAM	AC1 + AC2			
NISBET, JACK	1965	FIRST TEAM	AC1 + HM			
MARTINIUK, FRANK	1966	FIRST TEAM	AC1	VERMONT		
SALATI, ALDO	1966	SECOND TEAM	AC2 + HM			
MARTINIUK, TED	1968	FIRST TEAM	AC1 + HM	ST. PETER'S		
SANGER, SANDY	1969	SECOND TEAM	AC2	WILLIAM PATERSON	🏀	
FERNANDEZ, OSCAR	1972	SECOND TEAM	AC2 + HM		🏀	
FAZIO, BOB	1973	SECOND TEAM	AC2 + AC3	ST. PETER'S		
LYNAM, DENNIS	1974	SECOND TEAM	AC2	ST. THOMAS AQUINAS		
MACHADO, JORGE	1978	THIRD TEAM	AC3			
MORALES, GINO	1983	FIRST TEAM	AC1 + AC2 + HM	WILLIAM PATERSON		
OTERO, GEORGE	1984	FIRST TEAM	AC1 + AC3			
ROBERTS, ALEX	1984	FIRST TEAM	AC1	ST. PETER'S		
RAGONE, TONY	1987	SECOND TEAM	AC2 + HM		🏀	

EMERSON

PLAYER	YEAR	HIGHEST ALL COUNTY HONOR	NO. OF ALL COUNTY HONORS	COLLEGE	1000 PT SCORERS	2000 PT SCORERS
LUGO, MARIO	1998	FIRST TEAM	AC1 TWICE	RUTGERS NEWARK	🏀	
SURIEL, MANNY	2001	FIRST TEAM	AC1 TWICE		🏀	
POWELL, CHRIS	2003	FIRST TEAM	AC1 + HM			
DELUCA, DANNY	2004	FIRST TEAM	AC1			
CRUZ, BRYAN	2007	FIRST TEAM	AC1 + HM			
CRUZ, JAIRO	2008	FIRST TEAM	AC1 + AC2 TWICE		🏀	

FERRIS

PLAYER	YEAR	HIGHEST ALL COUNTY HONOR	NO. OF ALL COUNTY HONORS	COLLEGE	1000 PT SCORERS	2000 PT SCORERS
COLASURDO, RALPH	1940	FIRST TEAM	AC1			
POMPEO, JOE	1943	SECOND TEAM	AC2 + HM			
WIERZBICKI, HANK	1947	FIRST TEAM	AC1 + AC2 + HM			
CUNNINGHAM, TOM	1949	SECOND TEAM	AC2 + AC3 + HM			
RADZISZEWSKI, RAY	1952	HONORABLE MENTION	HM	ST. JOSEPH'S (PA)		
NICODEMO, TONY	1955	FIRST TEAM	AC1 + AC3 + HM	ST. MICHAEL'S (VT)	🏀	
COSTELLO, JOHN	1958	FIRST TEAM	AC1 + HM			
MALTA, NICK	1958	SECOND TEAM	AC2 + HM	FAIRLEIGH DICKINSON	🏀	
PICCILLO, RICHIE	1961	THIRD TEAM	AC3 + HM TWICE + HR		🏀	
UNGERMAN, JACK	1965	FIRST TEAM	AC1		🏀	
WELDON, MEL	1970	FIRST TEAM	AC1	BOSTON COLLEGE		
WELDON, WILLIE	1974	SECOND TEAM	AC2		🏀	
STRICKLAND, DARYL	1976	FIRST TEAM	AC1 + HM	RUTGERS	🏀	
ORTIZ, BILL	1977	FIRST TEAM	AC1			
SMITH, CHARLES	1983	FIRST TEAM	AC1	BLOOMFIELD		

FERRIS

PLAYER	YEAR	HIGHEST ALL COUNTY HONOR	NO. OF ALL COUNTY HONORS	COLLEGE	1000 PT SCORERS	2000 PT SCORERS
BRYANT, ADAM	1985	SECOND TEAM	AC2	MERCER COUNTY JC		
WILSON, DARYL	1985	FIRST TEAM	AC1 TWICE	UNIV. DISTRICT OF COLUMBIA		
BASH, JEROME	1987	FIRST TEAM	AC1 TWICE + HM		⊕	
TAYLOR, KEVIN	1987	SECOND TEAM	AC2 + HM	NEW HAVEN		
KING, NEIL	1988	SECOND TEAM	AC2	NJCU		
WILSON, LEROY	1988	FIRST TEAM	AC1	LIU		
MYRICK, BOBBY	1989	FIRST TEAM	AC1			
CRADLE, ANDRE	1990	HONORABLE MENTION	HM	LIU		
FLUELLEN, DAVID	1990	FIRST TEAM	AC1 + HM	NJCU		
DASHER, ANDRE	1993	FIRST TEAM	AC1 TWICE	FDU	⊕	
DARBY, FRANK	1994	HONORABLE MENTION	HM TWICE		⊕	
WILLIAMS, KORIE	1995	FIRST TEAM	AC1	SPRINGFIELD		
BUSH, JASON	1998	FIRST TEAM	AC1	MONTCLAIR STATE		
WRIGHT, AMIN	1998	FIRST TEAM	AC1 + HM	RAMAPO		
TUCKER, KEVIN	2002	FIRST TEAM	AC1			
ARCHIBALD, TYRELL	2003	FIRST TEAM	AC1 + HM THREE TIMES		⊕	
DASHER, ISIAH	2017	FIRST TEAM	AC1 + AC2 + HM	ST. PETER'S	⊕	
EMANUEL, BUSTER	2017	HONORABLE MENTION	HM			

PLAYER	YEAR	HIGHEST ALL COUNTY HONOR	NO. OF ALL COUNTY HONORS	COLLEGE	1000 PT SCORERS	2000 PT SCORERS
CARNEY, JACK	1947	SECOND TEAM	AC2 + HM		🏀	
DEVANEY, JIM	1978	FIRST TEAM	AC1 + AC3	MONMOUTH	🏀	
NICHIRCO, JERRY	1979	HONORABLE MENTION	HM TWICE		🏀	
FERRIERO, VINNIE	1981	HONORABLE MENTION	HM TWICE		🏀	
MULRENAN, DARRYL	1984	HONORABLE MENTION	HM		🏀	
ENRIGHT, RAY	1987	THIRD TEAM	AC3 + HM		🏀	
LUCAS, RAY	1991	FIRST TEAM	AC1 + HM TWICE	RUTGERS (FOOTBALL)		🏀
MCCAULEY, BRIAN	1997	HONORABLE MENTION	HM TWICE	FDU MADISON	🏀	
MCDONOUGH, TOMMY	2002	HONORABLE MENTION	HM TWICE	KEAN	🏀	
OLIVERA, FREDERICO	2014					
CAJIGA, ALEX	2015					
LEIRAS, JONATHAN	2017				🏀	
DANIELLIAN, TIMOTHY	2018				🏀	
FELIZ, ERIC	2020					
BURGOS, EDWARD	2023					
STOKES, REUBEN	2023					

PLAYER	YEAR	HIGHEST ALL COUNTY HONOR	NO. OF ALL COUNTY HONORS	COLLEGE	1000 PT SCORERS	2000 PT SCORERS
CRITIDES, CHARLES*	1940	FIRST TEAM	AC1			
MCKIBBIN, MARTY*	1946	FIRST TEAM	AC1 + HM			
SILLETH, JOHN*	1947	SECOND TEAM	AC2			

* DEMAREST

HOBOKEN

PLAYER	YEAR	HIGHEST ALL COUNTY HONOR	NO. OF ALL COUNTY HONORS	COLLEGE	1000 PT SCORERS	2000 PT SCORERS
RUBBINACCIO, JOE*	1952	SECOND TEAM	AC2 + HM			
RADOVICH, TONY*	1952	FIRST TEAM	AC1 TWICE	NORTH CAROLINA	🏀	
ROMANO, JOHN *	1953	FIRST TEAM	AC1 + HM	ND (FOOTBALL)		
DELAURO, FRANK*	1955	HONORABLE MENTION	HM			
SIES, JOE*	1956	HONOR ROLL	HR			
PENSARI, GENE*	1957	THIRD TEAM	AC3			
BELLO, MIKE*	1958	THIRD TEAM	AC3			
ALTAMURA, JOHN*	1960	HONORABLE MENTION	HM			
MONTECALVO, GEORGE*	1961	SECOND TEAM	AC2 + HM			
WENDELKEN, JOHN*	1961	FIRST TEAM	AC1 TWICE + AC2 + HM	HOLY CROSS	🏀	
D'ANDREA, KEN *	1962	SECOND TEAM	AC2			
LITTLE, DAVE*	1962	HONOR ROLL	HR			
GROOMES, ED	1963	SECOND TEAM	AC2			
MEEKS, JOHN	1964	FIRST TEAM	AC1	NJCU		
BARONE, JOHN	1965	SECOND TEAM	AC2 + AC3	MONMOUTH		
MATTESSICH, TONY	1969	THIRD TEAM	AC3	ST. MICHAEL'S (VT)		
FOSTER, JIM	1970	FIRST TEAM	AC1 + HM	UCONN		
MILLER, CHARLES	1979	FIRST TEAM	AC1 TWICE + HM	BOSTON COLLEGE	🏀	
DUBOIS, BOB	1979	SECOND TEAM	AC2 + HM TWICE	BOSTON COLLEGE	🏀	
ABRAMO, FRED	1986	FIRST TEAM	AC1 + AC3			
ALSTON, DERRICK	1990	FIRST TEAM	AC1	DUQUESNE		
FORBES, RON	1990	SECOND TEAM	AC2 + HM TWICE		🏀	

* DEMAREST

HOBOKEN

PLAYER	YEAR	HIGHEST ALL COUNTY HONOR	NO. OF ALL COUNTY HONORS	COLLEGE	1000 PT SCORERS	2000 PT SCORERS
EUSEBIO, ED	1991	FIRST TEAM	AC1 + HM	NEW HAMPSHIRE		
HUGGINS, DONNIE	1996	HONORABLE MENTION	HM THREE TIMES		🏀	
FERGUSON, VERNON	2000	HONORABLE MENTION	HM			
CASTELLANOS, EDDIE	2006	FIRST TEAM	AC1 TWICE + HM	STONY BROOK	🏀	
KAMARA, DUVAL	2007	SECOND TEAM	AC2 TWICE	ND (FOOTBALL)		
CANARY, EDDIE	2009	FIRST TEAM	AC1			
PURVIS, ANTHONY	2013	FIRST TEAM	AC1			
DAVIS, JUSTIN	2017	FIRST TEAM	AC1 TWICE + HM		🏀	
HANBERRY, TYSHON	2017	SECOND TEAM	AC2 TWICE		🏀	
ASSADORIUN, ARAM	2019	FIRST TEAM	AC1			
GOODWIN, AMIR	2019	FIRST TEAM	AC1			
FREEMAN, NYJON	2020	FIRST TEAM	AC1			
HENSON, DANNY	2020	SECOND TEAM	AC2			
MORRISON, DEVION	2020	SECOND TEAM	AC2			

HOLY FAMILY

PLAYER	YEAR	HIGHEST ALL COUNTY HONOR	NO. OF ALL COUNTY HONORS	COLLEGE	1000 PT SCORERS	2000 PT SCORERS
ST. JOHN, JOHN	1944	THIRD TEAM	AC3 TWICE			
KAWATERS, ALAN	1951	SECOND TEAM	AC2			
ROCHE, JIM	1955	HONORABLE MENTION	HM	ST. FRANCIS (NY)		
KELLY, FRAN	1956	SECOND TEAM	AC2	HOLY CROSS	🏀	
SCHNEIDER, FRED	1956	HONORABLE MENTION	HM	ST. FRANCIS (NY)		
BALDINI, AL	1957	THIRD TEAM	AC3	ST. MICHAEL'S (VT)		
FINKEL, HENRY	1960	THIRD TEAM	AC3	DAYTON		

HOLY FAMILY

PLAYER	YEAR	HIGHEST ALL COUNTY HONOR	NO. OF ALL COUNTY HONORS	COLLEGE	1000 PT SCORERS	2000 PT SCORERS
DESANTIS, PETE	1961	SECOND TEAM	AC2			
AFFUSO, GEORGE	1962	HONORABLE MENTION	HM	BELMONT ABBEY		
FRANGIPANE, JOE	1962	SECOND TEAM	AC2	FORDHAM		
GREELEY, TOM	1963	FIRST TEAM	AC1 TWICE + AC3	HOLY CROSS	●	
SCHAFFNER, TOM	1964	THIRD TEAM	AC3			
ZINKE, FRANK	1965	SECOND TEAM	AC2	BELMONT ABBEY		
REGAN, TIM	1966	THIRD TEAM	AC3	ST. MICHAEL'S (VT)		
BALZANO, MIKE	1968	THIRD TEAM	AC3	ST. MICHAEL'S (VT)	●	
MILLER, ED	1969	HONORABLE MENTION	HM	CW POST		
VOLK, RICHIE	1969	FIRST TEAM	AC1		●	
COVIELLO, TOM	1970	SECOND TEAM	AC2	CW POST	●	
CALDWELL, NORM	1970			FLORIDA		●

HUDSON CATHOLIC

PLAYER	YEAR	HIGHEST ALL COUNTY HONOR	NO. OF ALL COUNTY HONORS	COLLEGE	1000 PT SCORERS	2000 PT SCORERS
MCDONOUGH, JIM	1973	FIRST TEAM	AC1 + AC3	WILLIAM & MARY	●	
SPANARKEL, JIM	1975	FIRST TEAM	AC1 TWICE + HM	DUKE	●	
O'KOREN, MIKE	1976	FIRST TEAM	AC1 TWICE + HM	NORTH CAROLINA	●	
BIHUNIAK, MIKE	1979	HONORABLE MENTION	HM TWICE	COLGATE		
NIERSTEDT, ED	1981	FIRST TEAM	AC1 + AC2	COLLEGE OF CHARLESTON	●	
LEE, PAUL	1982	FIRST TEAM	AC1 + HM TWICE		●	
RYAN, MIKE	1983	SECOND TEAM	AC2 + HM	SETON HALL		
FURCH, JOHN	1985	SECOND TEAM	AC2 + HM	DUKE (BASEBALL)		
BROWN, CHRIS	1987	HONORABLE MENTION	HM TWICE	PACE		

HUDSON CATHOLIC

PLAYER	YEAR	HIGHEST ALL COUNTY HONOR	NO. OF ALL COUNTY HONORS	COLLEGE	1000 PT SCORERS	2000 PT SCORERS
LEWIS, EGON	1990	FIRST TEAM	AC1 + HM	MONTCLAIR STATE	🏀	
CORSO, MIKE	1993	HONORABLE MENTION	HM		🏀	
HEALY, JERRY	1994	FIRST TEAM	AC1 + HM	NJCU		
OKERULU, DARLINGTON	2002	FIRST TEAM	AC1 + HM TWICE	SAINT ANSELM	🏀	
JOHNSON, KIAMEER	2003	FIRST TEAM	AC1 + HM	UNIVERSITY RHODE ISLAND		
MIHALINEC, DANNY	2004	FIRST TEAM	AC1			
CORTEZ, JONATHAN	2008	SECOND TEAM	AC2	BERGEN COUNTY CC	🏀	
KELLY, RAKWAN	2012	SECOND TEAM	AC2 TWICE + AC3	MISSISSIPPI VALLEY STATE		
YOUNG, MIKE	2012	FIRST TEAM	AC1	PITTSBURGH		
CAMERON, REGGIE	2013	SECOND TEAM	AC2	GEORGETOWN	🏀	
HALL, JARED	2013	HONORABLE MENTION	HM	LIU	🏀	
MCLEGGAN, KYLE	2013	FIRST TEAM	AC1	ADELPHI		
STEWART, KAVON	2013	FIRST TEAM	AC1 TWICE	ROBERT MORRIS		
BARRINO, NASSIR	2015	FIRST TEAM	AC1 + HM		🏀	
FRIDAY, SAMMY	2015	FIRST TEAM	AC1 + HM	SIENA		
BURNO, TYHEEM	2016	FIRST TEAM	AC1	UNION COUNTY CC		
KING, LOUIS	2017	FIRST TEAM	AC1 + AC2	OREGON		
MUHAMMAD, LUTHER	2018	FIRST TEAM	AC1 TWICE	ARIZONA STATE	🏀	
QUINERLY, JAHVON	2018	FIRST TEAM	AC1 TWICE + HM	ALABAMA	🏀	
DEZONIE, SHANE	2019	FIRST TEAM	AC1	TEMPLE		
RODRIGUEZ, DANNY	2019	FIRST TEAM	AC1 + HM TWICE	FDU		
GLOVER, JUSTIN	2020	FIRST TEAM	AC1	DICKINSON		
GERTRUDE, ELIJAH	2022	FIRST TEAM	AC1	VIRGINIA		

PLAYER	YEAR	HIGHEST ALL COUNTY HONOR	NO. OF ALL COUNTY HONORS	COLLEGE	1000 PT SCORERS	2000 PT SCORERS
PINKNEY, ADAM	2000	HONORABLE MENTION	HM	RUTGERS NEWARK	🏀	
ALONSO, JERRY	2003	HONORABLE MENTION	HM TWICE		🏀	
JOHNSON, MATT	2006	HONORABLE MENTION	HM THREE TIMES		🏀	
BOCCIA, TONY	2007	HONORABLE MENTION	HM	KEAN		
SANDY, OWEN	2007	HONORABLE MENTION	HM			

PLAYER	YEAR	HIGHEST ALL COUNTY HONOR	NO. OF ALL COUNTY HONORS	COLLEGE	1000 PT SCORERS	2000 PT SCORERS
WARREN, FRANK	1940	FIRST TEAM	AC1			
KIRK, BOB	1944	FIRST TEAM	AC1 + AC2	UPSALA		
MCCORMICK, FRANNY	1946	SECOND TEAM	AC2			
KILCULLEN, WALT	1964	THIRD TEAM	AC3	STETSON		
HALICKI, ED	1968	HONORABLE MENTION	HM	MONMOUTH		
LANDI, RALPH	1972	HONORABLE MENTION	HM TWICE		🏀	
RETO, BOB	1975	HONORABLE MENTION	HM + SH	NJIT	🏀	
LATKA, JOHN	1977	SECOND TEAM	AC2	TENNESSEE TECH	🏀	
SMEDBERG, JEFF	1978	HONORABLE MENTION	HM TWICE	BERGEN COUNTY CC	🏀	
PEGUERO, ALEX	1982	THIRD TEAM	AC3			
MEOLA, TONY	1987	THIRD TEAM	AC3 TWICE	VIRGINIA (SOCCER)		
ROSAMILIA, SAL	1987	HONORABLE MENTION	HM TWICE	COLUMBIA		
GORESH, KEITH	1994	HONORABLE MENTION	HM		🏀	
AMADEO, ANDREW	2006	SECOND TEAM	AC2 + HM			
MCDERMOTT, TOMMY	2007	SECOND TEAM	AC2	NJIT		
BLUNT, TROY	2008	FIRST TEAM	AC1			
GURZAKOVIC, SEJDO	2009	SECOND TEAM	AC2 + HM	NJCU		

KEARNY

PLAYER	YEAR	HIGHEST ALL COUNTY HONOR	NO. OF ALL COUNTY HONORS	COLLEGE	1000 PT SCORERS	2000 PT SCORERS
HOCH, DYLAN	2013	HONORABLE MENTION	HM TWICE	PENN STATE HARRISBURGH	🏀	
BAEZ, JOSEPH	2015	SECOND TEAM	AC2 TWICE + HM	BERGEN COUNTY CC (BASEBALL)	🏀	
SMYTH, GEORGE JR.	2016	HONORABLE MENTION	HM TWICE	BARUCH		
VEREEN, GRALEN	2017	HONORABLE MENTION	HM THREE TIMES	CLARK		
MYERS, ROBERT	2019	FIRST TEAM	AC1			
SOUZA, NICK	2020	FIRST TEAM	AC1			

LINCOLN

PLAYER	YEAR	HIGHEST ALL COUNTY HONOR	NO. OF ALL COUNTY HONORS	COLLEGE	1000 PT SCORERS	2000 PT SCORERS
MACKNOWSKI, JOHN	1941	FIRST TEAM	AC1	SETON HALL		
FREIDEL, HARRY	1942	FIRST TEAM	AC1			
WINOGRAD, MICKEY	1951	FIRST TEAM	AC1 + AC3	DUQUESNE		
MCLAUGHLIN, JIMMY	1954	FIRST TEAM	AC1	DUQUESNE		
BOWLER, ED	1955	FIRST TEAM	AC1	LASALLE		
MCLOUGHLIN, BOB	1956	HONORABLE MENTION	HM	ST. MARY'S (KS)		
DONNELLY, RICHIE	1958	THIRD TEAM	AC3 + HM	ST. MARY'S (KS)	🏀	
WHITNEY, TIM	1959	HONORABLE MENTION	HM			
BROWN, CHARLIE	1960	HONORABLE MENTION	HM	NJSU		
GALLIARD, CLEM	1960	HONOR ROLL	HR	NYU		
KELLY, JOE	1963	HONORABLE MENTION	HM			
LAURIE, HARRY	1963	SECOND TEAM	AC2 + HM + HR	ST. PETER'S		
WILLIS, WILLIE	1964	FIRST TEAM	AC1 + AC3 + HM	NORFOLK STATE	🏀	
GLADSTONE, STEVE	1965	HONORABLE MENTION	HM			
HOOD, ANDY	1965	FIRST TEAM	AC1	NJCU		
WEBSTER, ELNARDO	1965	SECOND TEAM	AC2 + HM	ST. PETER'S		

LINCOLN

PLAYER	YEAR	HIGHEST ALL COUNTY HONOR	NO. OF ALL COUNTY HONORS	COLLEGE	1000 PT SCORERS	2000 PT SCORERS
MAINOR, BILL	1966	SECOND TEAM	AC2	FORDHAM		
ROUNDTREE, VINCE	1969	FIRST TEAM	AC1 + HM	RUTGERS	🏀	
STEWART, ARON	1969			RICHMOND		
MARTIN, BILL	1971	FIRST TEAM	AC1 + HM TWICE	HARTWICK COLLEGE	🏀	
CORBIN, GLEN	1974	FIRST TEAM	AC1	WEST VIRGINIA		
ROBERSON, SAM	1974	FIRST TEAM	AC1 + HM		🏀	
BEST, THOMAS	1979	FIRST TEAM	AC1 + HM	ST. PETER'S		
SUMTER, ALVIN	1981	THIRD TEAM	AC3 + HM			
BRYANT, ARKIM	1993	HONORABLE MENTION	HM			
FREDERICKS, JUSTIN	1994	FIRST TEAM	AC1			
NEAL, ISAAC	1996	FIRST TEAM	AC1			
DREW, DAWUD	1999	FIRST TEAM	AC1			
WESLEY, TIM	2000	FIRST TEAM	AC1	RAMAPO		
NELSON, DAMIEN	2003	FIRST TEAM	AC1			
MOORE, LEE	2005	HONORABLE MENTION	HM			
MCCORD, DERRICK	2007	FIRST TEAM	AC1 + AC2 TWICE			
ROBINSON, FAROD	2007	FIRST TEAM	AC1 TWICE + HM			
JACKSON, TYMEL	2008	FIRST TEAM	AC1 + HM TWICE		🏀	
PETTIFORD, DAQUAN	2009	FIRST TEAM	AC1 TWICE			
DARBY, FRANK	2015	FIRST TEAM	AC1 TWICE	ARIZONA STATE (FOOTBALL)		
DARBY, DONTE	2019	FIRST TEAM	AC1 + AC2 + HM			
PAYTON, PRIME	2020	FIRST TEAM	AC1			
MORELAND, WENDELL	2021	SECOND TEAM	AC2 TWICE			
MUNFORD, TORIANO	2021	FIRST TEAM	AC1 THREE TIMES			

MARIST

PLAYER	YEAR	HIGHEST ALL COUNTY HONOR	NO. OF ALL COUNTY HONORS	COLLEGE	1000 PT SCORERS	2000 PT SCORERS
KENNEDY, BILL	1959	THIRD TEAM	AC3 + HM			
DURAN, PHIL	1964	HONORABLE MENTION	HM THREE TIMES			
KOCMALSKI, BOB	1964	SECOND TEAM	AC2 + AC3			
WALL, MIKE	1966	HONORABLE MENTION	HM TWICE	SETON HALL		
MURPHY, ED	1973	THIRD TEAM	AC3 + HM	MERRIMACK		
BROWN, ED	1975	SECOND TEAM	AC2	MONTCLAIR STATE		
CANCRO, BLAISE	1978	SECOND TEAM	AC2 TWICE			
SHARKEY, JOE	1980	FIRST TEAM	AC1 + AC2	ST. FRANCIS (PA)		
DUNBAR, SYKES	1986	FIRST TEAM	AC1 + AC2 + HM	ST. BONAVENTURE		
EADY, KIRK	1986	FIRST TEAM	AC1 + AC2 + AC3	OLD DOMINION	🏀	
OSHUST, PAUL	1988	SECOND TEAM	AC2 + HM	BLOOMFIELD		
GEORGE, KEVIN	1989	FIRST TEAM	AC1 + HM			
DASHER, ANTWAN	1991	FIRST TEAM	AC1 TWICE	ROWAN		
GIRALDO, JOHN	1992	FIRST TEAM	AC1 + HM	MONMOUTH	🏀	
HARRIS, ROSCOE	1992	FIRST TEAM	AC1 THREE TIMES + HM	VILLANOVA		🏀
ANDERSON, WARREN	1993	FIRST TEAM	AC1	SETON HALL		
CARRASCO, PABLO	1993	HONORABLE MENTION	HM	FDU		
ENCARNACION, RANDY	1993	FIRST TEAM	AC1	MARIST		
WILLIAMS, DONNELL	1993	FIRST TEAM	AC1 TWICE + HM	SETON HALL	🏀	
BENNETT, JOHN	1994	FIRST TEAM	AC1	UNIVERSITY RHODE ISLAND		
MARTINEZ, CHRIS	1995	FIRST TEAM	AC1 TWICE + SM			
MEJIA, ALVARO	1995	FIRST TEAM	AC1 TWICE			
FELTON, JAMES	1996	FIRST TEAM	AC1 + HM TWICE			
CESPEDES, RAMON	1997	FIRST TEAM	AC1			

MARIST

PLAYER	YEAR	HIGHEST ALL COUNTY HONOR	NO. OF ALL COUNTY HONORS	COLLEGE	1000 PT SCORERS	2000 PT SCORERS
BETHEA, SIEAM	1998	HONORABLE MENTION	HM THREE TIMES			
DUNBAR, RASHID	1999	FIRST TEAM	AC1 + HM			
TATE, TONY	2001	FIRST TEAM	AC1			
WINCHESTER, JOHN	2001	FIRST TEAM	AC1			
BOARDS, DEMETRIUS	2008	FIRST TEAM	AC1 + AC2	RAMAPO	●	
WILLIAMS, MARVIN	2011	FIRST TEAM	AC1 + AC2	BLOOMFIELD	●	
SMITH, JARON	2013	FIRST TEAM	AC1 + HM	NYACK		
SUAREZ, MANNY	2013	FIRST TEAM	AC1 TWICE	FORDHAM	●	
SANTIAGO, LOGAN	2015	FIRST TEAM	AC1 + AC2			
THOMAS, MARK	2015	FIRST TEAM	AC1			
KARIOKI, BENJAMIN	2016	HONORABLE MENTION	HM			
SANTIAGO, ANGELO	2019	FIRST TEAM	AC1			
MENCY, KEITH	2020	FIRST TEAM	AC1			
TOHA, MANNY	2020	FIRST TEAM	AC1			
JACKSON, MICHAEL	2021				●	

MCNAIR ACADEMIC

PLAYER	YEAR	HIGHEST ALL COUNTY HONOR	NO. OF ALL COUNTY HONORS	COLLEGE	1000 PT SCORERS	2000 PT SCORERS
BLACKEN, GILL	1981	HONORABLE MENTION	HM TWICE	NJCU	●	
FAIR, KEVIN	1982	HONORABLE MENTION	HM THREE TIMES		●	
WHITE, DERRICK	1987	HONORABLE MENTION	HM THREE TIMES	HOWARD	●	
SMITH, DWAYNE	1988	HONORABLE MENTION	HM TWICE	NJCU	●	
BALDWIN, RADAMAS	1991	FIRST TEAM	AC1 + HM	CALDWELL		
MAPLES, JUSTIN	1991	HONORABLE MENTION	HM TWICE	NIAGARA	●	
GREEN, GREG	1993	HONORABLE MENTION	HM	DELAWARE STATE	●	

MCNAIR ACADEMIC

PLAYER	YEAR	HIGHEST ALL COUNTY HONOR	NO. OF ALL COUNTY HONORS	COLLEGE	1000 PT SCORERS	2000 PT SCORERS
HENRY, JAMAL	1995	HONORABLE MENTION	HM		🏀	
ISHMAN, TIM	2004	SECOND TEAM	AC2 + HM			
HENRY, FREDDIE	2009	SECOND TEAM	AC2 + HM	NJCU		
GHEBRIAL, MIRA	2014	FIRST TEAM	AC1 + HM			
CAMARA, ISMAEL	2019	FIRST TEAM	AC1	MONTCLAIR STATE	🏀	
HABOUCHE, ADAM	2019	FIRST TEAM	AC1		🏀	
CALDEJON, JULIAN	2020	SECOND TEAM	AC2		🏀	
ULOKAMEJE, JUDE	2020	SECOND TEAM	AC2			

MEMORIAL

PLAYER	YEAR	HIGHEST ALL COUNTY HONOR	NO. OF ALL COUNTY HONORS	COLLEGE	1000 PT SCORERS	2000 PT SCORERS
GASPAROVIC, FRANK	1940	FIRST TEAM	AC1			
WADDON, JAKE	1941	FIRST TEAM	AC1 + AC2			
MAHNKEN, JOHN	1942	FIRST TEAM	AC1 THREE TIMES	GEORGETOWN	🏀	
POVOLONY, TOM	1942	FIRST TEAM	AC1			
KONRAD, ANDY	1943	FIRST TEAM	AC1			
MULLER, TOMMY	1943	FIRST TEAM	AC1			
DAZZA, AL	1944	FIRST TEAM	AC1			
PROIETTI, TONY	1948	SECOND TEAM	AC2 + AC3			
POLJANIC, MATT	1949	THIRD TEAM	AC3			
CICIRELLI, BERNIE	1950	FIRST TEAM	AC1	ST. PETER'S		
ANTONOVICH, GEORGE	1952	SECOND TEAM	AC2 + HM			
MCNAMEE, RAY	1954	SECOND TEAM	AC2 TWICE			
SIMONOVICH, TOM	1956	FIRST TEAM	AC1 + HM			
O'BRIEN, JOHN	1957	FIRST TEAM	AC1 + AC3	SEATTLE	🏀	

PLAYER	YEAR	HIGHEST ALL COUNTY HONOR	NO. OF ALL COUNTY HONORS	COLLEGE	1000 PT SCORERS	2000 PT SCORERS
SWENSEN, CHARLES	1957	SECOND TEAM	AC2 + HM	COLBY		
PASSANTE, RALPH	1959	FIRST TEAM	AC1 + AC2	ST. JOHN'S		
BRUNNER, JACK	1963	SECOND TEAM	AC2	ST. JOHN'S		
KATZ, DON	1964	THIRD TEAM	AC3			
SOTTOSANTI, VINCE	1965	THIRD TEAM	AC3	QUINNIPIAC		
MARDY, MIKE	1966	FIRST TEAM	AC1	PRINCETON	●	
SILVESTRI, VIN	1966	THIRD TEAM	AC3	MONTCLAIR STATE		
BONACHEA, REINALDO	1967	THIRD TEAM	AC3 + HM	COLUMBIA		
SIRES, ALBIO	1970	FIRST TEAM	AC1 + AC2	ST. PETER'S	●	
VEGA, HARRY	1972	FIRST TEAM	AC1 + HM	ST. THOMAS AQUINAS		
PALOMEQUE, CESAR	1973	SECOND TEAM	AC2 TWICE	UNIVERSITY RHODE ISLAND		
GILLON, JACK	1974	FIRST TEAM	AC1 TWICE + HM	SOUTH CAROLINA	●	
ZIMMERMANN, GARY	1974	THIRD TEAM	AC3	WILLIAM PATTERSON		
MCCANN, BRIAN	1975	THIRD TEAM	AC3 + HM	MONTCLAIR STATE		
GARCIA, JORGE	1979	THIRD TEAM	AC3			
LOMBARDI, SCOTT	1980	FIRST TEAM	AC1 + SM			
ROBERTS, RONALD	1982	THIRD TEAM	AC3	OKLAHOMA		
RIVERA, JOHN	1986	SECOND TEAM	AC2 + HM		●	
MEJIA, JOSE	1991	HONORABLE MENTION	HM TWICE		●	
MANZANARES, AL	1999	FIRST TEAM	AC1			
MELENDEZ, RON	2000	FIRST TEAM	AC1			
VEGA, DAVID	2001	FIRST TEAM	AC1 + HM TWICE		●	
BURGOS, ISRAEL	2002	FIRST TEAM	AC1			
SURIEL, MANNY	2002	FIRST TEAM	AC1			

MEMORIAL

PLAYER	YEAR	HIGHEST ALL COUNTY HONOR	NO. OF ALL COUNTY HONORS	COLLEGE	1000 PT SCORERS	2000 PT SCORERS
SABINO, CESAR	2003	FIRST TEAM	AC1			
VIJANDE, ANDREW	2005	SECOND TEAM	AC2			
BAUTISTA, BYRON	2007	FIRST TEAM	AC1 + HM		🏀	
MUNOZ, JONATHAN	2009	SECOND TEAM	AC2 + HM		🏀	
RIVERA, MANNY	2013	FIRST TEAM	AC1 + HM			
MARTINEZ, ANTHONY	2017	SECOND TEAM	AC2 + HM		🏀	
FARHAT, HASSAN	2019	FIRST TEAM	AC1			
AVILES, AJ	2020	FIRST TEAM	AC1			

NORTH BERGEN

PLAYER	YEAR	HIGHEST ALL COUNTY HONOR	NO. OF ALL COUNTY HONORS	COLLEGE	1000 PT SCORERS	2000 PT SCORERS
PETERSEN, ED	1962	THIRD TEAM	AC3	NJCU		
THOMAS, JIM	1962	HONORABLE MENTION	HM			
ABRAMSON, RICHIE	1964	SECOND TEAM	AC2 + HM		🏀	
DEMELLIER, BUD	1966	HONORABLE MENTION	HM TWICE			
HARLIN, JOHN	1967	SECOND TEAM	AC2			
DEPASQUALE, RON	1969	SECOND TEAM	AC2	CLEMSON		
TAIBL, DENNIS	1971	FIRST TEAM	AC1 + AC3	FELICIAN	🏀	
DECEGLI, NICK	1973	FIRST TEAM	AC1			
FORENZA, JOE	1974	SECOND TEAM	AC2 + HM			
CRUZ, LOU	1977	SECOND TEAM	AC2			
DEVITO, CARL	1977	HONORABLE MENTION	HM			
MARANO, CHRIS	1977	THIRD TEAM	AC3			
PICCINICH, MATT	1977	FIRST TEAM	AC1	LIU		

NORTH BERGEN

PLAYER	YEAR	HIGHEST ALL COUNTY HONOR	NO. OF ALL COUNTY HONORS	COLLEGE	1000 PT SCORERS	2000 PT SCORERS
CALLANDRILLO, DAN	1978	FIRST TEAM	AC1 TWICE	SETON HALL	🏀	
GRIECO, STEVE	1979	FIRST TEAM	AC1			
HAVLICEK, GORDON	1981	SECOND TEAM	AC2 + HM			
O'DONNELL, WHITEY	1982	SECOND TEAM	AC1	MONMOUTH		
FERNANDEZ, JOSE	1986	HONORABLE MENTION	HM TWICE			
CASTRO, JOSE	1988	THIRD TEAM	AC3 + HM TWICE			
BROWN, TYLER	1989	HONORABLE MENTION	HM TWICE			
PINO, CARLOS	1989	THIRD TEAM	AC3			
APODACA, RICK	1999	FIRST TEAM	AC1 THREE TIMES + HM	HOFSTRA		🏀
WILLIAMS, PAUL	2001	FIRST TEAM	AC1 + HM	SIENA		
BADER, STEVE	2003	HONORABLE MENTION	HM TWICE			
FERNANDEZ, ANDY	2005	FIRST TEAM	AC1 + HM		🏀	
FELICES, GARY	2006	FIRST TEAM	AC1 + AC2		🏀	
RODRIGUEZ, EVAN	2006	FIRST TEAM	AC1			
SILVA, XAVIER	2007	FIRST TEAM	AC1			
ALLEN, NOEL	2010	FIRST TEAM	AC1 TWICE + HM		🏀	
GILL, ALEX	2013	FIRST TEAM	AC1 + HM			
DARLEY, KAYTON	2017	FIRST TEAM	AC1 + HM		🏀	
EL SALEH, ABDALLAH	2019	FIRST TEAM	AC1 TWICE	BLOOMFIELD	🏀	
ELLIS, DEAVION	2020	FIRST TEAM	AC1	BLOOMFIELD		
DOTEL, ESTABAN	2021	THIRD TEAM	AC3			

PLAYER	YEAR	HIGHEST ALL COUNTY HONOR	NO. OF ALL COUNTY HONORS	COLLEGE	1000 PT SCORERS	2000 PT SCORERS
LEVINE, HAROLD	1970	THIRD TEAM	AC3 + HM			
SENDER, SAUL	1973	HONORABLE MENTION	HM Twice			
GARFINKEL, JEFF	1973					
STAHL, JERRY	1974	HONORABLE MENTION	HM			
HOROWITZ, DAVE	1975	HONORABLE MENTION	HM			
ROSENBERG, LEN	1975	SPECIAL HONORS	SH			

PLAYER	YEAR	HIGHEST ALL COUNTY HONOR	NO. OF ALL COUNTY HONORS	COLLEGE	1000 PT SCORERS	2000 PT SCORERS
JASICZEK, LES	1977	SECOND TEAM	AC2	ST. FRANCIS (PA)		
O'BRIEN, JOE	1979	HONORABLE MENTION	HM TWICE	UPSALA	🏀	
BITTIGER, JEFF	1980	HONORABLE MENTION	HM			
MACK, KEN	1986	SECOND TEAM	AC2 + HM	ST. PETER'S	🏀	
KASHIAN, ALAN	1993	HONORABLE MENTION	HM	STEVENS	🏀	
FORD, JAMAAL	2002	FIRST TEAM	AC1 + HM	MONTCLAIR STATE	🏀	
SCHLEMM, ZAC	2010	SECOND TEAM	AC2 TWICE	WILLIAM PATERSON	🏀	
IYER, COLBY	2014					
MEDINA, AUSTIN	2015					
CAMACHO, ZACHARY	2015					
RAMOS, JOVIN	2017			CENTENARY	🏀	
MITCHELL, KERRY	2018					
SANCHEZ, GABE	2018					
KASHIAN, AARON	2019			FELICIAN	🏀	
LAMA, JAMLING	2021			FELICIAN	🏀	
KOKOMANI, KEVIN	2021					
PANTOLINO, PATRICK	2021					

SNYDER

PLAYER	YEAR	HIGHEST ALL COUNTY HONOR	NO. OF ALL COUNTY HONORS	COLLEGE	1000 PT SCORERS	2000 PT SCORERS
BARMAD, DUCKY	1943	SECOND TEAM	AC2			
GREENBERG, HANK	1945	FIRST TEAM	AC1 + AC2			
MULLER, ANDY	1947	THIRD TEAM	AC3 + HM			
SILVERMAN, TEX	1949	FIRST TEAM	AC1 + AC2 + AC3	GEORGE WASHINGTON		
GAYNOR, TOM	1953	HONORABLE MENTION	HM	ST. PETER'S		
HENRY, GEORGE	1954	FIRST TEAM	AC1 + HM			
GOVAN, GERALD	1959			ST. MARY'S (KS)		
DELISA, PETE	1961	FIRST TEAM	AC1 TWICE + HM		🏀	
ROONEY, MIKE	1961	FIRST TEAM	AC1 TWICE + HM	OKLAHOMA	🏀	
HEITNER, RICHIE	1962	HONORABLE MENTION	HM TWICE			
SZEIGIS, BOB	1964	HONORABLE MENTION	HM TWICE			
PRATHER, ED	1967	THIRD TEAM	AC3 + HM	MONTCLAIR STATE		
SMITH, HARVEY	1967	FIRST TEAM	AC1 + AC2 + HM	LIU	🏀	
DOUGLAS, WALT	1971	FIRST TEAM	AC1 + AC3	FORDHAM		
ALEXANDER, BILLY	1973	HONORABLE MENTION	HM TWICE	FDU		
JACOBS, FLOYD	1978	FIRST TEAM	AC1 + HM	EAST TEXAS STATE	🏀	
GIBBS, SHELTON	1981	SECOND TEAM	AC2	ST. PETER'S		
RICHARDSON, CLARENCE	1981	FIRST TEAM	AC1 + AC3	UNION COUNTY CC		
ADDISON, RAFAEL	1982	FIRST TEAM	AC1 + AC3 + HM	SYRACUSE		
FRAZIER, STEVE	1987	THIRD TEAM	AC3 + HM TWICE			
GARVIN, GARY	1988	THIRD TEAM	AC3 + HM			
BURGESS, RAHKIIM	1990	FIRST TEAM	AC1 + AC2	ST. PETER'S	🏀	
COLE, ALAN	1991	HONORABLE MENTION	HM	BROWN		
HAIRSTON, ROY	1991	FIRST TEAM	AC1 TWICE	PURDUE	🏀	

SNYDER

PLAYER	YEAR	HIGHEST ALL COUNTY HONOR	NO. OF ALL COUNTY HONORS	COLLEGE	1000 PT SCORERS	2000 PT SCORERS
LEWIS, JEFF	1993	FIRST TEAM	AC1	DELAWARE STATE		
RANDOLPH, JARMEL	1994	FIRST TEAM	AC1			
KING, RIYAD	1996	FIRST TEAM	AC1	HARTFORD		
JOHNSON, KIRENE	1997	FIRST TEAM	AC1	AKRON		
JENKINS, IRV	1998	FIRST TEAM	AC1 + HM		🏀	
MIDDLETON, FRED	1998	FIRST TEAM	AC1			
PHARMES, JEHRU	1999	FIRST TEAM	AC1			
CONYERS, WILLIAM	2013	FIRST TEAM	AC1			
RICHARDSON, JAMES	2013	FIRST TEAM	AC1 TWICE	NJCU	🏀	
HARRIS, D'VANTAY	2014	FIRST TEAM	AC1			
HILTON, JEROME	2014	FIRST TEAM	AC1	MONTCLAIR STATE		
COFFEE, CHRIS	2015	SECOND TEAM	AC2 + HM			
NEIL, ISAAC	2015	FIRST TEAM	AC1 + HM	RARITAN VALLEY CC		
WASHINGTON, RONALD	2016	FIRST TEAM	AC1	SOUTHWESTERN CHRISTIAN		
SMALL, ISIAH	2017	FIRST TEAM	AC1	TEXAS STATE		
EMANUEL, DAESHAWN	2019	FIRST TEAM	AC1 + AC3	NJCU		
MANNING-FLOYD, COREY	2019	FIRST TEAM	AC1 + AC2 + HM	NJCU	🏀	
JENKINS-FLOYD, SHY'HEED	2020	FIRST TEAM	AC1	RUTGERS NEWARK		

PLAYER	YEAR	HIGHEST ALL COUNTY HONOR	NO. OF ALL COUNTY HONORS	COLLEGE	1000 PT SCORERS	2000 PT SCORERS
BOSCO, JOE	1949	THIRD TEAM	AC3 + HM			
LONG, RICHIE	1952	FIRST TEAM	AC1 + AC3	SETON HALL	●	
THRUNK, BOBBY	1954	FIRST TEAM	AC1 + AC3	CANISIUS	●	
KAMINSKI, RICHIE	1957	FIRST TEAM	AC1 TWICE	VILLANOVA	●	
ERNST, VINNIE	1959	FIRST TEAM	AC1 TWICE + HM	PROVIDENCE	●	
SPONZA, BOB	1959	SECOND TEAM	AC2 + HM	FAIRFIELD	●	
RICHARDSON, DENNIS	1963	FIRST TEAM	AC1 + AC3 + HM			
GLEASON, BOB	1964	THIRD TEAM	AC3 + HM TWICE		●	
TRUDELL, BOB	1964	SECOND TEAM	AC2 + HM			
LARDINO, JOE	1967	HONORABLE MENTION	HM THREE TIMES			
PRENDERGAST, MARTY	1972	FIRST TEAM	AC1 + AC3 TWICE	TULANE	●	
HADDEN, KEN	1977	HONORABLE MENTION	HM	RAMAPO		
DICKSON, JOE	1980	HONORABLE MENTION	HM	MERRIMACK		
PLATTEN, JIMMY	1983	FIRST TEAM	AC1 + HM	ST. THOMAS (FLA)	●	
FERRULLI, VINNIE	1985	HONORABLE MENTION	HM TWICE	NJCU	●	
ALSTON, BRUCE	1986	HONORABLE MENTION	HM	MITCHELL (NH)	●	
CALICCHIO, TOM	1988	HONORABLE MENTION	HM TWICE	NJCU	●	
MITCHELL, TOM	1990	HONORABLE MENTION	HM TWICE	HUDSON COUNTY CC	●	
MORGAN, BOBBIE	1993	HONORABLE MENTION	HM	CENTENARY		
DANZEY, WILL	1994	HONORABLE MENTION	HM			
SIMMONS, JAMAR	1999	HONORABLE MENTION	HM		●	
WILLIAMS, HAROLD	2000	HONORABLE MENTION	HM	NJCU	●	
HICKS, CHRIS	2007	SECOND TEAM	AC2	MARYLAND EASTERN SHORE	●	

PLAYER	YEAR	HIGHEST ALL COUNTY HONOR	NO. OF ALL COUNTY HONORS	COLLEGE	1000 PT SCORERS	2000 PT SCORERS
MAJEWSKI, FRANK	1956	SECOND TEAM	AC2 + HM	ST. JOSEPH'S (PA)	🏀	
YATES, PAUL	1961	HONORABLE MENTION	HM TWICE	J.C. STATE	🏀	
MODOSKI, MIKE	1962	SECOND TEAM	AC2 + HM	J.C. STATE	🏀	
ZIELINSKI, STEVE	1966	FIRST TEAM	AC1 + AC3 + HM	SETON HALL	🏀	
KING, NEHRU	1968	FIRST TEAM	AC1 + HM	PROVIDENCE	🏀	
FREDA, RICHARD	1970	HONORABLE MENTION	HM	HARTWICK COLLEGE		
MARKOWSKI, KEN	1970	SECOND TEAM	AC2 + HM TWICE	ST. PETER'S	🏀	
CHARLES, DARYLE	1974	FIRST TEAM	AC1 + AC3	LASALLE	🏀	
ROBINSON, GARY	1975	FIRST TEAM	AC1	HARTWICK COLLEGE	🏀	
ROCHFORD, DAN	1976	FIRST TEAM	AC1 + HM TWICE			
WEJNERT, RICH	1977	FIRST TEAM	AC1	SOUTH CAROLINA	🏀	
RIVERA, FELIX	1980	FIRST TEAM	AC1 + AC2	ST. PETER'S		
ROBINSON, PHIL	1980	FIRST TEAM	AC1	NORTHEASTERN		
JOHNSON, CHARLES	1981	FIRST TEAM	AC1 THREE TIMES + HM	MARQUETTE	🏀	
KING, JARETT	1981	FIRST TEAM	AC1 + HM	MONMOUTH		
RIVERS, DAVID	1984	FIRST TEAM	AC1 TWICE + AC2	NOTRE DAME	🏀	
WILSON, KENNY	1985	FIRST TEAM	AC1 TWICE	VILLANOVA	🏀	
THOMAS, MIKE	1987	FIRST TEAM	AC1	PACE		
WALKER, JASPER	1987	FIRST TEAM	AC1	ST. PETER'S		
DAVIS, MONTY	1988	FIRST TEAM	AC1	WAGNER		
DEHERE, TERRY	1989	FIRST TEAM	AC1 + HM	SETON HALL		
HURLEY, BOBBY	1989	FIRST TEAM	AC1 TWICE	DUKE	🏀	
WALKER, JERRY	1989	FIRST TEAM	AC1 TWICE + AC3	SETON HALL	🏀	
HURLEY, DANNY	1991	FIRST TEAM	AC1 TWICE	SETON HALL	🏀	

PLAYER	YEAR	HIGHEST ALL COUNTY HONOR	NO. OF ALL COUNTY HONORS	COLLEGE	1000 PT SCORERS	2000 PT SCORERS
WRIGHT, JAMES	1991	FIRST TEAM	AC1 + HM	ALLEGHENY		
RHODES, RODRICK	1992	FIRST TEAM	AC1 THREE TIMES + HM	KENTUCKY	🏀	
CURRY, JAMAR	1993	FIRST TEAM	AC1	OREGON		
MCLEOD, ROSHOWN	1993	FIRST TEAM	AC1 TWICE	DUKE		
ROBERTS, JALIL	1993	FIRST TEAM	AC1 TWICE	WISCONSIN	🏀	
CUETO, CARLOS	1994	HONORABLE MENTION	HM TWICE	RICHMOND		
ATKINSON, EUGENE	1995	FIRST TEAM	AC1 TWICE	JAMES MADISON		
BASIT, AJMAL	1995	FIRST TEAM	AC1 TWICE	UMASS	🏀	
ARRINGTON, DELVON	1996	FIRST TEAM	AC1 TWICE	FLORIDA STATE		
BURNO, RASHON	1996	FIRST TEAM	AC1 TWICE + HM	DEPAUL		
WILLIAMS, IKE	1996	FIRST TEAM	AC1	FDU		
PERRY, ANTHONY	1997	FIRST TEAM	AC1 FOUR TIMES	GEORGETOWN	🏀	
CHEEKS, ROBERT	1998	FIRST TEAM	AC1 + HM	ST. BONAVENTURE		
NORRIS, AMIN	1998	FIRST TEAM	AC1	DELAWARE STATE		
JACKSON, MAURICE	1999	FIRST TEAM	AC1			
TATE, TONY	1999	FIRST TEAM	AC1 + HM			
COPELAND, DONALD	2002	FIRST TEAM	AC1 TWICE	SETON HALL		
INGRAM, ELIJAH	2002	FIRST TEAM	AC1 THREE TIMES + HM	ST. JOHN'S	🏀	
LEE, DWAYNE	2002	FIRST TEAM	AC1 TWICE	ST. JOSEPH'S (PA)		
ROBERTS, TERRENCE	2003	FIRST TEAM	AC1 + HM			
MCCURDY, SEAN	2004	FIRST TEAM	AC1	WILLIAM & MARY		
WILLIAMS, MARCUS	2004	FIRST TEAM	AC1 + HM	ST. FRANCIS (NY)		
ANDERSON, BARNEY	2005	FIRST TEAM	AC1 TWICE	RYDER		
MERCER, DERRICK	2005	FIRST TEAM	AC1 TWICE	AMERICAN		

ST. ANTHONY

PLAYER	YEAR	HIGHEST ALL COUNTY HONOR	NO. OF ALL COUNTY HONORS	COLLEGE	1000 PT SCORERS	2000 PT SCORERS
NIVINS, AHMAD	2005	FIRST TEAM	AC1 + HM	ST. JOSEPH'S (PA)		
BULLOCK, DAVID	2006	FIRST TEAM	AC1 + AC2	GLOBE JC		
GASTON, CHRIS	2007	FIRST TEAM	AC1	FORDHAM		
WOODALL, TRAVON	2007	FIRST TEAM	AC1 + AC2 TWICE	PITTSBURGH		
CHEEK, DOMINIC	2008	FIRST TEAM	AC1 TWICE	VILLANOVA		
ROSARIO, MIKE	2008	FIRST TEAM	AC1 TWICE + HM	RUTGERS		
TAYLOR, TYSHAWN	2008	FIRST TEAM	AC1	KANSAS		
CARTER, ELIJAH	2010	FIRST TEAM	AC1 + HM	RUTGERS		
COLLIER, DEVON	2010	FIRST TEAM	AC1	OREGON STATE		
WILLIAMS, DERRICK	2010	FIRST TEAM	AC1	RICHMOND		
JONES, LUCIUS	2011	FIRST TEAM	AC1	ROBERT MORRIS		
MACK, MYLES	2011	FIRST TEAM	AC1	RUTGERS		
ANDERSON, KYLE	2012	FIRST TEAM	AC1 TWICE	UCLA		
FRINK, JEROME	2012	FIRST TEAM	AC1 TWICE	LIU		
BROWN, JOSH	2013	FIRST TEAM	AC1	TEMPLE		
SMITH, TARAN	2014	FIRST TEAM	AC1	UCONN		
MCDUFFIE, MARKIS	2015	FIRST TEAM	AC1 TWICE	WICHITA STATE		
HAYES, JURVAIS	2016	FIRST TEAM	AC1	MERRIMACK		
GIST, ASANTE	2016	FIRST TEAM	AC1	IONA		
GIBBS, SHAYQUAN	2016	FIRST TEAM	AC1	NJIT		
MOSELY, JAGAN	2016	FIRST TEAM	AC1 TWICE	GEORGETOWN		
COLE, R.J.	2017	FIRST TEAM	AC1 TWICE	UCONN		

PLAYER	YEAR	HIGHEST ALL COUNTY HONOR	NO. OF ALL COUNTY HONORS	COLLEGE	1000 PT SCORERS	2000 PT SCORERS
TURRIE, RALPH	1954			ST. MICHAEL'S (VT)	🏀	
DOLIN, CHARLIE	1954			ST. MICHAEL'S (VT)	🏀	
MENARI, JIM	1955			MONTCLAIR STATE		
RAFTERY, BILL	1959	FIRST TEAM	AC1	LASALLE		🏀
REGAN, GEORGE	1959	HONORABLE MENTION	HM			
KOWALIK, TOM	1960	HONORABLE MENTION	HM			
CONNELL, BILL	1963	THIRD TEAM	AC3 TWICE + HM	NAVY		
MAZZA, FRANK	1965	HONORABLE MENTION	HM TWICE			
DEGNAN, BILL	1978	HONORABLE MENTION	HM TWICE			

PLAYER	YEAR	HIGHEST ALL COUNTY HONOR	NO. OF ALL COUNTY HONORS	COLLEGE	1000 PT SCORERS	2000 PT SCORERS
MARKEY, ED	1947	THIRD TEAM	AC3 + HM	ST. MICHAEL'S (VT)		
WHALEN, JACK	1956	THIRD TEAM	AC3 + HM			
MCLOUGHLIN, ROBERT	1958	FIRST TEAM	AC1	ST. MARY'S (KS)	🏀	
BROOKS, TOM	1963	FIRST TEAM	AC1 + HM TWICE	DAYTON	🏀	
BELLOTTI, JERRY	1963	HONORABLE MENTION	HM TWICE	VILLANOVA (FOOTBALL)		
ORTIZ, RAY	1968	SECOND TEAM	AC2 + HM TWICE	VERMONT		
DOLECKI, STEVE	1970	SECOND TEAM	AC2 + HM			
COSGROVE, RICHIE	1971	SECOND TEAM	AC2	NJCU		
FANELLI, DON	1972	FIRST TEAM	AC1 TWICE	CORNELL (FOOTBALL)	🏀	
HIGGINS, TOM	1974	SECOND TEAM	AC2	ST. THOMAS AQUINAS		
DEROJAS, SERGIO	1980	THIRD TEAM	AC3	ADELPHI		
SALABARRIA, JUAN	1980	THIRD TEAM	AC3			

ST. JOSEPH'S (WNY)

PLAYER	YEAR	HIGHEST ALL COUNTY HONOR	NO. OF ALL COUNTY HONORS	COLLEGE	1000 PT SCORERS	2000 PT SCORERS
MENDEZ, JOHN	1984	THIRD TEAM	AC3			
ORTIZ, JOSE	1991	HONORABLE MENTION	HM TWICE			
BROWN, KHALIL	2009	SECOND TEAM	AC2			
ISERN, LUIS	2009	FIRST TEAM	AC1			

ST. MARY'S

PLAYER	YEAR	HIGHEST ALL COUNTY HONOR	NO. OF ALL COUNTY HONORS	COLLEGE	1000 PT SCORERS	2000 PT SCORERS
CAMILLERY, JOE	1963	FIRST TEAM	AC1 + HM			
PIERCE, DON	1965	SECOND TEAM	AC2 + HM			
MAGUIRE, FRAN	1968	THIRD TEAM	AC3 + HM TWICE			
ROSS, CRAIG	1969	FIRST TEAM	AC1 + AC2		🏀	
BOYLAN, JIM	1973	SECOND TEAM	AC2 TWICE	MARQUETTE	🏀	
ANDERSON, PERCY	1975	THIRD TEAM	AC3 + HM	WEST VIRGINIA STATE	🏀	
GRIFFIN, LUKE	1976	FIRST TEAM	AC1 TWICE	ST. JOSEPH'S (PA)	🏀	
ORTIZ, RAY	1979	FIRST TEAM	AC1 + AC2	SETON HALL	🏀	
MOHLMANN, GEORGE	1982	FIRST TEAM	AC1 + AC3 TWICE	ST. PETER'S		
HAMPTON, TYRELL	1984	SECOND TEAM	AC2 + AC3 + HM			
LAGUERRE, PAT	1985	FIRST TEAM	AC1 + AC2	JACKSONVILLE		
WARD, EMORY	1985	SECOND TEAM	AC2	RUTGERS		
MADISON, NOVA	1988	SECOND TEAM	AC2 + HM			
MORIARTY, TOM	1989	SECOND TEAM	AC2 + HM			
GLOVER, ROBERT	1992	FIRST TEAM	AC1	NEW HAMPSHIRE		
GONZALEZ, MIKE	1994	FIRST TEAM	AC1			
ROBERTS, JASON	1994	FIRST TEAM	AC1 TWICE	WAGNER		

ST. MARY'S

PLAYER	YEAR	HIGHEST ALL COUNTY HONOR	NO. OF ALL COUNTY HONORS	COLLEGE	1000 PT SCORERS	2000 PT SCORERS
KEYES, DEMAN	1995	FIRST TEAM	AC1 + HM			
GARDENHIRE, BRIAN	2000	FIRST TEAM	AC1			
STANBERRY, DEVON	2003	FIRST TEAM	AC1 + HM			
GARDENHIRE, JUSTIN	2004	FIRST TEAM	AC1			
LOPEZ, JOSH	2006	FIRST TEAM	AC1 + AC2			

ST. MICHAEL'S (JC)

PLAYER	YEAR	HIGHEST ALL COUNTY HONOR	NO. OF ALL COUNTY HONORS	COLLEGE	1000 PT SCORERS	2000 PT SCORERS
TAYLOR, TOMMY	1948	FIRST TEAM	AC1 + HM			
BARRY, GEORGE	1949	SECOND TEAM	AC2 + HM			
O'DONNELL, TOM	1950	SECOND TEAM	AC2 + HM			
LUTZ, DICK	1953	FIRST TEAM	AC1 + HM			
BROWN, LOU	1957	FIRST TEAM	AC1	NORTH CAROLINA	🏀	
MCGOVERN, DENNIS	1959	SECOND TEAM	AC2 + HM	UNIVERSITY RHODE ISLAND		
DEPALMA, MIKE	1961	SECOND TEAM	AC2 + HM			
BROWER, RICKI	1964	THIRD TEAM	AC3 + HM	NJCU		
HORAN, ART	1967	THIRD TEAM	AC3 + HM	STONEHILL		
DOWNES, BRIAN	1974	THIRD TEAM	AC3 + HM			
SMITH, KEVIN	1979	HONORABLE MENTION	HM			
VIERA, RALPH	1979	HONORABLE MENTION	HM TWICE			
ALLEN, ANDREW	1980	SECOND TEAM	AC2	RAMAPO		
FIELDS, RODNEY	1982	SECOND TEAM	AC2 + HM			
SABB, ART	1983	FIRST TEAM	AC1	BLOOMFIELD		

ST. MICHAEL'S (UC)

PLAYER	YEAR	HIGHEST ALL COUNTY HONOR	NO. OF ALL COUNTY HONORS	COLLEGE	1000 PT SCORERS	2000 PT SCORERS
MACKEY, TOM	1948	THIRD TEAM	AC3 + HM			
HEINSOHN, TOM	1952	FIRST TEAM	AC1 + AC2	HOLY CROSS		
RUBBINACCIO, MIKE	1952	SECOND TEAM	AC2 + HM	ST. PETER'S		
CONSTANTINO, FRED	1958	HONORABLE MENTION	HM			
TAGLIABUE, PAUL	1958	FIRST TEAM	AC1 + HM	GEORGETOWN		
LEON, RAY	1959	SECOND TEAM	AC2			
WADDLETON, DAN	1960	FIRST TEAM	AC1 TWICE + HM	ST. JOHN'S		
DREYER, RICHIE	1962	HONORABLE MENTION	HM			
BRAKER, BILL	1964	HONORABLE MENTION	HM			
LOPEZ, AL	1964	HONORABLE MENTION	HM			
O'CONNOR, TOM	1964	SECOND TEAM	AC2 + HM	ASSUMPTION		
DEPIANO, SAM	1965	THIRD TEAM	AC3	ST. PETER'S		
KELLERT, BOB	1966	SECOND TEAM	AC2	FORDHAM		
CLARK, PAT	1969	HONORABLE MENTION	HM	SETON HALL		
O'CONNOR, RICHIE	1969	FIRST TEAM	AC1 TWICE + HM	FAIRFIELD		
VYZAS, RAY	1969	HONORABLE MENTION	HM	SACRED HEART		

ST. PETER'S

PLAYER	YEAR	HIGHEST ALL COUNTY HONOR	NO. OF ALL COUNTY HONORS	COLLEGE	1000 PT SCORERS	2000 PT SCORERS
PORTFOLIO, AL	1940	FIRST TEAM	AC1	NOTRE DAME		
COYLE, JOE	1941	FIRST TEAM	AC1	ST. PETER'S		
ULLMAN, DAN	1942	FIRST TEAM	AC1			
BARRY JR., DENNIS	1944	THIRD TEAM	AC3 + HM	ST. PETER'S		
O'KEEFE, TOM	1945	FIRST TEAM	AC1	GEORGETOWN		

ST. PETER'S

PLAYER	YEAR	HIGHEST ALL COUNTY HONOR	NO. OF ALL COUNTY HONORS	COLLEGE	1000 PT SCORERS	2000 PT SCORERS
SMITH, TOMMY	1945	THIRD TEAM	AC3			
MARCK, ED	1946	FIRST TEAM	AC1	ST. PETER'S		
DOHERTY, VINCE	1949	SECOND TEAM	AC2	JOHN CAROLL		
MARKEY, EARL	1949	FIRST TEAM	AC1	HOLY CROSS		
CLUNE, JOHN	1950	FIRST TEAM	AC1 + HM	NAVY		
FINN, DON	1950	SECOND TEAM	AC2 + HM	ST. PETER'S		
VAYDA, JERRY	1952	FIRST TEAM	AC1 + AC2	NORTH CAROLINA		
BURKE, TOM	1952	SECOND TEAM	AC2			
MORANO, HANK	1953	FIRST TEAM	AC1 + HM	ST. PETER'S		
WADDLETON, GEORGE	1953	FIRST TEAM	AC1 TWICE + AC2	HOLY CROSS	🏀	
NIES, JACK	1955	FIRST TEAM	AC1	ST. MARY'S (KS)		
CROTTY, JOHN	1956	FIRST TEAM	AC1 + AC2	NORTH CAROLINA		
PEDONE, MIKE	1956	FIRST TEAM	AC1 + HM	ST. JOHN'S	🏀	
UNGER, DON	1956			FDU		
BLANEY, GEORGE	1957	FIRST TEAM	AC1 + HM	HOLY CROSS		
POTYRALA, CHARLIE	1957			FDU		
BARRY, JIM	1961	FIRST TEAM	AC1 THREE TIMES	GEORGETOWN	🏀	
MCGUIRT, WAYNE	1961	SECOND TEAM	AC2 + HM	FORDHAM		
NICOLETTI, FRANK	1962	FIRST TEAM	AC1 TWICE + HM	SYRACUSE	🏀	
SHEERAN, BRIAN	1962	HONORABLE MENTION	HM TWICE	FORDHAM		
HESKIN, NEIL	1963	FIRST TEAM	AC1	GEORGETOWN		
HOCHSTEIN, KEITH	1964	FIRST TEAM	AC1	HOLY CROSS		
MERCIER, TIM	1967	FIRST TEAM	AC1	GEORGETOWN		
BOYLAN, MIKE	1969	FIRST TEAM	AC1 + AC3	ASSUMPTION		

ST. PETER'S

PLAYER	YEAR	HIGHEST ALL COUNTY HONOR	NO. OF ALL COUNTY HONORS	COLLEGE	1000 PT SCORERS	2000 PT SCORERS
LAWSON, ED	1983	FIRST TEAM	AC1 + AC2	MANHATTAN	🏀	
GORDON, JACK	1992	FIRST TEAM	AC1 TWICE + HM	MONMOUTH	🏀	
SMITH, TUQWUAN	1998	FIRST TEAM	AC1	RAMAPO		
CASTANON, JOSE	1999	FIRST TEAM	AC1	IONA		
ROBINSON, BRIAN	2001	FIRST TEAM	AC1 TWICE	ASSUMPTION		
THOMPSON, EMMANUEL	2001	FIRST TEAM	AC1			
O'ROURKE, PAT	2005	FIRST TEAM	AC1	BOSTON COLLEGE		
DAVIS, MYLES	2010	FIRST TEAM	AC1 TWICE	XAVIER		
ROBERTS JR., RONALD	2010	FIRST TEAM	AC1 TWICE	ST. JOSEPH'S (PA)		
WALKER, KEVIN	2011	FIRST TEAM	AC1 + AC2 + HM TWICE	CALDWELL	🏀	
LUMPKIN, KEITH	2011	FIRST TEAM	AC1 + AC3 + HM	RUTGERS (FOOTBALL)	🏀	
O'GARRO, TYRONE	2012	FIRST TEAM	AC1	FDU		
WYCHE, TREVIS	2012	FIRST TEAM	AC1			
CUMMINGS, SEAN	2013	FIRST TEAM	AC1 + HM	SCRANTON		
WHITE, AUSTIN	2014	FIRST TEAM	AC1 + AC2	HIGH POINT	🏀	
HUNTER, NAJAA	2014	FIRST TEAM	AC1	RICE		
SINGH, VEER	2014	FIRST TEAM	AC1	SETON HALL		
SIMON, SHAYNE	2018	SECOND TEAM	AC2	ND (FOOTBALL)	🏀	
THIELE, BRENDAN	2018	FIRST TEAM	AC1	WEST POINT	🏀	
WHITE, WILL	2020	FIRST TEAM	AC1			
FORD, RAY	2021	FIRST TEAM	AC1 TWICE			
ARMSTRONG, MARK	2022	FIRST TEAM	AC1 TWICE	VILLANOVA	🏀	

STEVENS ACADEMY

PLAYER	YEAR	HIGHEST ALL COUNTY HONOR	NO. OF ALL COUNTY HONORS	COLLEGE	1000 PT SCORERS	2000 PT SCORERS
VON HOLLEN, HENRY	1947	HONORABLE MENTION	HM TWICE	STEVENS TECH	🏀	
LEMATTY, GORDON	1952	HONORABLE MENTION	HM TWICE			
MOSKOWITZ, TED	1954	HONORABLE MENTION	HM			
MADDEN, BILL	1957	HONORABLE MENTION	HM	YALE	🏀	
GROSS, LARRY	1958	HONORABLE MENTION	HM TWICE			
SCHLOSSBERG, BEN	1959	HONORABLE MENTION	HM	CORNELL		
CAMPEN, GEORGE	1960	HONORABLE MENTION	HM	BROWN		
CALABRO, ART	1962	HONORABLE MENTION	HM TWICE			
MILANESI, AL	1962	FIRST TEAM	AC1 + HM	BROWN	🏀	
SCHAEFER, RON	1966	HONORABLE MENTION	HM TWICE			
OURY, DENNIS	1968	THIRD TEAM	AC3 + HM	ST. JOSEPH'S (IN)		
DONNELLY, TOM	1972	THIRD TEAM	AC3			

UNION CITY

PLAYER	YEAR	HIGHEST ALL COUNTY HONOR	NO. OF ALL COUNTY HONORS	COLLEGE	1000 PT SCORERS	2000 PT SCORERS
ARIAS, ANTHONY	2009	SECOND TEAM	AC2			
MATTA, JOSE	2009	FIRST TEAM	AC1	NJCU		
AGURTO, JONATHAN	2009	HONORABLE MENTION	HM	BERGEN COUNTY CC	🏀	
MARTINEZ, RAMON	2010	SECOND TEAM	AC2–HR	BERGEN COUNTY CC		
CORCORAN, XAVIER	2011	SECOND TEAM	AC2		🏀	
TIMPONE, ROCCO	2013	FIRST TEAM	AC1	RAMAPO		
SANCHEZ, JOHNNY	2014	FIRST TEAM	AC1			
FELIZ, ABRAHAM	2016	FIRST TEAM	AC1 + HM		🏀	
GOMEZ, ANTHONY	2016	FIRST TEAM	AC1 + AC2 + HM TWICE	KEAN		

UNION CITY

PLAYER	YEAR	HIGHEST ALL COUNTY HONOR	NO. OF ALL COUNTY HONORS	COLLEGE	1000 PT SCORERS	2000 PT SCORERS
JOHNSON, GABE	2019	FIRST TEAM	AC1	ARKANSAS BAPTIST		
JACKSON, MIKE	2021	FIRST TEAM	AC1	MONTCLAIR STATE		
JENKINS–FLOYD, SHY'HEED	2021	THIRD TEAM	AC3	RUTGERS NEWARK	🏀	
ODUM, MAURICE	2021	FIRST TEAM	AC1 THREE TIMES	PACIFIC	🏀	

UNION HILL

PLAYER	YEAR	HIGHEST ALL COUNTY HONOR	NO. OF ALL COUNTY HONORS	COLLEGE	1000 PT SCORERS	2000 PT SCORERS
PASCH, DICK	1940	FIRST TEAM	AC1			
PLANTEMURA, FRANK	1941	SECOND TEAM	AC2 TWICE			
DONOVAN, HARRY	1945	FIRST TEAM	AC1 + AC2	MUHLENBERG		
MORRISON, DAVE	1946	SECOND TEAM	AC2 + HM			
GOGLIN, WALDO	1947	FIRST TEAM	AC1			
BAIRD, BILLY	1948	FIRST TEAM	AC1	RHODE ISLAND COLLEGE		
INNIS, PETE	1949	SECOND TEAM	AC2 TWICE			
SHABEL, FRED	1949	HONORABLE MENTION	HM	DUKE		
PALAZZI, TOGO	1950	FIRST TEAM	AC1 + AC2 + HM	HOLY CROSS		
VON WEYHE, BILL NELSON	1953	FIRST TEAM	AC1 + HM			
ALTOMARE, DON	1955	THIRD TEAM	AC3 + HR	FORDHAM		
HOFFMAN, RICHIE	1955	FIRST TEAM	AC1 + AC2			
PERICOLA, RAY	1955	SECOND TEAM	AC2	CLEMSON		
ORLANDO, HARRY	1956	SECOND TEAM	AC2 + AC3	WAGNER		
RAMMING, GEORGE	1957	FIRST TEAM	AC1 TWICE + HM + HR	DARTMOUTH		
RICERETO, DAVE	1958	SECOND TEAM	AC2 + AC3	UNIVERSITY RHODE ISLAND		
INAUEN, ERIC	1965	FIRST TEAM	AC1 + HM	ASSUMPTION		

UNION HILL

PLAYER	YEAR	HIGHEST ALL COUNTY HONOR	NO. OF ALL COUNTY HONORS	COLLEGE	1000 PT SCORERS	2000 PT SCORERS
GARGANO, TONY	1966	THIRD TEAM	AC3 + HM			
KELLY, JOHN	1968	SECOND TEAM	AC2			
SCHADE, MARTY	1970	FIRST TEAM	AC1 + HM	ST. MICHAEL'S (VT)	🏀	
GALIS, NICK	1975	FIRST TEAM	AC1	SETON HALL	🏀	
BARDAJI, SERGIO	1977	FIRST TEAM	AC1 + HM	MANHATTAN	🏀	
DOWNEY, JOE	1980	THIRD TEAM	AC3 TWICE			
GAETA, BOBBY	1982	SECOND TEAM	AC2		🏀	
MOREJON, JOE	1987	FIRST TEAM	AC1 + AC3 + HM			
TORRES, WILMER	1997	FIRST TEAM	AC1 THREE TIMES + HM	RUTGERS NEWARK	🏀	
MENDEZ, RENE	1998	FIRST TEAM	AC1			
FALL, LAMINE	1999	FIRST TEAM	AC1 + HM			
BAUTISTA, HAROLD	2000	FIRST TEAM	AC1 + HM		🏀	
MARTINEZ, SHYAM	2003	FIRST TEAM	AC1			
CABRERA, ANDREW	2007	FIRST TEAM	AC1 TWICE + HM			
SANCHEZ, JUSTIN	2008	FIRST TEAM	AC1 + AC2 + HM		🏀	

WEEHAWKEN

PLAYER	YEAR	HIGHEST ALL COUNTY HONOR	NO. OF ALL COUNTY HONORS	COLLEGE	1000 PT SCORERS	2000 PT SCORERS
GABBIANELLI, DANNY	1940	FIRST TEAM	AC1			
SCHWAB, EDDIE	1943	FIRST TEAM	AC1	MUHLENBERG		
CANAVARI, JOHN	1944	FIRST TEAM	AC1 + AC2			
HOGAN, BILL	1946	FIRST TEAM	AC1 + HM			
KRUGER, ED	1946	FIRST TEAM	AC1 + AC3			
BOOTH, JOEY	1947	SECOND TEAM	AC2 + AC3	BUCKNELL		

WEEHAWKEN

PLAYER	YEAR	HIGHEST ALL COUNTY HONOR	NO. OF ALL COUNTY HONORS	COLLEGE	1000 PT SCORERS	2000 PT SCORERS
COSGROVE, LES	1947	FIRST TEAM	AC1 + HM	HOLY CROSS		
PELZER, FRANK	1948	FIRST TEAM	AC1			
STEWART, JACK	1948	THIRD TEAM	AC3 + HM			
MADREPERLA, STEVE	1953	FIRST TEAM	AC1 + HM			
GORMAN, RONNIE	1954	FIRST TEAM	AC1 + HM	UNIVERSITY RHODE ISLAND		
SABATO, JIM	1955	THIRD TEAM	AC3			
ANDERSON, BOB	1959	HONORABLE MENTION	HM THREE TIMES			
AULETTO, LEN	1959	THIRD TEAM	AC3	NYU		
HUGHES, RICHIE	1961	THIRD TEAM	AC3 + HM			
ROSEN, DANNY	1962	HONORABLE MENTION	HM	FDU		
HOLM, TONY	1967	SECOND TEAM	AC2 + HM	ST. PETER'S		
HOOVER, TOM	1967	SECOND TEAM	AC2 + HM			
HUELBIG, RAY	1967	FIRST TEAM	AC1 + HM	RHODE ISLAND COLLEGE		
ANDERSON, HARRY	1968	FIRST TEAM	AC1 + HM	ST. PETER'S	🏀	
HAUGH, GLEN	1970	THIRD TEAM	AC3 + SH			
BRADLEY, KEN	1971	SECOND TEAM	AC2			
MAIONE, SAL	1973	FIRST TEAM	AC1	RHODE ISLAND COLLEGE		
WILT, CHUCKIE	1976	FIRST TEAM	AC1 + AC2	RHODE ISLAND COLLEGE	🏀	
RENDINE, MIKE	1978	HONORABLE MENTION	HM	FDU		
COCCHIO, GARY	1981	HONORABLE MENTION	HM	DEVRY		
MANSO, PEPE	1982	THIRD TEAM	AC3	WILLIAM PATERSON		
SABATO, JON	1986	THIRD TEAM	AC3 + HM	BLOOMFIELD	🏀	
SABATO, JOE	1989	THIRD TEAM	AC3 TWICE + HM	APPLACHIAN STATE	🏀	
RENTAS, JOE	1990	HONORABLE MENTION	HM TWICE	DEVRY	🏀	

WEEHAWKEN

PLAYER	YEAR	HIGHEST ALL COUNTY HONOR	NO. OF ALL COUNTY HONORS	COLLEGE	1000 PT SCORERS	2000 PT SCORERS
PETROSINO, ANTHONY	1993	HONORABLE MENTION	HM TWICE	NJIT		
MARTINEZ, JOSE	1997	FIRST TEAM	AC1 + HM TWICE	NJCU	🏀	
CRUZ, WILKINS	1998	FIRST TEAM	AC1			
HERNANDEZ, CHRIS	2000	FIRST TEAM	AC1 + HM	ST. PETER'S (BASEBALL)	🏀	
KALLERT, KEVIN	2004	SECOND TEAM	AC2	ST. PETER'S (BASEBALL)		
CORREDOR, DAMIAN	2013	FIRST TEAM	AC1	KEAN (FOOTBALL)	🏀	
STRANDBERG, DAVIS	2013					
LEDUKE, MCKAY	2015					
RAVELO, ALAN	2015					
CIERI, DONTE	2016					
PADRON, BRYAN	2017	HONORABLE MENTION	HM	ROWAN (FOOTBALL)	🏀	
ROMANO, ALESSANDRO	2017					
MORALES, MOSES	2020	HONORABLE MENTION	HM	CALDWELL	🏀	
COLON, JAMES	2020					
DURAN, JONATHAN	2020					
RAY, KEANU	2023				🏀	
COLE, TRISTEN	2023					
GONZALEZ, JASON	2023					

HUDSON COUNTY PLAYERS OF DISTINCTION

1940-2023
—

GIRLS

We made a conscientous effort to obtain as much accurate information as possible. Unfortunately, in some cases, our attempt was hindered by older players, defunct schools and inability to contact appropriate school officials.

BAYONNE

PLAYER	YEAR	HIGHEST ALL COUNTY HONOR	NO. OF ALL COUNTY HONORS	COLLEGE	1000 PT SCORERS	2000 PT SCORERS
CARROL, ELAINE	1976	FIRST TEAM	AC1 TWICE	KEAN		
BROWN, NANCY	1977	HONORABLE MENTION	HM THREE TIMES	KEAN		
ROSS, SHARON	1979	FIRST TEAM	AC1 THREE TIMES + AC3		●	
GORMAN, THERESA	1980	SECOND TEAM	AC2 THREE TIMES		●	
CARUCCI, LIZ	1981	SECOND TEAM	AC2 + HM			
GOODSON, ADRIENNE	1984	FIRST TEAM	AC1 THREE TIMES + HM	OLD DOMINION		●
MARAFIOTI, DEBBIE	1984	SECOND TEAM	AC2 + HM	NJCU		
SILUK, JEAN	1985	SECOND TEAM	AC2 + HM			
SPIKES, GINA	1988	FIRST TEAM	AC1 + HM			
RYAN, PEGEEN	1988	FIRST TEAM	AC1 THREE TIMES + HM	ST. PETER'S	●	
BERA, MELANIE	1989	FIRST TEAM	AC1 + AC3 + HM			
GUAGLIDARDO, ANNETTE	1990	SECOND TEAM	AC2			
SZEMPLE, KERRY	1991	FIRST TEAM	AC1 TWICE	RIDER	●	
ZARICZNY, JANE	1992	THIRD TEAM	AC3 TWICE + HM	JCSC		
FINNERTY, JILL	1992	FIRST TEAM	AC1 TWICE	RUTGERS	●	
GRIFFITH, TRACEY	1993	FIRST TEAM	AC1 + AC2	DOWLING		
GRIFFITH, KERRI	1996	FIRST TEAM	AC1 TWICE + AC2		●	
DEROCCO, MELISSA	1996	FIRST TEAM	AC1 TWICE + HM	FDU MADISON		
ROSKOWSKI, ASHLEY	1997	FIRST TEAM	AC1 + HM TWICE			
VIDA, DAWN	1997	FIRST TEAM	AC1 + HM TWICE		●	
KUBIAK, EWA	2000	HONORABLE MENTION	HM TWICE		●	
MAYO, BETH	2003	SECOND TEAM	AC2 + HM	NORTHEASTERN	●	
DUGAN, DANIELLE	2002	FIRST TEAM	AC1 FOUR TIMES		●	
ALTIMIRANO, CHRISTY	2006	FIRST TEAM	AC1 + HM	FDU	●	

PLAYER	YEAR	HIGHEST ALL COUNTY HONOR	NO. OF ALL COUNTY HONORS	COLLEGE	1000 PT SCORERS	2000 PT SCORERS
SWEENEY, ALEXIS	2006	FIRST TEAM	AC1 + HM			
YOUNG, COURTNEY	2006	SECOND TEAM	AC2 TWICE			
MAYO, JEN	2005	FIRST TEAM	AC1 TWICE + AC3 + HM	PITTSBURGH	●	
DEVANEY, ASHLEY	2008	SECOND TEAM	AC2 TWICE			
CALLAWAY, CASSANDRA	2008	FIRST TEAM	AC1 TWICE	ALBANY	●	
MAGGIO, SAMANTHA	2010	SECOND TEAM	AC2 + HM			
ROVATSOS, LISA	2012	FIRST TEAM	AC1 FOUR TIMES	CALDWELL	●	
FLYNN, TARA	2012	FIRST TEAM	AC1 + AC3	ADELPHI	●	
WILLIAMS, ANELA	2014	FIRST TEAM	AC1 TWICE			
VAZQUEZ, DESERAI	2014	SECOND TEAM	AC2 + HM			
MCGLONE, MADISON	2016	FIRST TEAM	AC1 + AC2		●	
MARSHALL, NIAIMANI	2017	FIRST TEAM	AC1	FELICIAN		
DIAWARA, MAKOYE	2019	FIRST TEAM	AC1	NORFOLK STATE	●	
SEMENIAK, JESSE	2019			STONEHILL	●	
SCOTT, ENIYA	2022	FIRST TEAM	AC1 TWICE + AC2	FDU	●	
MEYERS, JANAYA	2023					
NEAL, MCKENZIE	2023					

PLAYER	YEAR	HIGHEST ALL COUNTY HONOR	NO. OF ALL COUNTY HONORS	COLLEGE	1000 PT SCORERS	2000 PT SCORERS
KELLY, MARISA	2003	FIRST TEAM	AC1 + HM TWICE		●	
FISHER, ERICA	2004	HONORABLE MENTION	SPECIAL MENTION + HM TWICE		●	
WILSON, KELLY	2005	SECOND TEAM	AC2			
DELFINO, DANIELLE	2007	HONORABLE MENTION	HM TWICE			
CASILLAS, AMANDA	2010	HONORABLE MENTION	HM TWICE			

DICKINSON

PLAYER	YEAR	HIGHEST ALL COUNTY HONOR	NO. OF ALL COUNTY HONORS	COLLEGE	1000 PT SCORERS	2000 PT SCORERS
STROTIAK, JUNE	1979	HONORABLE MENTION	HM TWICE			
FRENCH, ANN MARIE	1981	HONORABLE MENTION	HM TWICE			
HARRIS, JACKIE	1984	HONORABLE MENTION	HM TWICE			
BREADY, DESIREE	1985	THIRD TEAM	AC3 + HM			
GARCIA, TRACEY	1986	HONORABLE MENTION	HM TWICE			
BAILS, TRACY	1988	SECOND TEAM	AC2 + AC3			
GERTRUDE, MILLICENT	1989	FIRST TEAM	AC1 TWICE + HM	ST. PETER'S		🏀
CUFFY, CARLA	1990	SECOND TEAM	AC2		🏀	
GERTRUDE, TANYA	1993	FIRST TEAM	AC1 TWICE + AC2		🏀	
WHITE N'KENGA	2000	HONORABLE MENTION	HM		🏀	
RODRIGUEZ, JANIERIS	2017	FIRST TEAM	AC1			
CAMACHO, JADA	2018	SECOND TEAM	AC2 TWICE + AC3	NJCU	🏀	
NAGEEB, MAVI	2022	FIRST TEAM	AC1 + AC3			
DAVIS, SA'MAYA	2022	FIRST TEAM	AC1			

EMERSON

PLAYER	YEAR	HIGHEST ALL COUNTY HONOR	NO. OF ALL COUNTY HONORS	COLLEGE	1000 PT SCORERS	2000 PT SCORERS
AVOLETTA, LINDA	1976	HONORABLE MENTION	HM TWICE			
BAUMANN, DREW	1980	HONORABLE MENTION	HM THREE TIMES		🏀	
MANGIANTE, PAT	1981	THIRD TEAM	AC3 + HM			
BUNCE, MICHELLE	1984	FIRST TEAM	AC1 + HM			
PENA, RAYDERIS	2001	HONORABLE MENTION	HM THREE TIMES			
VARGAS, VANESSA	2002	FIRST TEAM	AC1 TWICE + HM TWICE		🏀	

FERRIS

PLAYER	YEAR	HIGHEST ALL COUNTY HONOR	NO. OF ALL COUNTY HONORS	COLLEGE	1000 PT SCORERS	2000 PT SCORERS
BRYANT, TANYA	1979	HONORABLE MENTION	HM THREE TIMES			
HEMINGWAY, MONIQUE	1982	SECOND TEAM	AC2 + HM TWICE	NJCU	🏀	
MARTINEZ, JACKIE	1986	HONORABLE MENTION	HM TWICE	MONTCLAIR STATE		
RILEY, LINDA	1986	FIRST TEAM	AC1 + AC2 + HM	ST. PETER'S	🏀	
MARTINEZ, MARITZA	1988	FIRST TEAM	AC1 + AC3	MONTCLAIR STATE	🏀	
BROWN, TAWANA	1990	FIRST TEAM	AC1 + HM TWICE	ST. PETER'S	🏀	
PARSONS, MAE	1993	HONORABLE MENTION	HM TWICE	UPSALA		
BORRERO, ADIL	1994	FIRST TEAM	AC1 TWICE	MONTCLAIR STATE		
GARCIA, IRIS	1995	FIRST TEAM	AC1 THREE TIMES + HM	CENTRAL CONNECTICUT	🏀	
SESSIONS, DANIELLE	1996	FIRST TEAM	AC1 + HM			
TURNER, YAFA	1996	FIRST TEAM	AC1 + AC2 + HM	RUTGERS NEWARK		
RODRIGUEZ, MARITZA	1996	FIRST TEAM	AC1 + AC2	RIDER		
ROJAS, LUCY	1997	HONORABLE MENTION	HM TWICE			
KIDD, SHLINDA	1997	FIRST TEAM	AC1			
LOPEZ, INDIA	2000	FIRST TEAM	AC1	ST. PETER'S		
MCKENZIE, KARIMA	2000	HONORABLE MENTION	HM TWICE	COLLEGE OF NEW JERSEY		
HEMINGWAY, DENAYA	2003	SECOND TEAM	AC2 + HM TWICE	NJIT	🏀	
GALLOWAY, SELENA	2006	FIRST TEAM	AC1 TWICE	DELAWARE STATE	🏀	
STANTON, ASHLEY	2008	SECOND TEAM	AC2 THREE TIMES			
BLAKE, KELELA	2008	FIRST TEAM	AC1 + HM TWICE	LEHIGH		
HINES, SAMANTHA	2015	FIRST TEAM	AC1			
FONSECA, NATALIE	2022	FIRST TEAM	AC1			

HARRISON

PLAYER	YEAR	HIGHEST ALL COUNTY HONOR	NO. OF ALL COUNTY HONORS	COLLEGE	1000 PT SCORERS	2000 PT SCORERS
GRAVES, ROZI	1983	FIRST TEAM	AC1		🏀	
BURGOS, ALICE	1986	FIRST TEAM	AC1 THREE TIMES	WAGNER	🏀	
KUTT, KRISSY	1986	FIRST TEAM	AC1 TWICE + AC3	PACE	🏀	
FERRIERO, DONNA	1988	FIRST TEAM	AC1	MONTCLAIR STATE	🏀	
HOEY, MICHELE	1988	SECOND TEAM	AC2 + AC3	RAMAPO	🏀	
KACZOR, ROBYN	1989	HONORABLE MENTION	HM TWICE	SETON HALL		
HILL, JODY	1990	FIRST TEAM	AC1 TWICE + HM	PACE		🏀
GILMORE, DANIELLE	1992	FIRST TEAM	AC1 + HM	MONTCLAIR STATE	🏀	
VILLALTA, LISA	1992	SECOND TEAM	AC2 + AC3	MONTCLAIR STATE		
FERRIERO, MICHELE	1992	FIRST TEAM	AC1 TWICE + AC2	ST. PETER'S	🏀	
MELO, ANDREA	1994	FIRST TEAM	AC1 TWICE	PACE		
PURZYCKI, JEN	1994	FIRST TEAM	AC1 + HM	STOCKTON	🏀	
CIPRIANO, KIM	1997	FIRST TEAM	AC1 + HM + SM	SETON HALL	🏀	
MCDONOUGH, KIM	1998	FIRST TEAM	AC1 FOUR TIMES	ST. PETER'S		🏀
MELO, DANIELLA	2000	HONORABLE MENTION	HM TWICE	CALDWELL	🏀	
QUINONEZ, GINGER	2001	FIRST TEAM	AC1 THREE TIMES	ST. PETER'S		🏀
MORALES, JENN	2005	HONORABLE MENTION	HM TWICE		🏀	
VASQUEZ, MICHELLE	2006	FIRST TEAM	AC1	NJCU		
O'DONNELL, BRIANNA	2012					
MARTINEZ, BIANCA	2012					
LUCAS, RAYVEN	2013					
RIVERA, SARAI	2014					
O'DONNELL, AMBER	2015					
FERREIRA, CYNTHIA	2017					

HARRISON

PLAYER	YEAR	HIGHEST ALL COUNTY HONOR	NO. OF ALL COUNTY HONORS	COLLEGE	1000 PT SCORERS	2000 PT SCORERS
MONTILLA, JAILYN	2018					
LUCAS, KIERRAH	2018					
LUCAS, KAYLA	2020					
O'DONNELL, HALEY	2021					

HIGH TECH

PLAYER	YEAR	HIGHEST ALL COUNTY HONOR	NO. OF ALL COUNTY HONORS	COLLEGE	1000 PT SCORERS	2000 PT SCORERS
LYKES, MONICA	2001	HONORABLE MENTION	HM TWICE			
QUIROGA, VANESSA	2004	FIRST TEAM	AC1		🏀	
WRIGHT, TERESA	2006	SECOND TEAM	AC2			
THOMPSON, ERIKA	2008	FIRST TEAM	AC1 + AC2		🏀	
RIVERA, KRISTINA	2009	SECOND TEAM	AC2			
LYNCH, SYBIL	2010	FIRST TEAM	AC1		🏀	

HOBOKEN

PLAYER	YEAR	HIGHEST ALL COUNTY HONOR	NO. OF ALL COUNTY HONORS	COLLEGE	1000 PT SCORERS	2000 PT SCORERS
CUTILLO, JEAN	1976	FIRST TEAM	AC1 TWICE		🏀	
PALUMBO, ANN MARIE	1978	HONORABLE MENTION	HM TWICE			
SERRIPIERRO, KATHY	1981	FIRST TEAM	AC1		🏀	
FULLAM, DEBBIE	1982	SECOND TEAM	AC2 TWICE + AC3 + HM		🏀	
PRINGLE, YVETTE	1984	HONORABLE MENTION	HM THREE TIMES			
GONZALEZ, MADELINE	1986	HONORABLE MENTION	HM TWICE			
RODRIGUEZ, MARIE	1987	SECOND TEAM	AC2 TWICE + AC3			
WHEELER, NIKKI	1992	HONORABLE MENTION	HM TWICE			

HOBOKEN

PLAYER	YEAR	HIGHEST ALL COUNTY HONOR	NO. OF ALL COUNTY HONORS	COLLEGE	1000 PT SCORERS	2000 PT SCORERS
MITCHELL, TARA	1992	FIRST TEAM	AC1 TWICE + AC3 + HM	NJCU	🏀	
FOSTER, SABRINA	2004	SECOND TEAM	AC2 + HM TWICE			
LYNCH, SYBIL	2012	FIRST TEAM	AC1 + AC3			
MATTESSICH, ZOE	2020	THIRD TEAM	AC3		🏀	
WHITE, ALEX	2022	FIRST TEAM	AC1			

HOLY FAMILY ACADEMY

PLAYER	YEAR	HIGHEST ALL COUNTY HONOR	NO. OF ALL COUNTY HONORS	COLLEGE	1000 PT SCORERS	2000 PT SCORERS
COLASURDO, PAT	1975	FIRST TEAM	AC1	MONTCLAIR STATE	🏀	
GOMEZ, LISA	1977	FIRST TEAM	AC1 TWICE + HM	MONTCLAIR STATE		
PARKS, CAROL	1978	HONORABLE MENTION	HM TWICE			
SMITH, SANDY	1978	FIRST TEAM	AC1 TWICE + AC3			
BURNS, KATHY	1979	SECOND TEAM	AC2			
ODENWALDER, LINDA	1979	FIRST TEAM	AC1 + AC3 + HM	FAIRFIELD	🏀	
MOSCA, CHRIS	1980	HONORABLE MENTION	HM TWICE	NJCU		
YELVERTON, AUDREY	1985	SECOND TEAM	AC2 + HM TWICE	NJCU		
O'HALLORAN, MONICA	1986	FIRST TEAM	AC1 TWICE + HM	MARIST	🏀	
MAKOWSKI, CINDY	1987	FIRST TEAM	AC1 + AC2 TWICE	UNC WILMINGTON		
REGAN, ALICE	1988	THIRD TEAM	AC3 + HM	KEAN		
SAVINO, JANINE	1988	SECOND TEAM	AC2 TWICE + HM	ST. PETER'S		
ALGERIA, ROBYN	1990	FIRST TEAM	AC1 TWICE	PRINCETON	🏀	
HOCK, NIKKI	1991	THIRD TEAM	AC3 + HM	ST. PETER'S		
O'DONNELL, SHANNON	1993	FIRST TEAM	AC1 + AC2 + HM			
HEALEY, SHANNON	1994	FIRST TEAM	AC1	FLORIDA ATLANTIC		

HOLY FAMILY ACADEMY

PLAYER	YEAR	HIGHEST ALL COUNTY HONOR	NO. OF ALL COUNTY HONORS	COLLEGE	1000 PT SCORERS	2000 PT SCORERS
GENTILE, CHERYL	1996	HONORABLE MENTION	HM THREE TIMES	NJCU		
HEALEY, ERIN	1996	FIRST TEAM	AC1 TWICE + HM		🏀	
QUINN, KATHLEEN	1997	HONORABLE MENTION	HM TWICE	NJCU		
O'REILLY, MELISSA	1997	FIRST TEAM	AC1 + HM	NJCU		
BUTURLA, JANINE	1999	FIRST TEAM	AC1 + AC2		🏀	
HANSEN, AMY	2000	HONORABLE MENTION	HM TWICE			
BUTURLA, DANA	2000	FIRST TEAM	AC1 + HM			
DOOLAN, MARY	2002	HONORABLE MENTION	HM TWICE	COLLEGE OF ST. ELIZABETH		
DUNDAS, DANIELLE	2008	FIRST TEAM	AC1 + AC2		🏀	
VEVERKA, CAITLIN	2008	HONORABLE MENTION	HM TWICE	CENTENARY (SOCCER)		
KELLER, GRACE	2008	SECOND TEAM	AC2 + HM TWICE	NJCU	🏀	
GILL, CHRISTINA	2010	FIRST TEAM	AC1 + HM TWICE	BOSTON COLLEGE	🏀	
FORKER, DIANE	2011	FIRST TEAM	AC1 TWICE + AC3		🏀	

HUDSON CATHOLIC

PLAYER	YEAR	HIGHEST ALL COUNTY HONOR	NO. OF ALL COUNTY HONORS	COLLEGE	1000 PT SCORERS	2000 PT SCORERS
STANTON, SYDNEY	2013	FIRST TEAM	AC1			
BROWN, MIKEERA	2014	SECOND TEAM	AC2 + HM			
SCOTT, TANIA	2016	SECOND TEAM	AC2	FELICIAN	🏀	
GOMEZ, ALYSSA	2017	SECOND TEAM	AC2			
RAMIREZ, HAYLEE	2020	FIRST TEAM	AC1 THREE TIMES + AC3	FELICIAN	🏀	
SURREL, INYESIAH	2020	THIRD TEAM	AC3 TWICE			
PACHECO, ADIANA	2021	FIRST TEAM	AC1	ESSEX COUNTY CC		
JONES ZANAI	2021	FIRST TEAM	AC1 TWICE	VILLANOVA	🏀	

HUDSON CATHOLIC

PLAYER	YEAR	HIGHEST ALL COUNTY HONOR	NO. OF ALL COUNTY HONORS	COLLEGE	1000 PT SCORERS	2000 PT SCORERS
BECKFORD, KAYLA	2021	FIRST TEAM	AC1			
MEYERS, JANAYA	2022	FIRST TEAM	AC1			
RAMIREZ KENDRA LEE	2023	FIRST TEAM	AC1			

KEARNY

PLAYER	YEAR	HIGHEST ALL COUNTY HONOR	NO. OF ALL COUNTY HONORS	COLLEGE	1000 PT SCORERS	2000 PT SCORERS
MASOTES, ALICE	1976	HONORABLE MENTION	HM		🏀	
SMITH, ANN MARIE	1981	SECOND TEAM	AC2 + HM			
HANSEN, ROBYN	1981	FIRST TEAM	AC1 + HM		🏀	
KERZIC, MARGIE	1985	HONORABLE MENTION	HM THREE TIMES			
BYRNES, MARYBETH	1992	THIRD TEAM	AC3 + HM			
GONZALEZ, MONICA	1992	HONORABLE MENTION	HM TWICE			
DAY, JEANINE	1999	FIRST TEAM	AC1			
MENDEZ, MARGIE	2000	HONORABLE MENTION	HM TWICE		🏀	
DEFRITAS, VANESSA	2000	FIRST TEAM	AC1			
MONTANEZ, MELINA	2002	FIRST TEAM	AC1 + HM	BLOOMFIELD	🏀	
BARTHOLOMEW, EMMA	2005	SECOND TEAM	AC2 TWICE	ESSEX COUNTY CC	🏀	
RUMINSKA, MARTYNA	2007	FIRST TEAM	AC1 + AC2	RUTGERS NEWARK	🏀	
DYL, ALLYSON	2008	HONORABLE MENTION	HM TWICE			
MCNALLY, JENNA	2008	FIRST TEAM	AC1			
AQUINO, JANITZA	2009	FIRST TEAM	AC1 + AC2	MONTCLAIR STATE	🏀	
GOMES, STEFANIE	2012	HONORABLE MENTION	HM		🏀	
JIANG, MANDY	2013	FIRST TEAM	AC1			

KEARNY

PLAYER	YEAR	HIGHEST ALL COUNTY HONOR	NO. OF ALL COUNTY HONORS	COLLEGE	1000 PT SCORERS	2000 PT SCORERS
FARIH, NOURA	2013	FIRST TEAM	AC1			
MCCLELLAN, MEAGAN	2017	FIRST TEAM	AC1	RUTGERS (SOCCER)	🏀	
HYAMS, AVA	2023	FIRST TEAM	AC1 + HM	WORCHESTER POLYTECH	🏀	
COVELLO, MACI	2023	THIRD TEAM	AC3 + HM	FELICIAN	🏀	

LINCOLN

PLAYER	YEAR	HIGHEST ALL COUNTY HONOR	NO. OF ALL COUNTY HONORS	COLLEGE	1000 PT SCORERS	2000 PT SCORERS
GADSEN, CAROLYN	1979	FIRST TEAM	AC1 TWICE	ST. PETER'S	🏀	
GADSEN, CARLA	1980	HONORABLE MENTION	HM TWICE			
JONES, BLANCHE	1981	FIRST TEAM	AC1 TWICE + AC2 + HM	ST. PETER'S	🏀	
MCCORMICK, GERRI	1982	FIRST TEAM	AC1			
GARNER, LETITIA	1982	SECOND TEAM	AC2 TWICE			
GARNER, TISH	1983	FIRST TEAM	AC1			
CUNNIFFEE, EILEEN	1985	FIRST TEAM	AC1 + HM TWICE			
WILLIAMS, MILDRED	1989	HONORABLE MENTION	HM THREE TIMES			
SPEAKS, SHAKEEMA	1996	HONORABLE MENTION	HM THREE TIMES			
GOODMAN, DENISE	2002	HONORABLE MENTION	HM TWICE			
GOODMAN, LATISHA	2004	FIRST TEAM	AC1 + HM		🏀	
JONES, SHANIQUA	2006	FIRST TEAM	AC1 + HM			
EDWARDS, KRISTAL	2008	FIRST TEAM	AC1 TWICE + AC2	ST. PETER'S		
DICKERSON, RAHQUANA	2008	FIRST TEAM	AC1 TWICE + HM			
WILLIAMS, ZIERRA	2010	FIRST TEAM	AC1			
BEY, BREANA	2013	FIRST TEAM	AC1 + AC2	STETSON	🏀	
CALAMITO, TIMIAH	2012	SECOND TEAM	AC2 + HM			

LINCOLN

PLAYER	YEAR	HIGHEST ALL COUNTY HONOR	NO. OF ALL COUNTY HONORS	COLLEGE	1000 PT SCORERS	2000 PT SCORERS
SUBER, SHE'KINAH	2014	FIRST TEAM	AC1 + AC2	NJCU	🏀	
WILLIAMS, ZHAN'E	2014	FIRST TEAM	AC1 + AC2 + AC3	LIU	🏀	
JOHNSON, KIANTE	2015	FIRST TEAM	AC1 THREE TIMES + AC3		🏀	
CORTES, NATALIE	2015	THIRD TEAM	AC3 + HM			
SCHULER, DESTINY	2016	FIRST TEAM	AC1 + AC3	UNION COUNTY CC		
MUMFORD, ALAISHA	2020	SECOND TEAM	AC2 THREE TIMES	BLOOMFIELD		
DARBY, DANIYA	2020	FIRST TEAM	AC1 THREE TIMES	BLOOMFIELD	🏀	
COAR, JAKIRA	2021	FIRST TEAM	AC1		🏀	

MARIST

PLAYER	YEAR	HIGHEST ALL COUNTY HONOR	NO. OF ALL COUNTY HONORS	COLLEGE	1000 PT SCORERS	2000 PT SCORERS
MCDONALD, MELANIE	1989	HONORABLE MENTION	HM TWICE			
DOHERTY, STEPHANIE	1993	FIRST TEAM	AC1			
RICHARDSON, TIFFANY	1994	FIRST TEAM	AC1			
HALSEY, DENENE	1997	FIRST TEAM	AC1 THREE TIMES + AC2		🏀	
SETTLE, SHAWNIKA	1998	HONORABLE MENTION	HM TWICE			
STOEBLING, ANN MARIE	2000	HONORABLE MENTION	HM TWICE			
GLEATON, MAKEDA	2001	FIRST TEAM	AC1 FOUR TIMES		🏀	
WALKER, TARA	2001	FIRST TEAM	AC1 FOUR TIMES	ST. JOHN'S		🏀
LEWANDOWSKI, JEN	2002	SECOND TEAM	AC2 + HM			
FITZGERALD, ANGELA	2004	FIRST TEAM	AC1 THREE TIMES		🏀	
SMITH, CHISTINA	2006	SECOND TEAM	AC2 TWICE + HM			
BIAMONTE, JANELLE	2006	FIRST TEAM	AC1 FOUR TIMES		🏀	
CENTENO, CRISTINA	2008	FIRST TEAM	AC1 TWICE	SIENNA	🏀	

MARIST

PLAYER	YEAR	HIGHEST ALL COUNTY HONOR	NO. OF ALL COUNTY HONORS	COLLEGE	1000 PT SCORERS	2000 PT SCORERS
THOMAS, EBONY	2008	FIRST TEAM	AC1 + AC2	CALDWELL	⦿	
BLUE, LYNEA	2008	SECOND TEAM	AC2 + HM	ST. PETER'S	⦿	
BENITEZ, BERNIE	2009	FIRST TEAM	AC1 + HM			
VASQUEZ, ASHLEY	2010	SECOND TEAM	AC2 + HM			
DENMARK, DESIREE	2010	FIRST TEAM	AC1 + AC2		⦿	
BLAKE, ANTOINETTE	2011	SECOND TEAM	AC2 THREE TIMES		⦿	
WILSON, ALEXIS	2013	FIRST TEAM	AC1 + HM			
MITCHELL, DENESIA	2014	THIRD TEAM	AC3 + HM			
REESE, JASMINE	2015	THIRD TEAM	AC3 TWICE	NJCU		
JEAN-BAPTISTE, STEPHANIE	2019	SECOND TEAM	AC2 + AC3			
FRAZIER, BREYANNA	2020	FIRST TEAM	AC1 THREE TIMES + AC3	JACKSONVILLE	⦿	

MCNAIR ACADEMIC

PLAYER	YEAR	HIGHEST ALL COUNTY HONOR	NO. OF ALL COUNTY HONORS	COLLEGE	1000 PT SCORERS	2000 PT SCORERS
POTTER, PAM	1981	HONORABLE MENTION	HM THREE TIMES		⦿	
PADILLA, DOMINGA	1989	HONORABLE MENTION	HM TWICE	DREW		
TAYLOR, JACKIE	1994	SECOND TEAM	AC2 + HM	COLLEGE OF NEW JERSEY	⦿	
CONKLIN, KIM	1996	HONORABLE MENTION	HM		⦿	
ANDREWS, NATASHA	1997	HONORABLE MENTION	HM TWICE	NJCU		
CIPRIANO, SUZIE	1997	HONORABLE MENTION	HM TWICE			
GOURDLER, TAMIKA	1997	FIRST TEAM	AC1		⦿	
HENRY, BAHIYYAH	1998	SECOND TEAM	AC2		⦿	
HAGGENMILLER, TIFFANY	2000	FIRST TEAM	AC1 TWICE		⦿	
OMILLO, CHIARRA	2001	HONORABLE MENTION	HM TWICE		⦿	

PLAYER	YEAR	HIGHEST ALL COUNTY HONOR	NO. OF ALL COUNTY HONORS	COLLEGE	1000 PT SCORERS	2000 PT SCORERS
MCGARRY, CHRISTIAN	2008	SECOND TEAM	AC2			
PHILIPPE, CATHYLEE	2009	SECOND TEAM	AC2			
CARTER, JALIA	2014	FIRST TEAM	AC1		🏀	
ROJAS, KRISTEN	2022	FIRST TEAM	AC1			
BROWN, MOLLY	2022	FIRST TEAM	AC1			

PLAYER	YEAR	HIGHEST ALL COUNTY HONOR	NO. OF ALL COUNTY HONORS	COLLEGE	1000 PT SCORERS	2000 PT SCORERS
SINISI, CAROL	1978	SECOND TEAM	AC2 TWICE + SH		🏀	
DIBISCEGLIE, LISA	1979	THIRD TEAM	AC3 TWICE			
EWENS, MARIBEL	1980	FIRST TEAM	AC1 + AC3 + HM	ST. PETERS	🏀	
DIBISCEGLIE, JOANNE	1982	HONORABLE MENTION	HM TWICE			
GONZALEZ, MARILA	1983	THIRD TEAM	AC3 + HM			
PORRO, MERCY	1983	FIRST TEAM	AC1 TWICE + HM		🏀	
PASSERO, SUSY	1984	SECOND TEAM	AC2 + AC3 TWICE		🏀	
URBAY, ELSIE	1985	HONORABLE MENTION	HM TWICE			
WEGNER, MARGARET	1987	HONORABLE MENTION	HM TWICE			
BAILEY, PAULA	1989	HONORABLE MENTION	HM TWICE			
DIAZ, SUSIE	1993	THIRD TEAM	AC3 + HM TWICE		🏀	
BATISTA, RAYZA	2000	HONORABLE MENTION	HM THREE TIMES	ST. THOMAS AQUINAS	🏀	
DEMBY, ALEXIS	2004	FIRST TEAM	AC1 + AC2 + HM TWICE		🏀	
NUNEZ, MERCEDES	2004	FIRST TEAM	AC1 + HM	WILLIAM PATTERSON	🏀	
CABRERA, INDHIRA	2005	HONORABLE MENTION	HM TWICE		🏀	
CARRALERO, CYNTHIA	2009	FIRST TEAM	AC1 + HM TWICE	RUTGERS		

MEMORIAL

PLAYER	YEAR	HIGHEST ALL COUNTY HONOR	NO. OF ALL COUNTY HONORS	COLLEGE	1000 PT SCORERS	2000 PT SCORERS
MELO, CAOLANY	2010	FIRST TEAM	AC1			
QUITO, TANIA	2010	FIRST TEAM	AC1			
ALCANTARA, ELAINE	2022	FIRST TEAM	AC1			

N. BERGEN

PLAYER	YEAR	HIGHEST ALL COUNTY HONOR	NO. OF ALL COUNTY HONORS	COLLEGE	1000 PT SCORERS	2000 PT SCORERS
KLAUBE, PAT	1977	HONORABLE MENTION	HM THREE TIMES			
COVINO, FRAN	1982	THIRD TEAM	AC3 TWICE + HM			
GRIERSON, MARGARET	1983	FIRST TEAM	AC1 + AC2 + HM			
GESAULDI, MARGARET	1988	FIRST TEAM	AC1 + AC2 + AC3 + HM		🏀	
RODRIGUEZ, MONICA	1988	HONORABLE MENTION	HM		🏀	
DURANGO, NANA	1996	FIRST TEAM	AC1 + HM TWICE		🏀	
WALL, KELLY	1998	HONORABLE MENTION	HM TWICE			
CASTILLO, LISA	1998	HONORABLE MENTION	HM THREE TIMES			
LIZANO, LILLY	2000	FIRST TEAM	AC1 + HM			
DIPAOLO, DENISE	2001	FIRST TEAM	AC1 TWICE + HM	UMASS		
MENDIETA, BETTY	2003	FIRST TEAM	AC1 + AC2 + HM	ADELPHI	🏀	
MOORE, MELISSA	2003	FIRST TEAM	AC1 + HM	WILLIAM PATERSON		
CORTORREAL, LIZ	2005	FIRST TEAM	AC1			
CHENET, CASSANDRA	2007	FIRST TEAM	AC1 + HM			
RIVERA, CYNTHIA	2007	FIRST TEAM	AC1 + HM	RAMAPO		
JIMENEZ, LAUREN	2007	FIRST TEAM	AC1 FOUR TIMES	JAMES MADISON	🏀	
MURIEL, LAURA	2010	HONORABLE MENTION	HM TWICE			

N. BERGEN

PLAYER	YEAR	HIGHEST ALL COUNTY HONOR	NO. OF ALL COUNTY HONORS	COLLEGE	1000 PT SCORERS	2000 PT SCORERS
VAZONNA, ASHLEY	2011	FIRST TEAM	AC1 TWICE + AC2 TWICE		🏀	
ILIC, DORIS	2013	FIRST TEAM	AC1	RAMAPO		
HAMMER, ICIES	2015	FIRST TEAM	AC1 THREE TIMES + AC2	FDU	🏀	
JOVER, JILLIAN	2016	SECOND TEAM	AC2 + AC3 + HM	COLLEGE OF NEW JERSEY		

SACRED HEART ACADEMY

PLAYER	YEAR	HIGHEST ALL COUNTY HONOR	NO. OF ALL COUNTY HONORS	COLLEGE	1000 PT SCORERS	2000 PT SCORERS
SPANO, STACEY	1991	HONORABLE MENTION	HM TWICE		🏀	
COLLAZO, MILLIE	1994	FIRST TEAM	AC1 + HM			🏀

SECAUCUS

PLAYER	YEAR	HIGHEST ALL COUNTY HONOR	NO. OF ALL COUNTY HONORS	COLLEGE	1000 PT SCORERS	2000 PT SCORERS
SMITH, LUANN	1977	HONORABLE MENTION	HM TWICE			
ACERRA, SANDY	1979	SECOND TEAM	AC2 TWICE + HM		🏀	
REHBELN, ALLYSON	1985	SECOND TEAM	AC2 + AC3 + HM			
CORRADINO, CONNIE	1986	HONORABLE MENTION	HM TWICE			
ULRICH, SHEILA	1987	SECOND TEAM	AC2 + HM		🏀	
KENNY, LAURA	1989	HONORABLE MENTION	HM THREE TIMES			
ACIZ, TIFFANY	2001	HONORABLE MENTION	HM TWICE			
ACIZ, HEATHER	2003	HONORABLE MENTION	HM THREE TIMES		🏀	
KOLAR, SAMANTHA	2005	SECOND TEAM	AC2 + HM			
ROESING, CORY	2007	FIRST TEAM	AC1 THREE TIMES + HM	CALDWELL (VOLLEYBALL)	🏀	
TOTARO, JENNA	2008	FIRST TEAM	AC1 + AC2	MONTCLAIR STATE	🏀	

SECAUCUS

PLAYER	YEAR	HIGHEST ALL COUNTY HONOR	NO. OF ALL COUNTY HONORS	COLLEGE	1000 PT SCORERS	2000 PT SCORERS
INNIS, ANDREA	2011	FIRST TEAM	AC1 TWICE + AC2	CENTENARY	🏀	
WATERS, SHANNON	2011	FIRST TEAM	AC1 + AC2 + HM		🏀	
LYNGHOLM, ALYSSA	2012					
PERO, ZOE	2013					
ROESING, DANIELLE	2013					
MITCHELL, DANIELLE	2013					
TOMAN, ALYSON	2014					
LENNON, ANDIE	2015	FIRST TEAM	AC1 TWICE + AC2	CALDWELL	🏀	
MCCLURE, JULIA	2015	FIRST TEAM	AC1 THREE TIMES	TAMPA	🏀	
CARUSO, KENDALL	2015					
ULRICH, KRISTINA	2016	FIRST TEAM	AC1 + AC2	WILLIAM PATERSON	🏀	
PESCHETTI, JULIA	2016					
MACK, LINDSEY	2018	FIRST TEAM	AC1 TWICE + AC2	YOUNGSTOWN STATE	🏀	
DEHNERT, AMANDA	2018					
ULRICH, AMANDA	2019	FIRST TEAM	AC1 THREE TIMES + AC2	ST. LEO'S		🏀
INTINDOLA, PAYTON	2019					
MOJICA, HAILEY	2019					
RODRIGUEZ, DAMARIS	2020	SECOND TEAM	AC2 THREE TIMES	NJCU	🏀	
BUJARI, JASMIN	2020					
SZABO, MACKENZIE	2020					
GALANG, SABINA	2020					
ROSS, LINDSEY	2021					
PARISE, NICOLE	2021					
FERATI, NURISHA	2022					

SECAUCUS

PLAYER	YEAR	HIGHEST ALL COUNTY HONOR	NO. OF ALL COUNTY HONORS	COLLEGE	1000 PT SCORERS	2000 PT SCORERS
CRAIGWELL, ALYSSA	2023				🏀	
PESCHETTI, DANIELA	2023					
SCHNEIDER, KATIE	2023					
CRUZ, MIA	2023					
TORILLO, GABRIELLA	2023					
D'AVANZO, GIANNA	2023					

SNYDER

PLAYER	YEAR	HIGHEST ALL COUNTY HONOR	NO. OF ALL COUNTY HONORS	COLLEGE	1000 PT SCORERS	2000 PT SCORERS
MOORE, VAL	1979	HONORABLE MENTION	HM TWICE			
TAYLOR, SHARON	1980	FIRST TEAM	AC1	CHEYNEY STATE	🏀	
PRIDGEN, ANTOINETTE	1982	SECOND TEAM	AC2 + AC3			
SIMMONS, TONYA	1987	HONORABLE MENTION	HM TWICE			
DAVIS, CONSUELO	1991	FIRST TEAM	AC1 + AC2		🏀	
DAVIS, HILLARY	1991	SECOND TEAM	AC2	NJCU	🏀	
ENGLISH, LATISHA	1993	HONORABLE MENTION	HM TWICE	UPSALA		
TAYLOR, TIA	1994	HONORABLE MENTION	HM TWICE			
MILLER, VICKY	1994	FIRST TEAM	AC1 TWICE + HM	ST. JOHN'S		
MCCLINTON, CRYSTAL	1995	FIRST TEAM	AC1 + AC2 + HM TWICE			
LEWIS, BARBARA	2003	FIRST TEAM	AC1 + AC2 + HM		🏀	
VAN DOREN, KHADIJAH	2007	HONORABLE MENTION	HM TWICE			
OVERTON, LASHAWN	2008	FIRST TEAM	AC1 + AC2	NJCU	🏀	
DANIELS, DEIDRE	2010	SECOND TEAM	AC2 + HM			

SNYDER

PLAYER	YEAR	HIGHEST ALL COUNTY HONOR	NO. OF ALL COUNTY HONORS	COLLEGE	1000 PT SCORERS	2000 PT SCORERS
EVERETT, KADECHA	2010	FIRST TEAM	AC1			
TYRE, TAMARA	2011	FIRST TEAM	AC1 TWICE			
GATHERS SASHA	2013	FIRST TEAM	AC1			
LEWIS, JAH'NEL	2022	FIRST TEAM	AC1 + AC2	CALDWELL		
THOMAS, KARINE	2022	HONORABLE MENTION	HM TWICE	RARITAN VALLEY CC		
ROSE, KYRA	2022	FIRST TEAM	AC1	COLLEGE OF STATEN ISLAND		

ST. ALOYSIUS ACADEMY

PLAYER	YEAR	HIGHEST ALL COUNTY HONOR	NO. OF ALL COUNTY HONORS	COLLEGE	1000 PT SCORERS	2000 PT SCORERS
MCDONALD, MIMI	1975	THIRD TEAM	AC3			
COLON, ELIA	1976	SECOND TEAM	AC2 + HM			
CHEECHIA, MARYBETH	1976	SECOND TEAM	AC2			
REGAN, MARGARET	1977	HONORABLE MENTION	HM			
BRADLEY, GLORIA	1980	SECOND TEAM	AC2			
MITCHELL, LINDA	1980	FIRST TEAM	AC1 + HM		🏀	
CERUTTI, PAM	1980	HONORABLE MENTION	HM		🏀	
ZUROWSKI, CHRIS	1982	HONORABLE MENTION	HM TWICE			
COUTILLO, LORRAINE	1983	THIRD TEAM	AC3			
CASEY, JEANETTE	1985	HONORABLE MENTION	HM TWICE			
RODGERS, ALICIA	1987	FIRST TEAM	AC1 + AC2 + AC3			
CASEY, PATTI	1989	HONORABLE MENTION	HM TWICE			
MITCHELL, TRACY	1995	HONORABLE MENTION	HM TWICE			
CUBILE, ERIKA	2001	HONORABLE MENTION	HM TWICE		🏀	

ST. ALOYSIUS HIGH

PLAYER	YEAR	HIGHEST ALL COUNTY HONOR	NO. OF ALL COUNTY HONORS	COLLEGE	1000 PT SCORERS	2000 PT SCORERS
CONNELLY, KARIN	1976	SECOND TEAM	AC2 + AC3			
MOHLMANN, MARY	1980	THIRD TEAM	AC3 TWICE + HM		🏀	
DELPIANO, FRAN	1981	HONORABLE MENTION	HM THREE TIMES			
CUMMINGS, JOANNE	1982	SECOND TEAM	AC2			
ROBBINS, JEAN	1985	SECOND TEAM	AC2			
CARROLL, JACKIE	1986	HONORABLE MENTION	HM THREE TIMES			
VAGG, DINA	1988	HONORABLE MENTION	HM THREE TIMES			
FURCH, SUSAN	1988	THIRD TEAM	AC3			
O'NEILL, KERRI ANN	1989	HONORABLE MENTION	HM TWICE			
WIDEJKO, CHRIS ANNE	1994	SECOND TEAM	AC2 + HM		🏀	
ALLEN, EVANGELYN	1996	HONORABLE MENTION	HM TWICE			
PERKINS, BONITA	2005	SECOND TEAM	AC2			

ST. ANTHONY

PLAYER	YEAR	HIGHEST ALL COUNTY HONOR	NO. OF ALL COUNTY HONORS	COLLEGE	1000 PT SCORERS	2000 PT SCORERS
SCHIMDT, ALICE	1975	FIRST TEAM	AC1		🏀	
LUKACHYK, CHRIS	1976	HONORABLE MENTION	HM TWICE			
MEYERS, KATHY	1976	FIRST TEAM	AC1 TWICE	MONTCLAIR STATE	🏀	
CASELLA, DIANE	1979	FIRST TEAM	AC1 TWICE		🏀	
ASHE, DIANE	1980	FIRST TEAM	AC1 + AC2 + AC3 + HM			
CANNON, TERRI	1983	HONORABLE MENTION	HM TWICE		🏀	
RODRIGUEZ, DIANE	1984	FIRST TEAM	AC1 THREE TIMES + AC3	GEORGETOWN	🏀	
WALL, SHEILA	1985	FIRST TEAM	AC1 + AC2 + HM	LASALLE	🏀	

ST. ANTHONY

PLAYER	YEAR	HIGHEST ALL COUNTY HONOR	NO. OF ALL COUNTY HONORS	COLLEGE	1000 PT SCORERS	2000 PT SCORERS
D'AMBROSIO, ANDREA	1986	SECOND TEAM	AC2 + HM			
DEFAZIO, MISSY	1988	HONORABLE MENTION	HM TWICE			
LEE, KIM	1990	FIRST TEAM	AC1 TWICE + AC2 + AC3			
SIMPSON, LYSSA	1993	FIRST TEAM	AC1 + AC3			
ROBERTS, NYREE	1994	FIRST TEAM	AC1 + AC4 + HM TWICE			
JOHNSON, ANTOINETTE	1995	HONORABLE MENTION	HM TWICE			
LLOYD, CANDACE	1997	FIRST TEAM	AC1 THREE TIMES + HM			
ABDULLAH, HASSANAH	1998	FIRST TEAM	AC1 + HM TWICE			
MCLEOD, MELONIE	1998	HONORABLE MENTION	HM THREE TIMES			
HARRIS, CRYSTAL	2002	THIRD TEAM	AC3 + HM TWICE			
RICKETTS, NAEEMAH	2005	FIRST TEAM	AC1 TWICE + HM	IONA		
BERMUDEZ, ANGELICA	2007	FIRST TEAM	AC1	KEAN		
HILL, TIFFANY	2007	FIRST TEAM	AC1			
ONDAH, REGINA	2008	HONORABLE MENTION	HM TWICE			
ALLEN, ADRIANNA	2010	FIRST TEAM	AC1			
HAWKINS, SHANICE	2010	FIRST TEAM	AC1			
TAYLOR-GASTON, ZYEARAH	2018	FIRST TEAM	AC1 TWICE + AC3 TWICE	NJCU		

ST. DOMINIC ACADEMY

PLAYER	YEAR	HIGHEST ALL COUNTY HONOR	NO. OF ALL COUNTY HONORS	COLLEGE	1000 PT SCORERS	2000 PT SCORERS
MELLANO, LOUISE	1969					
QUILTY, PAT	1976	FIRST TEAM	AC1 + HM	RUTGERS		
PHILLIPS, KATHY	1977	FIRST TEAM	AC1	ST. PETERS		
VENNER, ROBYN	1978	FIRST TEAM	AC1 TWICE			

ST. DOMINIC ACADEMY

PLAYER	YEAR	HIGHEST ALL COUNTY HONOR	NO. OF ALL COUNTY HONORS	COLLEGE	1000 PT SCORERS	2000 PT SCORERS
WESTERVELT, HELEN	1980	HONORABLE MENTION	HM TWICE		🏀	
POZNANSKI, GINA	1988	SECOND TEAM	AC2 + AC3	NJCU	🏀	
DOHERTY, STEPHANIE	1992	SECOND TEAM	AC2 TWICE + AC3	MARIST		
MCANDREW, BETH	1994	SECOND TEAM	AC2 + HM THREE TIMES	PROVIDENCE	🏀	
MILLER, JESSICA	1995	FIRST TEAM	AC1 + AC2	COLLEGE OF NEW JERSEY	🏀	
ZAMPELLA, ANGELA	1996	FIRST TEAM	AC1 FOUR TIMES	ST. JOSEPHS (PA)	🏀	
LARACY, CLARE	1997	HONORABLE MENTION	HM THREE TIMES	DESALES UNIVERSITY		
MILLER, RORY	2000	HONORABLE MENTION	HM TWICE			
VUCETAJ, SOPHIA	2001	FIRST TEAM	AC1 TWICE	KUTZTOWN	🏀	
LAZZARINI, PATRICIA	2001	FIRST TEAM	AC1 + HM		🏀	
TERRIOGO, RACHEL	2002	HONORABLE MENTION	HM TWICE			
COSSOLINI, ANNIE	2003	FIRST TEAM	AC1 THREE TIMES	MOUNT ST MARY'S	🏀	
HUSSEY, ELIZABETH	2004	FIRST TEAM	AC1		🏀	
ROMANO, ALYSSA	2010	SECOND TEAM	AC2 + HM	MONTCLAIR STATE		
CALLAHAN, KIERSTYN	2010	HONORABLE MENTION	HM TWICE	ST. MICHAEL'S (VT)		
SMITH, BRIA	2011	FIRST TEAM	AC1 TWICE + AC2 + HM	NJCU	🏀	
NIEVES, ARIANNA	2012	THIRD TEAM	AC3 + HM			
LEWIS, AMANDA	2013	FIRST TEAM	AC1	JOHNSON & WALES		
JOHNSON, HANNAH	2015	FIRST TEAM	AC1 + AC2 TWICE	NJCU	🏀	

PLAYER	YEAR	HIGHEST ALL COUNTY HONOR	NO. OF ALL COUNTY HONORS	COLLEGE	1000 PT SCORERS	2000 PT SCORERS
CREANGE, RENEE	1975	THIRD TEAM	AC3			
LANNACONNI, JANE	1976	SECOND TEAM	AC2			
COLEMAN, MARY	1976	THIRD TEAM	AC3 + HM			
ROTTNER, JEANNE	1979	SECOND TEAM	AC2 + HM TWICE		●	
KELLY, MAUREEN	1979	SECOND TEAM	AC2 TWICE + HM	MONTCLAIR STATE	●	
NITTING, BARBARA	1981	HONORABLE MENTION	HM THREE TIMES		●	
SPATUCCI, PAULA	1985	HONORABLE MENTION	HM TWICE			
ALVAREZ, ELAINE	1986	HONORABLE MENTION	HM TWICE		●	
STALTER, DONNA	1988	FIRST TEAM	AC1 + AC3		●	
SERRANO, TAVIA	1992	HONORABLE MENTION	HM THREE TIMES		●	
PICINIC, DIANE	2005	HONORABLE MENTION	HM		●	
RIVERA, GABRIELLE	2009	FIRST TEAM	AC1 + HM		●	

PLAYER	YEAR	HIGHEST ALL COUNTY HONOR	NO. OF ALL COUNTY HONORS	COLLEGE	1000 PT SCORERS	2000 PT SCORERS
OLSZEWSKI, RONNIE	1977	HONORABLE MENTION	HM TWICE			
ALVARADO, LISETTE	1984	SECOND TEAM	AC2 + HM			
SIMS, KHALLIAH	1995	HONORABLE MENTION	HM TWICE			
SMITH, APRIL	2001	HONORABLE MENTION	HM TWICE			
MCLEAN, ALISHA	2003	HONORABLE MENTION	HM TWICE			
COATES, RAVEN	2009	FIRST TEAM	AC1 + HM TWICE		●	

UNION CITY

PLAYER	YEAR	HIGHEST ALL COUNTY HONOR	NO. OF ALL COUNTY HONORS	COLLEGE	1000 PT SCORERS	2000 PT SCORERS
MATEO, JEN	2009	FIRST TEAM	AC1	KEAN		
ESTRADA, ANGELA	2011	THIRD TEAM	AC3			
RODRIGUEZ, SHAELA	2012	SECOND TEAM	AC2			
WOOD, EBONI	2013	FIRST TEAM	AC1	KEAN		
GARCIA, KARINA	2013	FIRST TEAM	AC1			
CEDENO, NELLASIA	2016	SECOND TEAM	AC2 TWICE	GEORGIAN COURT		
PICHARDO, ELAINY	2022	HONORABLE MENTION	HM	CENTENARY		
MERCEDES, ERIKA	2022	FIRST TEAM	AC1 TWICE	BLOOMFIELD		
GUERRA, JAIDA	2023					
OREFICE, JAYLYN	2024	FIRST TEAM	AC1 + AC2			

UNION HILL

PLAYER	YEAR	HIGHEST ALL COUNTY HONOR	NO. OF ALL COUNTY HONORS	COLLEGE	1000 PT SCORERS	2000 PT SCORERS
KELLY, SHARON	1975	THIRD TEAM	AC3			
LIMA, JUNE	1976	HONORABLE MENTION	HM TWICE			
NAHREBNY, LINDA	1980	THIRD TEAM	AC3 + HM			
DOUGHTY, KATHY	1984	HONORABLE MENTION	HM TWICE			
DULACK, TRACY	1984	THIRD TEAM	AC3 + HM			
GONZALEZ, ELIZABETH	1985	HONORABLE MENTION	HM TWICE			
SHERAMN, ELIZABETH	1985	THIRD TEAM	AC3			
FITZPATRICK, GERRI	1987	HONORABLE MENTION	HM TWICE			
MORALES, TERRI	1989	HONORABLE MENTION	HM TWICE			
ROJAS, CHRISTINA	1997	FIRST TEAM	AC1			

UNION HILL

PLAYER	YEAR	HIGHEST ALL COUNTY HONOR	NO. OF ALL COUNTY HONORS	COLLEGE	1000 PT SCORERS	2000 PT SCORERS
CRUZ, ARACELY	2000	HONORABLE MENTION	HM TWICE	STEVENS TECH	🏀	
FERNANDEZ, SHIRLEY	2004	SECOND TEAM	AC2 + HM THREE TIMES			
BEYRUTI, MELISSA	2005	FIRST TEAM	AC1	KEAN	🏀	
GUZMAN, ISA	2007	HONORABLE MENTION	HM THREE TIMES			

WEEHAWKEN

PLAYER	YEAR	HIGHEST ALL COUNTY HONOR	NO. OF ALL COUNTY HONORS	COLLEGE	1000 PT SCORERS	2000 PT SCORERS
FRANCO, LAURA	1977	HONORABLE MENTION	HM TWICE		🏀	
WILT, EILEEN	1979	HONORABLE MENTION	HM		🏀	
SPINOSA, LISA	1980	SECOND TEAM	AC2 + HM TWICE		🏀	
BEHRENS, DIANE	1981	SECOND TEAM	AC2 + AC3		🏀	
HANDEL, DONNA	1984	HONORABLE MENTION	HM THREE TIMES		🏀	
DEBARI, ANN MARIE	1985	HONORABLE MENTION	HM		🏀	
REA, VICKI	1986	HONORABLE MENTION	HM TWICE			
HILTON, DONNA	1990	THIRD TEAM	AC3 + HM THREE TIMES		🏀	
CUELRVO, LEYLA	1991	THIRD TEAM	AC3			
MCLAUGHLIN, KAREN	1994	HONORABLE MENTION	HM TWICE			
MARTINIUK, JADE	1995	HONORABLE MENTION	HM TWICE			
JAVIER, MARIA	1998				🏀	
CORREDOR, CRYSTAL	2008	FIRST TEAM	AC1 + AC2		🏀	
OSPINA, VALENTINA	2013					
LENTINI, CAITLYN	2014					
LENTINI, ANNA	2017					

WEEHAWKEN

PLAYER	YEAR	HIGHEST ALL COUNTY HONOR	NO. OF ALL COUNTY HONORS	COLLEGE	1000 PT SCORERS	2000 PT SCORERS
PRIMERO, NICOLE	2017					
CHONG, SAMANTHA	2017					
CHONG, SOPHIE	2017					
RODRIGUEZ, AMANDA	2017					
ORDONEZ, NATALIA	2018			NJCU		
MOLANO, NICOLE	2019	THIRD TEAM	AC3	KEAN		
SATORA, SAHIBA	2019			PENN STATE HARRISBURG		
RUIZ, ALEXSA	2019					
PURCELL, ERIN	2019					
EID, MARIE	2020			RAMAPO		
LOFTIN, ZIONNA	2021					
MENDEZ, SOFIA	2022			CENTENARY		
MENDEZ, VIVIANA	2022			CENTENARY		
WILLIAMS, SYDNEY	2022					
TOMLINSON, MORGAN	2022					
LAMAR, MIKAELA	2023					

I'm very pleased to salute three
Hudson County and Syracuse University
standouts who contributed greatly
to my Naismith Basketball Hall of Fame career...

— Frank Nicoletti (Class of 1966, teammate and friend) —

— Rafael Addison (Class of 1986) —

— Terrence Roberts (Class of 2007) —

with a special shoutout to the Hurleys,
The First Family of Hudson County Basketball.

Congratulations on their worthy inclusion
in *"Hoops Hotbed on the Hudson."*

All the Best,
Jim Boeheim

'HOOPS HOTBED' POTPOURRI

Expressing our appreciation for Dick Vitale's strong support of the 'Hoops Hotbed' project, Jersey Bounce Basketball Academy is pleased to present the Hudson County All-Paisan squad (all passing the high standards of Dickie V). With the substantial number of Italian–heritage figures who've excelled in Hudson basketball over the years, we had a hard time paring it down to 30 players, one head coach and six assistants.

So, without further ado, here's our list of grandi giocatori e allenatori.

Needing to draw the line somewhere, we apologize to the numerous list of other worthy candidates that didn't make the final cut.

JERSEY BOUNCE

Basketball Academy

PRESENTER OF HUDSON COUNTY ALL–PAISAN TEAM
(alphabetically)

Phil Baccarella, '68, Bayonne	*Dr. Al Milanesi, '62, Stevens Academy*	*Head Coach*
Al Baldini, '57, Holy Family	*Hank Morano, '53, St. Peter's Prep*	*Joe Palermo – St.Cecelia (K)*
Nick Barbato,'63, Ferris	*Tony Nicodemo, '55, Ferris*	
John Barone, '65, Hoboken	*Frank Nicoletti, '62, St. Peter's Prep*	*Assistant Coaches*
Art Calabro, '62, Stevens Academy	*Mike O'Koren, '76, Hudson Catholic*	
Dan Callandrillo, '78, North Bergen	*Togo Palazzi, '50, Union Hill*	*Gordie Chiesa – Manhattan*
Pete Capitano, '58, Bayonne	*Ralph Passante, '59, Memorial*	*Tom Favia – Ferris*
Bernie Cicirelli, '50, Memorial	*Mike Pedone, '56, St. Peter's Prep*	*Larry Mangino – Virginia*
Sam DePiano, '65, St.Michael's (UC)	*Ray Pericola, '55, Union Hill*	*Nick Mariniello – Hudson Catholic*
Pete DeLisa, '61, Snyder	*Perry del Purgatorio, '46, Emerson*	*Steve Ricciardi Sr. – Hudson Catholic*
Denis DiFeo, '63, St. Peter's Prep	*Steve Ricciardi, Jr., '97, Seton Hall Prep*	*Matty Sabello – North Bergen*
Dr.Don Fanelli, '72, St.Josephs (WNY)	*Tony Romano, '43, Ferris*	
Bob Fazio, '73, Emerson	*Mike Rubinaccio, '52, St. Michael's (UC)*	
Richie Freda, 70, St. Anthony	*Paul Tagliabue, '58, St. Michael's (UC)*	
Tony Holm, '67, Weehawken	*John Wendelken, '61, Demarest*	

It was just a small Jersey City Catholic school in the city's Marion section.

But as Rich Freda remembers, there were only five rows of bench seats and a balcony that was always filled with kids.

And every year, from the late 1950s to 1969, from late April to May, the gym was always packed to the rafters for the annual Mount Carmel Tournament.

The great Jersey Journal sports columnist Cas Rakowski wrote of the tournament: "Jersey City has generally been regarded as the basketball capital of the East and it's not too far-fetched to call Dom Matticola's Mt. Carmel Invitation Basketball Tournament the basketball showplace of the East."

As for the assembly of talent at the tournament, Rakowski wrote, "Jersey City and Hudson County are proving that the basketball capital of the world is right here."

Freda was the ballboy, official scorer and sometimes announcer during the tournament.

"There were 12 teams in the tournament, and I think it expanded to 16 after it got popular" said Freda. In the last few years of the tournament, it hit 20 teams. "There would be teams from Newark, Elizabeth, Harlem, Philadelphia, Long Island, Westchester County and a couple from Jersey City such as the Buddy Boyle Assn., Simonetti Bondsmen and Willie Wolfe Assn."

And the players were like a who's who of basketball, with several such as Bob Love and Mike Riordan earning NBA contracts after their performance in the tournament.

The deep talent pool on many teams was the result of several factors:

The NBA was only an eight-team league and many players cut by the NBA continued to play in the Eastern League and were, of course, recruited by teams in the tournament. These players included Walt Simon, Bruce Spraggins and Hank Whitney of the ABA's N.J. Americans, Stacey Arcenaux and former college players Dick Gaines (Seton Hall), Alan Seiden (St. John's) and Floyd Lane (CCNY).

Also, players barred from the NBA because of their involvement in the 1951 betting scandal participated, such as Jack Molinas, third pick in the first round of the 1953 NBA by Ft. Wayne, Sherman White, the No. 1 scorer in NCAA during the 1950-1951 season with a 27.7 points per game average, who had to leave team with several games remaining in the college season due to being charged with being involved in the scandal, as well as Ed Warner – a star on the 1950 CCNY team that won both the NIT and NCAA tournaments.

Moreover, the tournament boasted a strong contingent of local players such as Mike Rooney, Vinnie Ernst, Dan Waddleton, Elnardo Webster, Harry Laurie, Gerald Govan, George Blaney, John Wendelken, Ed Petersen, Paul Tagliabue and Harry Brooks to name just a few.

On five occasions, Snookies Sugar Bowl from Harlem and host team Mt. Carmel played in the finals, with Snookies prevailing three times.

According to Freda, the games had a lot of scoring but hardly any defense.

One game that fans talked about for years was Rooney's 57 point outburst as the Boyle Association defeated Snookies in the 1968 semifinals.

It was a great tournament for the fans as the small gym put them close to the action and you not only had a great view, but you could hear everybody talking and arguing.

Al Eschbach, the "king of sports talk radio in Oklahoma" remembers attending the games as a kid growing up in Jersey City.

"I'm watching this team with great players, guys that will be pretty famous later on." he said. "And The Jersey Journal did an amazing, amazing job covering the tournament."

Former St. Michael's (JC) and North Carolina star Lou Brown was forced to quit the Tar Heels team when he was charged for introducing players to Jack Molinas, the central figure in the 1951 scandal.

Brown's brother Lenny, before a Saturday night game at Mt. Carmel, made the comment to friends, "Something must be up with my brother's situation because my father had been a nervous wreck the last two months fearing my brother would be going to prison, but the last few days he seemed much calmer."

Shortly after making that comment, his brother Lou arrived at the gym, signaled to Jack Molinas to come over to him in front of the wall across from the bleacher seats, and had a 10- to 12-minute conversation in which both had big smiles and laughed often.

It turned out Brown had become a prosecution witness and wore a wire that night, which led, three weeks later, to Molinas being indicted and eventually convicted and receiving a sentence of 10 to 15 years. He was paroled in 1968 after serving five years.

The tournament was founded by Matticola and, according to Rakowski, it took two months of preparation and hundreds of phone calls by Matticola before he had the teams set for his tournament. Over the years, the tournament raised more than $40,000, which in the 1960s sufficiently supported all of Mt. Carmel's CYO activities.

In 1996 Matticola received the community service award when he was inducted into the Hudson County Sports Hall of Fame.

In one of the tournament's most memorable moments, Snookies coach John Walker stunned the crowd at the 13th annual tournament when he turned over his team's championship trophy to Matticola and asked him to present it to Matticola's wife Lillian, who was ill at the time and unable to attend the tournament as she normally did.

—

By, Caroline Wills and Harvey Zucker

To the many dedicated coaches, teachers and mentors, particularly my friends Dominic Bellefimine, Bob Hurley and Steve Riciardi, who've helped develop our young players, accept my gratitude and appreciation.

Nick Petruzzelli
Managing Partner, The Taurasi Group

Q & A ON THEIR HUDSON HOOPS DNA

**"1949 Annual Hudson Dispatch All-County Game
Silverman's Whites Won 46-39"**

Larry Silverman #6 White, Bob Budd #7 White, Earle Markey #3 White, Fred Shabel #8 White,
Togo Palazzi #9 White, Vinnie Doherty #9 Black, George Faltings Top Row 3rd. from left,
Harry Brooks #8 black, Pete Innis #6 black, Pete Caruso standing 3rd from the right,
Jerry Molloy Standing second from the right.

"Nostalgia is the only friend that stays with you forever."

–

Damien Echols

REV. EARLE MARKEY | ST. PETER'S PREP, 1949

I learned the game at : PS 6 in West New York, N.J.

I was taught the game by : I wasn't taught the game by anybody, I learned it by playing as much as I could, whenever I could.

First organized competition : 7th Grade League in West New York, NJ. This led to a team of youngsters, called, I think, The West New York Hub team. We played a 10-minute game in Madison Square Garden, between games of a College Double Header - which was a tradition then at the Garden Double Headers. We won 10-8 but what a thrill it was to play on the Madison Square Garden court "under the lights" before a big crowd.

This was first time I thought I was good : When I won the scoring title of the 8th grade league in West New York sponsored by the HUB.

I was patterning my game after : I Don't think I patterned my game after any one particular player - but tried to imitate the moves of many college players I saw play in the Garden.

Toughest player I faced in the county : I believe Harry Brooks ("Hurricane Harry") of Emerson High School in Union City.

Most influential person in my basketball career : was Lester "Buster" Sheary, my coach at Holy Cross. A close second was Pete Caruso, who took a losing junior year team and made them county and State Champions (and ESCIT runnerups) in my senior year. We went from "Worst to Best" in Hudson County in one year under Pete with a 30-6 record for the senior year.

Greatest basketball memory : was the overtime victory in 1949 over Union Hill HS (Union City) to win the Hudson County Championship - the first in the history of St. Peter's Prep and one of the first for a South Hudson team to win it. Other memorable victories over St. Louis University when they were in the top 20 in the country, and victories over Seattle U. and the O'Brien twins in the NIT in 1952 and the victories over Navy and Wake Forest in the 1953 NCAA Elite Eight part of the NCAA tournament.

When not on the court, I was seen hanging out at :
Doing homework at home when in high school or in the library when in college.

Favorite place for pizza in high school : A pizza place at a bar in West New York. The name of which escapes me at this time.

Something about me no one (or few people) know(s) : I only got one day of jug in my 4 years at St. Peter's Prep.

FRED SHABEL | UNION HILL, 1949

I learned the game at : P.S. 12 and Roosevelt School.

I was taught the game by : George Faltings.

First organized competition : Freshman at Union Hill.

This was first time I thought I was good : During my freshman year.

I was patterning my game after : No particular player.

Toughest player I faced in the county : Harry Brooks.

Most influential person in my basketball career : Vic Bubas & George Faltings.

Greatest basketball memory : Scoring the winning basket for Union Hill to defeat Emerson in the 1949 North Hudson Final to qualify to play St. Peter's Prep in county championship.

When not on the court, I was seen hanging out at : Boy Scout meetings at YMHA.

Favorite place for pizza in high school : Don't remember.

SANDY ADER | DICKINSON, 1955

I learned the game at : Jersey City YMHA

I was taught the game by : Sam Kaplan.

First organized competition : The Pierce Club in J.C.

This was first time I thought I was good : Playing at Kutshers in the Catskills between junior and senior years in high school.

I was patterning my game after : Adolph Schayes.

Toughest player I faced in the county : Rich Hoffman, Union Hill.

Most influential person in my basketball career : Bernie (Red) Sarachek, coach at Yeshiva U.

Greatest basketball memory : Playing the Israeli Olympic Team in Madison Square Garden to a full house in 1957.

When not on the court, I was seen hanging out at : Jersey City YMHA.

Favorite place for pizza in high school : Franks in the Marion section of J.C.

Something about me no one (or few people) know(s) : I aspired to become a sportscaster.

JACK NIES | ST. PETER'S PREP, 1955

JOHN CROTTY | ST. PETER'S PREP, 1956

I learned the game at : Horace Mann Grade School in Bayonne in the 8th grade. I wasn't very good, I was 5' 1".

I was taught the game by : Joe O'Brien, former player at the Prep, former coach of Assumption College and Director of the Basketball Hall of Fame.

First organized competition : 8th-grade team.

This was first time I thought I was good : Senior year at the Prep when we won the Parochial A State Championship and I was selected to the All-State Team with a quote that I was the best rebounder in the State of New Jersey – pound for pound – inch for inch – at 5' 11" and 168 lbs.

I was patterning my game after : Hank Morano, Prep '53; also admired the way that Bobby Knight and Mike Krzyzewski played defense in a tenacious manner that I tried to emulate.

Toughest player I faced in the county : Harry Brooks; others included Tony Nicademo (Ferris), Tommy Gaynor (Snyder), George Ramming (Union Hill), Eddie Bowler (Lincoln).

Most influential person in my basketball career : Roy Leenig, my high school coach.

Greatest basketball memory : Winning the State championship.

When not on the court, I was seen hanging out at : Other basketball courts and playgrounds.

Favorite place for pizza in high school : Ilventos in Jersey City - an Italian restaurant that had great mussels and pizza.

Something about me no one (or few people) know(s) : My mother forced me to take the entrance exam for Prep because I wanted to go to Bayonne High School and be with my friends. I soon made new friends at Prep.

I learned the game at : St. Vincent's Grammar School, 57th, Avenue D, Bayonne.

I was taught the game by : My cousin Warren Buehler and Ken Stibler.

First organized competition : 5th grade at St. Vincent's.

This was first time I thought I was good : at 12 years old competing against much older players.

I was patterning my game after : No one in particular.

Toughest player I faced in the county : Tony Nicodemo.

Most influential person in my basketball career : Warren Bueller and Ken Stibler.

Greatest basketball memory : Winning basket in last 5 seconds to win '56 County Championship vs Memorial.

When not on the court, I was seen hanging out at : Bayonne.

Favorite place for pizza in high school : Dido's 51st & Ave. D, Bayonne.

AL BALDINI | HOLY FAMILY, 1957

I learned the game at : Weehawken Recreation.

I was taught the game by : Schoolyard games and in high school by Coach Matt Sabello.

First organized competition : Sixth grade.

This was first time I thought I was good : 8th grade.

I was patterning my game after : Heinshon, Peracola and Brooks.

Toughest player I faced in the county : George Blaney.

Most influential person in my basketball career : Matt Sabello.

Greatest basketball memory : Winning College Divisional Regional as college sophomore in Burlington to go to Evansville and New York Knicks Rookie Camp.

When not on the court, I was seen hanging out at : The schoolyards and 32nd Street.

Favorite place for pizza in high school : Christina's, Union City.

MAUREEN WENDELKEN | ST. DOMINIC ACADEMY, 1957

I learned the game at : Joe Kelly's yard & Hoboken YMCA.

I was taught the game by : Father Leo McLaughlin.

First organized competition : St. Peter & Paul CYO.

This was first time I thought I was good : Playing against boys.

I was patterning my game after : Dick McGuire, Jerry West, Oscar Robinson.

Toughest player I faced in the county : Pat Devlin – St. Michael, J.C.; Maureen Dolan, St. Michael, UC.

Most influential person in my basketball career : Father & husband (John).

Greatest basketball memory : Coaching at Madison Square Garden, the Spectrum and Pauley Pavillion.

When not on the court, I was seen hanging out at : Abel's Ice Cream Parlor.

Favorite place for pizza in high school : Blue Point, Hoboken.

Something about me no one (or few people know(s) : I'm a gym rat (Planet Fitness), play golf.

GERALD GOVAN | SNYDER, 1959

I learned the game at : PS #14.

I was taught the game by : Mr. Lefkanes, teacher.

First organized competition : PS #14.

This was first time I thought I was good :
When Harry Brooks used to arrange to pick me up
so we could play together at the CYO & other venues.

I was patterning my game after : Nobody.

Toughest player I faced in the county : Jim Barry.

Most influential person in my basketball career :
Jerry Degnan.

Greatest basketball memory : Junior year leading
the nation in rebounding (NAIA).

When not on the court, I was seen hanging out at :
In Snyder locker room playing cards (tonk).

Favorite place for pizza in high school : No favorite
place.

DENNIS MCGOVERN | ST. MICHAEL'S (J.C.), 1959

I learned the game at : St. Peter's Prep school yard,
Audobon Park, 10 Street Playground and various camps. Also
St. Peter's Gymnasium on York Street.

I was taught the game by : My brother, CYO Coaches, Jim
Duane CYO Biddy basketball All Stars International Tourney
and Mike Pedone, former Prep star and later at St. John's.

First organized competition : CYO Leagues, Rec Leagues,
Jersey City Biddy basketball League

This was first time I thought I was good : Named to R.I.
Basketball Hall of Fame, Hudson County Basketball Hall of
Fame, R.I. Legends Award, New England Basketball Hall of
Fame, MVP New England All-Star Game, drafted by N.Y. Knicks

I was patterning my game after : Richie Guerin, Bill
Bradley, Sam Jones.

Toughest player I faced in the county : Raftery, Ernst,
Rooney, Waddleton, Wendelken.

Most influential person in my basketball career :
My family, Ernie Calverley, Dave Gavitt and Joe Mullaney.

Greatest basketball memory : Scoring 47 and 35 points in
State tourney.

When not on the court, I was seen hanging out at :
My places of P/T employment and active in church

Favorite place for pizza in high school : Erks on Newark
Ave J.C. and Jerry's in Italian Town, J.C.

Something about me no one (or few people) know(s) :
I would have liked to play football, but St. Mike's did not have
football. I would have liked to hit a three and am jealous
because I did not have the three; but a lot of mine were threes.

CHARLIE BROWN | LINCOLN, 1960

I learned the game at : P.S. #14 and Salem Baptist Church.

I was taught the game by : George Lefcanidos, Phys Ed teacher at P.S. #14; Ollie Gelston, Jersey City State.

First organized competition : P.S. #14 basketball team & Salem Baptist Church League.

This was first time I thought I was good : My senior year I scored 16 points against South Side H.S. and their All-State player Lonnie Wright.

I was patterning my game after : Oscar Robinson, only I'm lefty.

Toughest player I faced in the county : Mike Rooney.

Most influential person in my basketball career : John Stallworth, coach Jersey City Bondsmen.

Greatest basketball memory : Winning the N.A.I.A. District 31 Championship in 1964 and going to Kansas City for the National Championships.

When not on the court, I was seen hanging out at : Harry Massey's house.

Favorite place for pizza in high school : Pizza Parlor on Jackson & Wilkerson Aves.

Something about me no one (or few people) know(s) : When I was 4 years old I had pneumonia three times and after spending a lot of time in the hospital I had to learn to walk all over again.

HANK FINKEL | HOLY FAMILY, 1960

I learned the game at : Holy Family as a sophomore.

I was taught the game by : Matty Sabello.

First organized competition : Holy Family JV.

This was first time I thought I was good : End of senior year started scoring in 30 pts. per game.

I was patterning my game after : No one in particular.

Toughest player I faced in the county : Mike Rooney, Pete DeLisa and John Wendelken.

Most influential person in my basketball career : Matty Sabello.

Greatest basketball memory : Playing on same team with Hall of Famers Jojo White, Dave Cowens, Don Nelson.

When not on the court, I was seen hanging out at : Robert Walters School on 27th Street.

Favorite place for pizza in high school : 38th Street & Bergenline Avenue. (Don't remember the name).

Something about me no one (or few people) know (s) : Had no intent or desire to play basketball.

JOHN WENDELKEN | DEMAREST, 1961

I learned the game at : Hoboken YMCA, 4th Street Park Court.

I was taught the game by : Father, 8th Bloomfield kids.

First organized competition: Hoboken Rec Biddy League, Hoboken Grammar School League (Brandt School).

This was first time I thought I was good : Hoboken Biddy League, State Biddy Tournament (Jersey City YMCA).

I was patterning my game after : Frank Selvy, George Blaney.

Toughest player I faced in the county : Vinny Ernst, Danny Waddleton.

Most influential person in my basketball career : Coach Frank Chiocco at Demarest H.S., coaches Bob Curran & Frank Oftring (Holy Cross).

Greatest basketball memory : Winning North Hudson H.C.I.A.A. Championship (1961) 20-game winning streak.

When not on the court, I was seen hanging out at : Fourth Street courts and 8th Bloomfield Street lot (now gone).

Favorite place for pizza in high school : Blue Point Restaurant (now gone).

Something about me no one (or few people) know(s): Loved tennis (played) and golf (still playing).

MIKE ROONEY | SNYDER, 1961

I learned the game at : St. Aloysius School JC.

I was taught the game by : Mr. Breell, Mr. Lyon & Claude Pickett.

First organized competition : St. Aloysius Biddy Team.

This was first time I thought I was good : HS.

I was patterning my game after : Vinnie Ernst.

Toughest player I faced in the county : Vinnie Ernst.

Most influential person in my basketball career : Jerry Degnan, coach Snyder HS.

Greatest basketball memory : score 50 points in Eastern Basketball League.

When not on the court, I was seen hanging out at : McGinley Sq.– JC.

Favorite place for pizza in high school : Roma DC.

Something about me no one (or few people) know(s): Score 59 point against Niagara while at St. Bonaventure. Also had games of 50 & 57 points in the Eastern League.

YORKIE CALABRO | STEVEN ACADEMY, 1962

I learned the game at : Hoboken Recreation Center.

I was taught the game by : My father.

First organized competition : Hoboken Biddy League.

This was first time I thought I was good :
I was selected to Biddy All Stars.

I was patterning my game after : Bob Cousy.

Toughest player I faced in the county : George Montecalvo Demarest HS.

Most influential person in my basketball career : My father (great player and very successful coach at Demarest HS).

Greatest basketball memory : Being selected to the Lakewood HS Athletic Hall of Fame for our success in winning Three State Sectional Group III Girls Basketball Championships.

When not on the court, I was seen hanging out at : The Jersey Shore.

Favorite place for pizza in high school :
Blue Point Restaurant in Hoboken.

Something about me no one (or few people) know(s) : I am a singer songwriter and have a DooWop group. The group is called Yorke and the Actuals and we've been played on Sirius XM Cool Bobby B's 50's on 5.

ED PETERSEN | NORTH BERGEN, 1962

I learned the game at : The age of 10 playing Biddy Basketball & CYO in Union City and North Bergen.

I was taught the game by : My father.

First organized competition : Biddy Basketball.

This was first time I thought I was good :
When I made the All-Star Team in Biddy Basketball.

I was patterning my game after : Randy Chave.

Toughest player I faced in the county : Tom Greely- Holy Family HS

Most influential person in my basketball career : Matty Sabello, HS Coach at NB; Ollie Gelston, JCSC, Coach.

Greatest basketball memory : Making the winning basket in the NAIA Regional Tournament sending our team, JCSC to Kansas City.

When not on the court, I was seen hanging out at : The school yard.

Favorite place for pizza in high school :
Christina's Pizza - Union City.

Something about me no one (or few people) know(s) : Always wanted to be an FBI Agent

JIMMY FOSTER | HOBOKEN, 1970

I learned the game at : In the Hoboken youth recreation center while in the 6th grade.

I was taught the game by : My freshman high school coach, Bert Pierce

First organized competition : Was in the intramural 7th and 8th grade Jr. High School League.

This was first time I thought I was good : Was when I scored 40 pts in a intramural game in the 10th grade.

I was patterning my game after : Tiny Nate Archibald because he was my height and left-handed.

Toughest player I faced in the county : Was Rich O'Connor, who I was assigned to cover as a junior in High School.

Most influential person in my basketball career : Was my collegiate head coach at the University of Connecticut, Dee Rowe.

Greatest basketball memory : When we defeated the Tournament favored St. John's University in the NIT

When not on the court, I was seen hanging out at : In the ball field around the corner from my house playing pickup games.

Favorite place for pizza in high school : in Hoboken was Benny Tudino's Pizzeria on 622 Washington St.

Something about me no one (or few people) know(s) : I held the most H.S. Football interceptions in a single game (5) in school history.

ALBIO SIRES | MEMORIAL, 1970

I learned the game at : Washington Park. I just picked it up.

I was taught the game by : Charlie Swenson, my freshman coach at Memorial..

First organized competition : 8th grade at PS 4.

I was patterning my game after : Jerry West. I used to go to park and pretend I was Jerry West and release the ball fast.

Toughest player I faced in the county : Richie O'Connor (St. Michael's (U.C.) and Jimmy Foster (Hoboken) were the toughest players I faced in my high school career. Other players in the county I was impressed with were Mike Rooney and Jackie Gilloon who played at Memorial after me. Rooney was such a great shooter that if they had the three-point shot when he played for Snyder, he would have scored three thousand points. I know a lot of people would agree with me that Jackie Gilloon was the Pete Maravich of Hudson County.

Greatest basketball memory : Winning the county championship in 1970 when we defeated Dickinson, which was undefeated at the time.

When not on the court, I was seen hanging out at : Memorial Park on 57th Street. I practically lived there. At 10 P.M. they would close the park and I'd be bouncing the ball while walking toward my home and my mother would usually meet me halfway and say she was worried about me returning so late. I told her I was 6'4" and would be OK. She then would say she could not be at ease until I returned home safely. I appreciate that more now than ever.

Something about me no one (or few people) know (s): I never thought I would be going into politics. A friend ran for commissioner and he was against the administration and I became persona non grata. I had always wanted to be a coach at Memorial but that situation made it seem unlikely for the time being.

BOB FAZIO | EMERSON, 1973

I learned the game at : Union City Recreation biddy basketball league on Saturdays in the winter of 1967.

I was taught the game by : Nick Mastorelli, Frank McGovern, Vito D'Orio, Joe 'Pep' Novotny were my first coaches.

First organized competition : Union City biddy basketball where we were state champions in 1968 and played for the National title in Augusta, Georgia.

This was first time I thought I was good : In 1969 when I started varsity basketball at Holy Family High School in Union City where I played for Al Baldini.

I was patterning my game after : I wanted to be like Dave Cowens of the Boston Celtics, a tough, hard working undersized player.

Toughest player I faced in the county : Greg Ballard, a power forward from the University of Oregon. We played them in the N.I.T. in Madison Square Garden in 1975.

Most influential person in my basketball career : Al Baldini who coached me in my freshman year at Holy Family High School.

Greatest basketball memory : Scoring my 1000th point at 15th ranked Georgetown University in my junior year at St. Peter's college against a John Tompson coached team and upsetting them.

When not on the court, I was seen hanging out at : Playing darts, pool and 3 on 3 games in a small gym at St. Joseph Men's Catholic Club in Union City, where Tom Heinson perfected his hook shot.

Favorite place for pizza in high school : Christina's Restaurant on 17th St. Bergenline Ave. in Union City where everybody went after our games.

Something about me no one (or few people) know(s) : I was featured on 60 Minutes, the news show hosted by Leslie Sthal where I was called Mr. Fazio, an Urban leader of education. Also, visited by President Bill Clinton and Vice President Al Gore, and called an effective instructional leader, in 1996 at Christopher Columbus Middle School in Union City.

MIKE O'KOREN | HUDSON CATHOLIC, 1976

I learned the game at : Saint Joe's School Yard.

I was taught the game by : Ron Steinmetz.

First organized competition : Biddy basketball 5th grade, YMCA on Bergen Avenue.

This was first time I thought I was good : Picked first in pickup game when I was a freshman at Saint Joseph school yard.

I was patterning my game after : Never imitated any player.

Toughest player I faced in the county : Ray Vyzas.

Most influential person in my basketball career : My brother Ron.

Greatest basketball memory : County championship vs. Saint Anthony in 1975.

When not on the court, I was seen hanging out at : Kennedy Boulevard.

Favorite place for pizza in high school : Three Brother's Pizza in Journal Square.

Something about me no one (or few people) know(s) : My mother was born in Italy and I am Italian.

SERGIO BARDAJI | UNION HILL, 1977

I learned the game at : Jefferson School at the age of 9.

I was taught the game by : My cousin, Roger Bardaji

First organized competition: St. Augustine Biddy Basketball with Coach Clayton Morrell.

This was first time I thought I was good : Union Hill HS Freshman Year.

I was patterning my game after : Jackie Gilloon.

Toughest player I faced in the county : Lou Cruz North Bergen.

Most influential person in my basketball career : Nick Galis.

Greatest basketball memory : Winning JV Championship against Lincoln at the J.C. Armory after losing to them by 25 earlier in the year.

When not on the court, I was seen hanging out at : I had no real hangout … just hooping or with my high school sweetheart.

Favorite place for pizza in high school : Summit Pizza Downtown U.C.

Something about me no one (or few people) know(s): I was a better in football than basketball!

WILMER TORRES | UNION HILL, 1977

I learned the game at : St. Michael's.

I was taught the game by : Steve Ricciardi.

First organized competition: St. Michael's.

This was first time I thought I was good : Grammar school 8th grade.

I was patterning my game after : Jordan.

Toughest player I faced in the county : Damon Tucker (Snyder).

Most influential person in my basketball career : Steve Ricciardi.

Greatest basketball memory : Union Hill all-time scorer 1,931 pts.

When not on the court, I was seen hanging out at : 39th street park.

Favorite place for pizza in high school : Tremeori.

Something about me no one (or few people) know(s): I actually played defense.

TOM BEST | LINCOLN, 1979

I learned the game at : Lafayette Park, Teen Post, Jersey City Recreation

I was taught the game by : Charlie Brown, Eugene Terry, PS #22 gym teachers.

First organized competition : St. Peter's Prep H.A.P.

This was first time I thought I was good : 7th grade gym class.

I was patterning my game after : Magic Johnson.

Toughest player I faced in the county : Lester Harris.

Most influential person in my basketball career : Charlie Brown.

Greatest basketball memory : Hitting a buzzer beater against Bob Hurley's St. Anthony Friars.

When not on the court, I was seen hanging out at : No particular place.

Favorite place for pizza in high school : No particular place.

Something about me no one (or few people) know(s): I can juggle.

GREG HERENDA | ST. PETER'S PREP, 1979

I learned the game at : playing in James J. Braddock Park on 79 and 82nd Street in the early 1970's.

I was taught the game by : My first coach was Ken Bellani at Our Lady of Fatima in North Bergen.

First organized competition : was the Biddy League at Horace Mann School.

This was first time I thought I was good : In the summer league at the St. Paul's parish in Jersey City which was run by Coach Bob Hurley and I was playing against Brian Lee.

I was patterning my game after : North Bergen/Seton Hall legend Danny Callandrillo and on the pro level, Walt "Clyde" Frazier.

Toughest player I faced in the county : It's tough to narrow it down, but Danny Callandrillo, Ashley Walker (Snyder and Minnesota Vikings) and Phil Robinson (St. Anthony's) were the toughest competition I faced.

Most influential person in my basketball career : Mel Logan, who passed my name to the coaches at Merrimack College, and that is how I received a scholarship offer.

Greatest basketball memory : Coaching FDU in the school's first NCAA Tournament victory in 2019.

When not on the court, I was seen hanging out at : Hashways Deli on Kennedy Boulevard in North Bergen.

Favorite place for pizza in high school : Nick's and Sole' pizza in uptown North Bergen.

Something about me no one (or few people) know(s): I was the least talented player in my family. My younger brother Bill and older brother Anthony are far better athletes than me.

BOBBY HURLEY | ST. ANTHONY, 1989

I learned the game at : The gym where my dad was coaching teams as far back as I can remember.

I was taught the game by : My dad and all the great players I watched at St. Anthony.

First organized competition : Pee Wee Basketball at Our Lady of Mercy, grades 1–4, was where I got my introduction. They had 8-foot baskets!

This was first time I thought I was good : Was at a camp before eighth grade when I was named to the all-star team.

I was patterning my game after : Guys who played for my dad. They were my role models, especially Mandy Johnson, who went on to Notre Dame; David Rivers, who played at Marquette; & Ken Wilson, who went to Villanova.

Toughest player I faced in the county : Antoine Dasher of Marist and FDU. He was a big guard and really good, very underrated.

Most influential person in my basketball career : My dad. He shaped my basketball career by teaching me something about the game every single day.

Greatest basketball memory : My second Final Four, 1992 in Indianapolis, when we defeated UNLV for our first national championship.

When not on the court, I was seen hanging out at : The Country Village playground.

Favorite place for pizza in high school : Not just for pizza, Laico's on Terhune Avenue, Jersey City, one of my all-time favorite restaurants. In fact, it's very definitely in my top 5 all-time, and I've eaten all over the country, all over the world.

Something about me no one (or few people) know(s) : That I've developed skills in cooking. I like to make dinner for the family on weekends. I watch a lot of Gordon Ramsey on TV. In fact, my style of coaching is like his style of yelling at his students.

Bonus question: Rate the Final Fours you've been involved in: Well, it's definitely got to be a 1 & 1A situation: No. 1 is my first NCAA championship in Indianapolis and No. 1A was watching my brother Danny coach UConn to the championship last season in Houston. That was so crazy great! Then comes the '93 Final Four in Minneapolis where we won our second title, followed by '91 in Denver, where we lost to UNLV in the final.

Parting shot: There are five former Hudson players who still hold the career assist records at their r espective universities (plus one who is No. 2 at his school, Jack Gilloon at South Carolina). The five are Ed Lawson at Manhattan, Jasper Walker at St. Peter's, Delvon Arrington at Florida State, Kenny Wilson at Villanova and the NCAA career assist leader, a fella by the name of Bobby Hurley. Then there's Vinnie Ernst, who holds the single-game record at 17 but isn't listed among career leaders because season and career assist stats weren't kept in the early '60s. "Wow, that's something," Bobby said. "Four of those guys – Kenny, Delvon, Jasper and I – played for my dad, who always talked about Jackie Gilloon. Jackie didn't play for him but my dad sure liked his game."

JODY HILL | HARRISON, 1990

I learned the game at : Harrison High School and Washington Middle School.

I was taught the game by : Jack Rodgers.

First organized competition : 7th grade at Washington Middle School in Harrison.

This was first time I thought I was good : When I made a no-look pass on a 3 on 2 break.

I was patterning my game after : Alice Burgos and Krissy Kurt.

Toughest player I faced in the county : Brenda Milano and Kristen Simoji.

Most influential person in my basketball career : My high school coach, Jack Rodgers.

Greatest basketball memory : Beating St Peter's and Kristen Simojis team.

When not on the court, I was seen hanging out at : THE COURTS.

Favorite place for pizza in high school : Gina's pizzeria.

Something about me no one (or few people) know(s): I loved watching rocky movies before my basketball games.

DANNY HURLEY | ST. ANTHONY, 1991

I learned the game at : A very, very, very young age at White Eagle Hall.

I was taught the game by : My dad and all the great players I watched at St. Anthony.

First organized competition : On the Bucks in the OLM (Our Lady of Mercy) CYO League . . . an outdoor league with 8-foot metal rims . . . my brother and I were in the backcourt together . . . I was in the 1st grade, he was in the 3rd .

This was first time I thought I was good : When I was probably 8, 9 or 10 , anytime there was a timeout in a St. Anthony game, I would take the ball from the ref, dribble around and take shots . . . I could get off 10, 12 shots during the timeouts . . . layups, jump shots, move farther outside and shoot again . . . hearing all the "Ooohs!" and "Ahhhs!" from the fans in the stands told me I might be pretty good . . . and Bobby was doing the same thing at the other end of the court!

I was patterning my game after : Chris Mullen, because I was a lefty and fancied myself as a shooter, and Mark Price who played for Georgia Tech and then NBA.

Toughest player I faced in the county : Antoine Dasher of Marist and FDU . . . He was a big guard and really good, very underrated and then NBA.

Most influential person in my basketball career : My dad, with brother Bob right behind him.

Greatest basketball memory : Prior to winning the NCAA championship this spring, it was my senior year at St. Anthony beating Seton Hall Prep to win the TOC (Tournament of Champions) for my dad . . . we lost only once that season and finished 2nd overall in the country.

When not on the court, I was seen hanging out at : Always hanging out with the guys, the boys, the players . . . on the Country Village courts and playgrounds.

Favorite place for pizza in high school : I can't recall their names but there were these two pizzerias right next door to each other about two blocks from St. Anthony. A slice of pizza at either place was giant-sized . . . they were competing pizzerias . . . one place would charge 50 cents for huge slice, so the other place would lower their price and make their slices even bigger . . . and whenever we'd order pizza delivered, it was from Vinnie's ll.

Something about me no one (or few people) know(s): Growing up watching Mandy Johnson, David Rivers, Mike O'Koren, Jim Spanarkel and the impact of my dad and the pro-am he ran at Pershing Field . . it was pretty cool.

CARLOS CUETO | ST.ANTHONY, 1994

I learned the game at : St. Michael's and White Eagle Hall.

I was taught the game by : Frank McGovern and Steve Ricciardi.

First organized competition : St. Michael's Parish League.

This was first time I thought I was good : Coach Steve had Doc Miller work on my sprained ankle to get me ready for 8th grade championship.

I was patterning my game after : Larry Bird.

Toughest player I faced in the county : John Giraldo at Marist.

Most influential person in my basketball career : Steve Ricciardi and Bob Hurley.

Greatest basketball memory : Winning 2022 Sectional Championship with my daughter.

When not on the court, I was seen hanging out at : Emerson High School.

Favorite place for pizza in high school : Summit Pizza.

Something about me no one (or few people) know(s) : I met my wife in Kindergarden.

ANGELA ZAMPELLA | ST. DOMINIC, 1996

I learned the game at : 6 yrs playing for St. Francis in Hoboken.

I was taught the game by : John Clemente.

First organized competition : Playing for St. Francis Grammar School in Hoboken.

This was first time I thought I was good : My 1st varsity game as Freshman when I realized I could compete with other top varsity players.

I was patterning my game after : I didn't pattern my game after one player.

Toughest player I faced in the county : Denene Halsey, Marist.

Most influential person in my basketball career : My family.

Greatest basketball memory : Winning the A10 championship in college.

When not on the court, I was seen hanging out at : Didn't hang out much, was either playing basketball or baseball/softball.

Favorite place for pizza in high school : Filippos on 1st.

STEVE RICCIARDI JR. | SETON HALL PREP, 1997

I learned the game at : St. Michael's – Union City.

I was taught the game by : Steven Ricciardi Sr.

First organized competition : St. Michael's Parish League.

This was first time I thought I was good : Starting on the 12-year old BBA team at 10 years old.

I was patterning my game after : John Stockton.

Toughest player I faced in the county : Anthony Perry.

Most influential person in my basketball career : Steven Ricciardi Sr.

Greatest basketball memory : Winning 6 State Championships, Biddy, AA, HS.

When not on the court, I was seen hanging out at : I was at Gregory Park, Weehawken.

Favorite place for pizza in high school : Pinos Pizzeria.

Something about me no one (or few people) know(s) : I worked out at St. Michael's during high school and college during the season 45–90 minute shooting sessions - working out at Gregory Park in the rain.

MARIO LUGO | EMERSON HIGH SCHOOL, 1998

I learned the game at : St. Michael's.

I was taught the game by : Steve Ricciardi.

First organized competition : St. Mike's CYO.

This was first time I thought I was good : 7th Grade.

I was patterning my game after : Magic Johnson.

Toughest player I faced in the county : Wilmer Torres.

Most influential person in my basketball career : Steve Ricciardi.

Greatest basketball memory : In Oklahoma for an A.A.U. game and forgot my uniform.

When not on the court, I was seen hanging out at : Steve's house.

Favorite place for pizza in high school : Tino's Pizza.

Something about me no one (or few people) know(s): Used to sleep with a basketball.

RICK APODACA | NORTH BERGEN, 1999

I learned the game at : New York East Side.

I was taught the game by : Steve Ricciardi.

First organized competition : Horace Mann Elementary, North Bergen.

This was first time I thought I was good : Freshman scoring 30 pts. in St. Michael's H.S. League.

I was patterning my game after : Penny Hardaway.

Toughest player I faced in the county : Jerome Bash (Ferris).

Most influential person in my basketball career : Steve Ricciardi & Tom Peterson.

Greatest basketball memory : 2004 – Puerto Rico Olympic team that defeated U.S.

When not on the court, I was seen hanging out at : 82nd Park in North Bergen.

Favorite place for pizza in high school : Roma Pizza 86th & Kennedy Blvd.

Something about me no one (or few people) know(s) : I currently own 3 businesses.

ALEX MIRABEL | DICKINSON, 2002

I learned the game at : The Jersey City Boys and Girls Club

I was taught the game by : Donald Copeland Sr.

First organized competition : I played at the Jersey City Boys Club.

This was first time I thought I was good : I got selected to participate in the All-Star Team at the Boys and Girls Club.

I was patterning my game after : Jason Kidd, Ed Cota, Chris Paul.

Toughest player I faced in the county : Tony Tate (Marist).

Most influential person in my basketball career : Donald Copeland Sr., Charlie Brown.

Greatest basketball memory : Winning the Hudson County Title as head coach St. Peter's Prep 2020.

When not on the court, I was seen hanging out at : The house watching college and NBA games.

Favorite place for pizza in high school : Larry & Joe's.

Something about me no one (or few people) know(s) : My favorite sport to watch in the summer live is baseball.

BETTY MENDIETA | NORTH BERGEN, 2003

I learned the game at : Corner of 53rd and Columbia Ave in North Bergen. A double basketball courtyard that has now been converted into the Franklin School Annex.

I was taught the game by : My big brother, Freddy.

First organized competition : North Bergen recreation basketball league at the age of 8 where I scored my first basket for the opposite team.

This was first time I thought I was good : When the boys were scared to play against me at the courtyard.

I was patterning my game after : Michael Jordan, Chamique Holdsclaw, Cynthia Cooper, Rebecca Lobo.

Toughest player I faced in the county : Tara Walker from Marist.

Most influential person in my basketball career : After my parents, it would be Walter Welsh, my Gauchos AAU coach.

Greatest basketball memory : Cutting down the nets after winning the NYCAC Championship my freshman year at Adelphi.

When not on the court, I was seen hanging out at : Movies.

Favorite place for pizza in high school : Nick's on 77th St & Kennedy Blvd, North Bergen.

Something about me no one (or few people) know(s) : I come from a family of farmers in Ecuador.

LAUREN JIMINEZ | NORTH BERGEN, 2007

I learned the game at : The park and North Bergen recreation center.

I was taught the game by : Originally my dad, he was my first coach and taught me how to be a true post player. I had great AAU coaches along the way.

First organized competition : North Bergen rec games. I was on the Comets.

This was first time I thought I was good : Summer league game in high school I was a freshman, Bob Hurley went to my dad and told him this is just the beginning for me that I would go places a lot of people don't. Even then I wasn't sure I was always hard in myself.

I was patterning my game after : Shaquille O'Neal, Charles Barkley. They were dominant post players that were nasty on the court. I wanted that.

Toughest player I faced in the county : Tina Charles.

Most influential person in my basketball career : My dad. He made me watch games of great post players. Kept stats of my games, shooting percentage was important.

Greatest basketball memory : Winning two CAA Championships with James Madison University and going to the NCAA Tournament.

When not on the court, I was seen hanging out at : Home or a friends house, I have always been a homebody.

Favorite place for pizza in high school : Palermo's in North Bergen.

Something about me no one (or few people) know(s) : I'm artistic, although I was always in the gym in HS you could find me in the art department in the ceramics room or in sculpture.

We at The Nicoletti Law Firm legally laud our firm's founding partner, Frank Nicoletti, recognized by **"Hoops Hotbed on the Hudson"** on his illustrious basketball career.

IN SUMMATION...

1962 Dell Second Team High School All-American (St. Peter's Prep, Jersey City)

Syracuse University teammate (1963-66) of Naismith Basketball Hall of Famers Dave Bing and Jim Boeheim, when the Orangemen's 3 season record was 52-24

"Hoops Hotbed" Hudson County All-Decade Team (1960s)

Whether the basketball court or legal courts
— IT'S BEEN EXCELLENCE —
Verdict was unanimous.
Way to go, Frank!

Congratulations to a trio of distinguished Syracuse University
'Heroes of the Hardwood':

Frank Nicoletti (my teammate), Raf Addison and Terrance Roberts.

Also each and everyone whose accomplishments are recognized
in 'Hoops Hotbed on the Hudson'.

Best Regards,
George Hicker

'HOOPS HOTBED' HODGE-PODGE

During the course of researching this book and developing the content to be included, we came across a number of items, comments and anecdotes that didn't really fit into one of the articles or sections of the book. Since we felt they were either interesting, amusing or entertaining enough, we decided to include them as miscellaneous items. Think of them the way you would regard "team rebounds" in a basketball boxscore: Not worthy of their own category but important enough to be official.

Over the years, there have been cases of Hudson County players who started slow with little or no production on their high school teams but later proved their mettle at a future stop. This could be the result of players being on deep, talented teams and not getting a sufficient amount of playing time or just being "late bloomers" and needing the extra time to develop their game.

Bob Hurley has often stated this is a major a factor with the development of big men in particular.

One of the primary examplesof Hudson players "breaking out"after high school are Charlie Potyrala and Don Unger of St. Peter's Prep as described in a clip from The Advocate:

"RUTHERFORD – St. Peter's Prep alumni led both the varsity and freshmen basketball teams in scoring at Fairleigh Dickinson this past winter.
"Charlie Potyrala set a new season scoring mark of 440 with the varsity while Don Unger hit 420 with the frosh. Neither was a regular in his high school days."

———

Two examples of Bob Hurley's thesis on big men taking longer to develop are Snyder's Gerald Govan and Bayonne's Dan O'Sullivan.

Neither received any All-County recognition in their high school careers but both excelled afterward. Gerald blossomed at St. Mary's (Kan.), where he was aided by other Hudson teammates (Jack Nies, Richie Donnelly and Robert McLaughlin) and then in the Italian League and finally on to a season career in the ABA where he retired as the league's 2nd all-time leading rebounder behind Mel Daniels.

In Dan O'Sullivan's case, he had little production and sparse playing time at Bayonne but Fordham took a flyer on him and his career there validated Bob Hurley's belief about big men requiring a longer period to develop. Dan progressed from freshman stats of 1.6 points and 1.4 rebounds to senior season production of 12.5 points and 7.5 rebounds. After starting off in 1990 with the Omaha Racers of the Continental Basketball Association, he played with five different NBA teams from the 1990-91 to the '95-96 season, then concluded his career with three premier teams in Italy and Greece.

Perhaps the slowest of the "late bloomers" was Aron

Stewart, who only made the varsity at Lincoln as a senior year and started just one game. He then enrolled at Essex County Community College and gave folks a good look at things to come as he averaged 19.9 points in his freshman year and, as a sophomore, led all junior college players in the U.S. with an average of 36.6 points per game. Aron continued his high scoring feats at Richmond, where he averaged 30.2 points in 1972-72 and 26.5 in 1973-74 on his way to scoring 1,237 career points.

Finally, Snyder's Rafael Addison was an example of a "late bloomer" on the same team or school. Addison did not start on the varsity until his junior year and went from starter to star in his senior year by achieving All-County First-Team honors. After earning All-Big East honors at Syracuse, he played six seasons in the NBA and three seasons in Italy.

In the early research of this project, the great Jed D'Matteo of 'Jedsey Journal' fame was invited to chime in on his pal Richie Donnelly's place among the all-time great players out of Lincoln High School. Jed reacted very quickly by stating that was a "no-brainer" because Jugger (Richie's knickname) was Lincoln's first 1,000-point scorer – then quickly added with a laugh that he was also Lincoln's first 5,000-shot taker!

At the time of Togo Palazzi's passing in August 2022, highly respected former St. Al's coach Bob O'Conner praised Togo as a player and man, then commented on the plethora of Hudson County players who continued their schooling and basketball careers at Holy Cross.

"In the '50s and '60s, Holy Cross was a suburb of Hudson County," he said. And rightly so, as a partial list of Hudson/Holy Cross players shows:

George Blaney

Tom Heinsohn

Greg Hochstein

Keith Hochstein

Joe Kelly

Earle Markey

Joe O'Brien

Togo Palazzi

George Waddleton

John Wendelken

Interest in basketball in Hudson County surged in the 1950s and the All-Decade Team listed earlier was proof of the high level of the sport in Hudson. As basketball was "in the blood" of many former players, a number of them looked for avenues to continue in the sport in some role such as coaching, refereeing, sports writing, etc.

As far as high school coaching, the traditional appointments were teachers in a particular school or from the school system. In a departure from the norm, Dr, Hugh Doherty, a former St. Peter's Prep player, was appointed head coach by Essex Catholic High School in Newark. Hughie, brother of 'colorful character' Vince, maintained a busy dental practice in a two-story building on Summit Avenue near Pavonia and arranged his schedule so in most cases he could finish by 3 p.m. and depart for practice. Wonder if he brought his drills for those drills on the hardwood!!

Dr.Hugh Doherty and brother Vince Doherty

HONORED PLAYERS

Several Hudson County basketball players and personalities have been memorialized over the years with facilities and statues named in their honor:

KYLE ANDERSON
ST. ANTHONY

Kyle Anderson Court
Fairview Middle School
Fairview, NJ
Dedicated Sept. 23, 2023

JOHN CLUNE
ST. PETER'S PREP

Clune Arena
U.S. Air Force Academy
Colorado Springs, CO
Dedicated Dec. 6, 1993

ED FORD
SCHOOL OF HARD KNOCKS

Caven Point Athletic Complex
Jersey City, NJ
Dedicated June 14, 2012

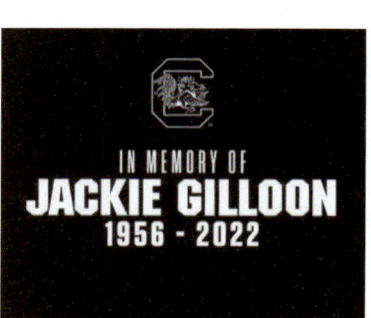

JACKIE GILLOON
MEMORIAL

Jackie Gilloon Memorial Courts
Washington Park
Union City, NJ
Dedicated Oct. 15, 2022

MIKE O'KOREN
HUDSON CATHOLIC

Mike O'Koren Courts
St. Joseph's Schoolyard
Jersey City, NJ
Dedicated June 17, 2022

MIKE ROONEY
SNYDER

Mike Rooney Gymnasium
Snyder High School
Jersey City, NJ
Dedicated Feb. 25, 2022

TEX SILVERMAN
SNYDER

Tex Silverman Court
George Washington U.
Washington, D.C.
Dedicated May 3, 2011

ALBIO SIRES
MEMORIAL

Albio Sires Elementary School
West New York
Dedicated Oct. 4, 2013

CHUCK WEPNER
BAYONNE

Chuck Wepner Statue
Dennis P. Collins Park
Bayonne, NJ
Dedicated Nov. 12, 2022

HUDSON PASSES MUSTER

In the course of compiling 'Hoops Hotbed on the Hudson,' there was much checking and rechecking regarding any number of common-knowledge facts, stats and figures that were already out there.

Sometimes, however, there was a discovery, a bona fide nugget so unique, perhaps a copyright or patent would've been appropriate....despite the voluminous love which has been accorded to New York City's roster of point guards (Bob Cousy, Dick McGuire, Lenny Wilkens, Nate 'Tiny' Archibald,, Mark Jackson, Rod Strickland and Stephon Marbury to lead that list), it's five 'distributors' out of Hudson County who are career assist leaders at their respective schools.

...so there.

PLAYER	SCHOOL	ASSISTS
BOBBY HURLEY*	DUKE (1989–1993)	1,706
DELVON ARRINGTON	FLORIDA STATE (1998–2002)	688
JASPER WALKER	ST. PETER'S (1987–1991)	672
KENNY WILSON	VILLANOVA (1985–1989)	627
ED LAWSON	MANHATTAN (1983–1988)	447

* NCAA ALL-TIME ASSIST LEADER

PLAYER NO. 2 IN SCHOOL'S CAREER ASSISTS

PLAYER	SCHOOL	ASSISTS
JACK GILLOON	SOUTH CAROLINA (1974–1978)	518*

* ONE-GAME RECORD (17)

(...including some special mentions to Vinnie Ernst [St. Aloysius], whose pair of 16-assist games set a [since-matched] Providence College record, and Juvaris Hayes [St. Anthony], whose split-division [I and II] tenure at Merrimack College [Mass.] ended with the NCAA steals record of 457)

ROY LEENIG
EX- ST. PETER'S PREP COACH

Jack "The Shot" Foley was best known as an unbelievable shot maker and All-American for the College of the Holy Cross back in the 1960's. But in his hometown of Worcester MA, Jack was also a highly regarded prankster.

He would often stroll in a bar after a summer league game at Crompton Park with an enormous snake wrapped casually around his neck and shoulders. And within minutes horrified hoopsters would dart for the exit. Jack would linger sipping on his Tadcaster beer.

Yet the greatest example of Jack's off-beat humor occurred in December 1960 when Holy Cross was playing in the Hurricane Classic in which HC beat Tennessee by one point and lost to host Miami 77-70 the following night.

Roy Leenig, a well-known coach out of New Jersey from his days at St. Peter's Prep, was in his final season coaching Holy Cross. While addressing HC after the Miami loss, he looked on in horror as Jack "The Shot" calmly pulled out a handgun and aimed it straight at Leenig. "No Jack...don't!" Leenig screamed, dropping to his knees for mercy. Jack calmly pulled the trigger. A flag in his fake gun dropped down. "Bang!" said Jack.

Witnesses in the locker room later recalled Leenig turned white. He did not laugh. But Jack and his Crusader teammates did.

At season's end Leenig left HC with a 22-6 record in his final season. And with a memory never to be forgotten.

–

By, John Gearan

HUDSON HARDWOOD AND BEYOND

Judging and evaluating ability in most sports is subjective and can result in provocative barroom or street corner discussions. Although we feel a very strong and compelling case has been made throughout this book on the claim of Hudson County producing more top-level basketball players than any other similarly sized area, in many cases that matter can be open to a legitimate debate and discussion. However, when reviewing the resumes of Hudson hoopsters, first on the court, then in subsequent sports-related endeavors, any unbiased observer would be hard-pressed to name other areas close to Hudson's size that even approach Hudson's success on this basis.

JOHN CLUNE   **FRED SHABEL**   **PAUL TAGLIABUE**

The following list of Hudson County hoopsters who were leaders or excelled in other sports – related endeavors certainly bears this claim out:

- Sports Administration, Professional – Paul Tagliabue, NFL Commissioner

- Sports Administration, College – John Clune, Director of Athletics, U.S. Air Force Academy

- Sports Administration, Museums – Joe O'Brien, President & CEO, Naismith Hall of Fame

- Sports Broadcasting, Television – Bill Raftery, popular CBS and Fox Sports basketball color commentator

- Sports Broadcasting, Radio – Al Eschbach, J.C. native is the pioneer of sports talk radio in Oklahoma

- Sports Coaching, Professional – Tom Heinsohn, guided Boston Celtics to 2 NBA titles

- Sports Coaching, High School – Bob Hurley, Sr., one of three H.S. coaches in Naismith Hall of Fame

- Sports Coaching, College – George Blaney, 28 seasons Head Coach at Dartmouth, Holy Cross, Seton Hall

- Sports Coaching, College – Dan Hurley, head coach of UConn Huskies 2023 National Champs

- Sports Coaching, International – Jim Boylan, led Vevey Basket to 1st ever Swiss League Championship

- Sports Corporation Executive – Fred Shabel, Vice-Chairman, Comcast-Spectacor

- Sports Dinner Speaker – Jerry Malloy, Toastmaster General of N.J., in class by himself at sports dinners

- Sports Filmmaker – Leon Gast, 1996 Academy Award Winner for Best Documentary

- Sports Journalism – Richard O'Connor, his articles have appeared in Sports Illustrated, Esquire, Playboy

- Sports Officiating – Jack Nies, at time of retirement in April 2009, refereed 3rd highest number of NBA Games (2046)

- Sports Ownership – Dan Silna, Co-Owner - Spirits of St. Louis (ABA), basketball's most profitable team

- Sports Participation, Non-Basketball, Individual – Chuck Wepner, fought Ali in 1975 World Title Fight

- Sports Participation, Non-Basketball, Team – Ray Lucas, QB for Rutgers University, New York Jets

- Sports Philanthropy – Larry "Tex" Silverman, court at George Washington Univ. bears his name

- Sports Public Address Announcer – Dom Alagia, long-time P.A. Announcer at St. Peter's College, West Point and Meadowlands Arena who worked 15 Army-Navy football games

- Sports Representation, NBA Players – Bill Madden, clients included NBA champ Jim McMillian, NBA champ/MVP/Hall of Famer Bob McAdoo and Elnardo Webster

- Sports Representation, International – Richard Kaner, pioneer in placement of American players abroad.

Eddie Ford also known as "The Faa" and known to me as Mr. Ford had a profound influence on my baseball playing career. He saw something in my game that he liked. He encouraged and inspired me to achieve success in the game that I loved. Whether coaching, scouting Major League Baseball prospects, umpiring baseball games or his colorful antics as a Hudson County Basketball Referee he brought a passion and commitment to whatever he did. Like so many other young athletes he mentored in baseball and basketball he will never be forgotten.

Mr. Ford would take the time to travel to Bergen County to see me play in high school games, baseball tournaments, as well as at Columbia University for my college games. He was honest and consistent in both his criticism and praise. He was always teaching me not only about the game of baseball, but valuable lessons in life.

I have taken many of the things he taught me to run successful youth baseball programs. I will forever remember him for his kindness, his caring, his generosity and for the good that he did for me and so many others.

Sean Callagy
Callagy Law
Paramus, NJ

CALLAGY LAW
Caring · Urgent · Aggressive

THE BROTHERS OF THE
SYRACUSE UNIVERSITY CHAPTER OF
SIGMA ALPHA MU FRATERNITY SALUTE THEIR FELLOW
FRAT BROTHER FRANK NICOLETTI, AND ALL OF THE OTHER
"HOOPS HOTBED ON THE HUDSON" HONOREES

DAVE BING	RICHIE FRANK
RICK BRUDNER	FRED KLEIN
RICH CHADAKOFF	LOREN KROLL
DON CRONSON	STANLEY RUBIN
BOB FAGENSON	JACK SCHERBAN
BERNIE FINE	NEIL SCHLESINGER
MICHAEL FRANK	KEN WURTENBERGER

APPENDIX

—

GRASSROOTS BASKETBALL

Listed below are some of the many selfless coaches, officials and volunteers instrumental in developing the skills of Hudson's players, along with the venues which were second homes.

SOUTH HUDSON

The Hurley Family Foundation

Coach Bob Hurley & Mrs. Chris Hurley, Melissa Hurley, John Bernardo, Kerry Miller, John Pignataro, Jay & Barby Lumang

NJ Triple Threat, Inc.

Dom Bellifemine, Alex Bynum, Pete Delgado, Anthony McIntosh, Damel Ling, George Rotundo

Jersey Bounce Basketball Academy

Dom Bellifemine, Damel Ling, Shelton Gibbs, Nick Gallo, Vito Gigante, Max Bracero, Jerome Davis, Willie Oquendo, Chaquan Scott, Brent Burgess, Shyquan Gibbs, Marvin Williams

The Dan Finn Classic

Ed Finn, Bob Lauterhan, Bob Hurley Sr., Steve Ricciardi Sr.

St. Al's CYO

Paul Keogh, Eddie Webster, Coach Romano (Coaches/Ref)

Duncan Projects

Harry Hilliard

JC PAL

Jim Hague, Frank Williams, Bobby McDonnell

Bayonne PAL

Jerry Clougher, Cliff Jacobsen, Marty Reed, Norman Elam, Mike Elam, Jim Mock, Kim "KT" Turello, Moe Kazazian, Walt Farley, Jeff Farley, Jerry Hogan, Dave Kobryn, John Calloway, Jim Davaney

Bayonne Rec / Board of Education

Tom Jacobsen, Mike Lynch, Steve Russell, Jack Hladik, Don Ahern, Phil Baccarella, Pete Amadeo, JJ Hladik, Kevin Walker, Cal Limig, Billy Zasowski, Dave Kobryn, Kenny Kopacz, Tim Mercier, Matt Allen, Artie Levan, Bob Leahy

Bayonne Mean Machine

John Calloway

Bayonne Junior Bees

James Turner, Tyler Rickard, Ashley Devaney, Tara Flynn, Courtney Young, Ben Gamble, Ed Malloy, Kevin Walker, Dom Bellifemine, Josh Lane

Hoboken Church Square Park (4th St.)

Gary White

Hoboken YMCA

Mike Granelli, Charles "Buddy" Matthews, Jesus Morales, John Ciriello

JC PAL

Jim Hague, Frank Williams, Bobby McDonnell

Hoboken Rec

Joe Pullano, Mike Rubbinaccio, Ed Miller, Charles Rozzi, Victor Chirichella, Max Bracero, Walter "Binky" LeBrink, Frank Cappolla, Ed Madigan, John Madigan, Gary White, Anthony Raccuia, Joe Palermo, Doug Peterson, Eddie Groomes, John Catallano, Tony Calland, Angela Zampella, Jason Blanks, Joe Casetta, Mas Forte, Davey Little, Michael Pellechia, Willie Oquendo, Dom Bellifemine, Damel Ling, John "Diddle" McDonald BoBo Toomey, Danny Burrell, Dennis McMullin, Vinny Johnson, William "Chubby" James, Joe DellaFave, Nick Lisa, Joe Petrillo, Nick Feola Jr.

Hoboken PAL

Joe Reinhart, Dom Lucignano, Tim McCourt,

Enrico Gnassi, William Truppner, Bobby Gohde, Cowboy Lucignano, Marion Kennedy, Mary Ellen Gallo, William "Chubby" James, Christopher LaBruno, Willie Oquendo, Tom Kennedy, Mr. Havens

Hoboken Board of Education

Madeline Gonzalez, Marquis Hanberry, Gene Spata, Maurice DeGennaro, Donnie Huggins, Frank Chicco Shawn Kolmer, Robert "Juice" Debois, Charles "Buddy" Matthews, Mike Donofrio, Bill & Jim Connor, Pete Costello

St. Francis

Joe Rabbia, John Clemente, Bobby Carrillo, Mike Taglieri, Tom Finnerty, Nick Feola Sr., Lou Zampella Sr., Ray Munch Vitale, Charlie Tortorella, Bill "Red" Murray, Victor Chirichella Sr.

Our Lady of Grace

Joe Walsh, Julian Castellanos, Ed Garland, Tom Calligy

Sts. Peter & Paul

Billy Culhane, Tony Cardino, Terrence Hayes

Hoboken Catholic Academy

Grace Sciancalepore, Harold "Junior" Milne, Roger Corrado, Mark Toscano

Our Lady of Grace

Joe Walsh, Julian Castellanos, Ed Garland, Tom Calligy

Brandt School

John Hildemann

Jersey City Boys & Girls Club

Gary Greenberg, Frank Burno, Eric McGinnis, Joe Whalen, Brian Whalen, Scott Jenks, Donald Copeland Sr., Joe Macchi, Jack Leahy, Dom Bellifemine, Alex Bynum, Kevin Reed, Steve Ricciardi Sr. Jim Hague, Eddie Groomes

St. Joseph's, Jersey City

Ronald O'Koren, Ronald Steinmetz, Gibby Lewis

Bayside Park

Donald Copeland Sr.

The Jersey City Bondsmen – Marion Neighborhood

Donald Copeland Sr., John Stallworth, Gene Terry (Sponsor), Tom Lalicato

Dickinson

Gordy Moore, Howie Fink, Shawn Drennan

St. Mary's

Tom Lalicato

Dickinson

Gordy Moore, Howie Fink, Shawn Drennan

Ferris

Richie Piccillo, Tom Favia

Hamilton Park

Pat Devaney, Regina Terriogo, Coach Bob Hurley

St. Patrick's, Jersey City

Roy Oller CYO, Pat Devaney Jr.

KEG / All-Saints/ Assumption All-Saints CYO/ St. Pat's

Greg Sharperson, Kevin Taylor, Eric Ragland, Ed Lawson

St. Peter's Prep Camps

Alex Mirabel

Marist Camps

Mike Leonardo, Ben Gamble, Frank Burno, Chris Chavannes, Jyron Brooks, Damel Ling William "Red" Drennan

St. Aedan's

Pete Romano

Our Lady of Mercy

Bob McDonnell, Wayne McCarthy

Mount Carmel Tournaments- Jersey City

Dom Matticola, Rich Freda

The Jersey City Rec / Armory

Joe Macchi, Mandy Johnson, Tommy Best, Flash Gordon, Gibby Lewis, Jim Hague, Ed "Faa" Ford, Charlie Brown Sr., Donald Copeland Sr.

Jersey City Board of Education

Rafael Addison, Charlie Brown

Lincoln-JC Rec

Flash Gordon, Willie Willis

Team Walker/Baby Rucker/Lena Edwards Park

Jerry Walker

Pershing Field

Charlie Straub

St. Nicholas

Charlie Straub

YMCA/JC

Mandy Johnson, Brian Hurley, Mike Bratton, Pop Russell

Bayonne Jewish Community Center

Bill Broderick

Basketball Courts & Gyms South Hudson

Hoboken Church Square Park
Bayonne 50th Street and Ave E
The Multi-Service Center
Sacred Heart
Our Lady of Victories
Bayonne 53rd Street
Our Lady of Mercy
Audubon Park
St. Paul of the Cross
Ege Avenue
Hamilton Park

Kearny

John Millar, Jody Hill, Ron Kirby, Sandy Juliano, Bobby McDonnell, Bill Raftery, Bill Mullins, Phil Kutt

Harrison

Kim McDonough Huaranga, Jack Rodgers,

Larry Bennett, Bill Mullin,. Jody Hill, George Glasgow, Phil Kutt, Tom McDonough, Raymond McDonough, Tom Ferreiro, Fred Confessore

Secaucus

Mike Piro, Guy Pascarello, John Schwartz, Nick Biamonte, Dennis McCaffery, Paul Logan, Joey O'Brien, Gary Wohlrab

Basketball Courts & Gyms-North Hudson

Elysian Park, Hoboken
Buchmuller Park, Secaucus
Charlie's Park, Weehawken
High Point Avenue, Weehawken 22nd St. / Gregory Avenue
Gilmore School, Union City 16th Street
Edison School, Union City Third Street
Hudson School, Union City 16th Street
St. Michael's Monastery, Union City 22nd Street
St, Augustine, Union City 39th Street
39th Street projects, Union City
North Bergen Recreation Center, 64th Street
Hudson County Park, North Bergen 70th Street
66th St. Park, West New York/Guttenberg
West New York Recreation Center, 59th Street and
Park Avenue, 88th Street Park, North Bergen
Anna L. Klein School, 70th Street, Guttenberg
School #2 West New York, Park Avenue
Robert Waters School, 28th Street, Union City
Washington School, 39th Street, Union City
17th Street Park, Union City, Robert Fulton
School, North Bergen, JFK School, North Bergen

Dickinson

Gordy Moore, Howie Fink, Shawn Drennan

Ferris

Richie Piccillo, Tom Favia

Hamilton Park

Pat Devaney, Regina Terriogo, Coach Bob Hurley

North Hudson Grass Roots CYO & Biddy Gyms

St. Michael's, Union City CYO/Biddy
Holy Family, Union City High School League
Holy Rosary, Union City Grammar/Biddy
Our Lady of Libera, West New York Grammar/ High School League

Hamilton Park

Pat Devaney, Regina Terriogo, Coach Bob Hurley

VOLUNTEER COACHES NORTH HUDSON

Turk Jordan -Weehawken Rec Lincoln Tunnel, Jack Gallo, Lou Ferrulo

North Bergen Rec

John Barone. Kevin Bianco, Frank Benna, Ray Janssen, Randy Chave, Matty Sabello, John"Digger" O'Dell, John Cellini, Tom Hopkins, Jimmy Avella, Phil Moretti

Our Lady Of Fatima

Joe Salvetti, Ken Bellani, Bob Mason, Bo Leone

St. Anthony Union City

Al Martinelli, Joe Zenko, Rafe Amato

Our Lady of Libera

Mikey Salvetti, Jim Souza

WNY Rec

Dennis Cooney, Bruce Gallasso, Ron Schurle, Bob Smith 30, Bill Dillon 30

St. John's Guttenberg

Frank Koetieror

St. Josephs, West New York

Jim McDonald 20, Ed D'Angelo

St. Francis Union City

Geo Campen, Frank Rieman, Bill Lynch, Nick Fargo 15

Anna L. Klein

Joe Forenza, Bob Tholen

St. Augustine's

Clayton Morrell, Mike Garcia , Luis Jiminez, Ivan Carvajal

St. Michael's

Frank McGovern, Steve Ricciardi Sr. 36 yrs Carlos Cueto, Steve Ricciardi Jr., Steve Rubbinaccio, John O'Donnell, Liz Rivetti, Augie Ricciardi

Union City Rec

Carlos Cueto, Drew Mora

NORTH HUDSON VOLUNTEER TEAMS

CYO/BIDDY

St. Michael's, Union City

St. Augustine, Union City

St. Francis, Union City

Holy Rosary, Union City

Holy Family, Union City

OLL, West New York

St. Joseph's, West New York

St. Mary's, West New York

OLF, North Bergen

St. John's, Guttenberg

St. Lawrence Weehawken

Anna L. Klein, Guttenberg

AAU

Jersey City Boys & Girls Club

St. Michael's, Union City

Team NJ Triple Threat

Cas Comets

Bayonne Mean Machine

TALLY BY SCHOOL OF HUDSON COUNTY CHAMPIONSHIPS AND RUNNERS UP

BOYS

ST. PETER'S
- **16 CHAMPIONSHIPS** (1949, 1950, 1952, 1956, 1957, 1959, 1961, 1962, 1963, 2001, 2008, 2009, 2010, 2011, 2020, 2023)
- **10 RUNNERS-UP** (1953, 1971, 2005, 2012, 2013, 2014, 2016, 2017, 2018, 2022)

HUDSON CATHOLIC
- **9 CHAMPIONSHIPS** (1975, 2012, 2013, 2014, 2015, 2016, 2017, 2018, 2022)
- **2 RUNNERS-UP** (2004, 2023)

MARIST
- **8 CHAMPIONSHIPS** (1989, 1991, 1992, 1993, 1994, 1995, 1997, 1999)
- **7 RUNNERS-UP** (1986, 1990, 2001, 2011, 2015, 2019, 2020)

BAYONNE
- **8 CHAMPIONSHIPS** (1951, 1954, 1958, 1964, 1965, 1968, 2003, 2005)
- **10 RUNNERS-UP** (1940, 1941, 1942, 1944, 1948, 1985,1988, 2002, 2006, 2009)

MEMORIAL
- **7 CHAMPIONSHIPS** (1940, 1941, 1942, 1943, 1944, 1970, 1973 – game stopped by police)
- **7 RUNNERS-UP** (1956, 1957, 1963, 1965, 1972, 1974, 2003)

SNYDER
- **5 CHAMPIONSHIPS** (1976, 1978, 1981, 1990, 1996)
- **6 RUNNERS-UP** (1960, 1967, 1980, 1982, 1991, 1993)

EMERSON
- **4 CHAMPIONSHIPS** (1945, 1948, 1966, 2004)
- **8 RUNNERS-UP** (1946, 1950,1951, 1954, 1968, 1984, 1987, 2000)

FERRIS
- **4 CHAMPIONSHIPS** (1983, 1985, 1986, 1998)
- **5 RUNNERS-UP** (1973, 1977, 1989, 1992,1995)

ST. ANTHONY
- **4 CHAMPIONSHIPS** (1980, 1982, 1987, 1988)
- **2 RUNNERS-UP** (1975, 1983)

NORTH BERGEN
- **3 CHAMPIONSHIPS** (1977, 1979, 2006)
- **7 RUNNERS-UP** (1969, 1976, 1978, 1981, 1997, 1998, 2010)

UNION HILL
- **2 CHAMPIONSHIPS** (1953, 1955)
- **5 RUNNERS-UP** (1945, 1947, 1949, 2007, 2008)

LINCOLN
- **3 CHAMPIONSHIPS** (1969, 1974, 2007)
- **2 RUNNERS-UP** (1979, 1996)

WEEHAWKEN
- **3 CHAMPIONSHIPS** (1946, 1947, 1967)
- **1 RUNNER-UP** (1943)

DICKINSON
- **3 CHAMPIONSHIPS** (1972, 2000, 2002)
- **4 RUNNERS-UP** (1955, 1966, 1970, 1999)

ST. MICHAEL'S (UC)
- **1 CHAMPIONSHIP** (1960)
- **3 RUNNERS-UP** (1952, 1958, 1959)

ST. MARY'S
- **1 CHAMPIONSHIP** (1984)
- **1 RUNNERS-UP** (1994)

ST. JOSEPH'S (WNY)
- **1 CHAMPIONSHIP** (1971)

UNION CITY
- **1 CHAMPIONSHIP** (2019)

HOBOKEN (DEMAREST)
- **2 RUNNERS-UP** (1961, 1964)

HOLY FAMILY
- **1 RUNNER-UP** (1962)

TALLY BY SCHOOL OF HUDSON COUNTY CHAMPIONSHIPS AND RUNNERS UP

GIRLS

BAYONNE
- **25 CHAMPIONSHIPS** (1975, 1976, 1977, 1980, 1984, 1986, 1987, 1988, 1989, 1990, 1991, 1992, 1995, 1997, 1998, 2002, 2003, 2006, 2009, 2010, 2011, 2016, 2020, 2022, 2023)
- **11 RUNNERS-UP** (1974, 1978, 1985, 1996, 1999, 2000, 2005, 2007, 2008, 2012, 2014)

NORTH BERGEN
- **6 CHAMPIONSHIPS** (1972, 1973, 1974, 2004, 2005, 2007)
- **5 RUNNERS-UP** (1975, 2001, 2003, 2006, 2011)

LINCOLN
- **6 CHAMPIONSHIPS** (1979, 1981, 2012, 2013, 2014, 2018)
- **5 RUNNERS-UP** (2009, 2010, 2015, 2016, 2019)

MARIST
- **4 CHAMPIONSHIPS** (1998, 1999, 2001, 2008)
- **3 RUNNERS-UP** (1998, 2004, 2017)

ST. ANTHONY
- **3 CHAMPIONSHIPS** (1982, 1983, 1985)
- **2 RUNNERS-UP** (1984, 1986)

FERRIS
- **3 CHAMPIONSHIPS** (1993, 1994, 1996)
- **1 RUNNER-UP** (1995)

SECAUCUS
- **2 CHAMPIONSHIPS** (2015 AND 2017)
- **3 RUNNERS-UP** (2013, 2018, 2023)

MEMORIAL
- **1 CHAMPIONSHIP** (1978)
- **5 RUNNERS-UP** (1972, 1973, 1977, 1982, 1983)

ST. DOMINIC
- **1 CHAMPIONSHIP** (2000)
- **2 RUNNERS-UP** (1994, 2002)

HUDSON CATHOLIC
- **1 CHAMPIONSHIP** (2019)
- **1 RUNNER-UP** (2020)

HOLY FAMILY
- **4 RUNNERS-UP** (1987, 1988, 1990, 1997)

HOBOKEN
- **3 RUNNERS-UP** (1980, 1981, 1992)

ST. JOSEPH
- **3 RUNNERS-UP** (1975, 1976, 1979)

SNYDER
- **2 RUNNERS-UP** (1991, 1993)

DICKINSON
- **1 RUNNER-UP** (1989)

UNION CITY
- **1 RUNNER-UP** (2022)

HUDSON COUNTY CHAMPIONSHIP GAMES – BOYS

Year	Winner	Score	Loser	Score
1940	MEMORIAL	41	BAYONNE	25
1941	MEMORIAL	41	BAYONNE	32
1942	MEMORIAL	45	BAYONNE	32
1943	MEMORIAL	35	WEEHAWKEN	18
1944	MEMORIAL	27	BAYONNE	25
1945	EMERSON	40	UNION HILL	36
1946	WEEHAWKEN	39	EMERSON	35
1947	WEEHAWKEN	46	UNION HILL	44
1948	EMERSON	38	BAYONNE TECH	26
1949	ST. PETER'S	45	UNION HILL	46 OT
1950	ST. PETER'S	49	EMERSON	42
1951	SWEENEY	77	EMERSON	44
1952	ST. PETER'S	60	ST. MICHAELS (UC)	37
1953	UNION HILL	48	ST. PETER'S	39
1954	BAYONNE	76	EMERSON	61
1955	BAYONNE	61	DICKINSON	47
1956	UNION HILL	47	MEMORIAL	46
1957	ST. PETER'S	60	MEMORIAL	48
1958	ST. PETER'S	63	ST. MICHAEL'S (UC)	55
1959	BAYONNE	65	ST. MICHAEL'S (UC)	55
1960	ST. PETER'S	59	SNYDER	58
1961	ST. MICHAEL'S (UC)	75	DEMAREST	40
1962	ST. PETER'S	58	HOLY FAMILY	53
1963	ST. PETER'S	52	MEMORIAL	32
1964	ST. PETER'S	54	HOBOKEN	53
1965	BAYONNE	65	MEMORIAL	53
1966	BAYONNE	61	DICKINSON	44
1967	EMERSON	64	SNYDER	49
1968	WEEHAWKEN	69	EMERSON	68
1969	BAYONNE	64	N. BERGEN	55
1970	UNION HILL	57	FERRIS	54
1971	ST. JOSEPH (WNY)	61	ST. PETER'S	57
1972	ST. PETER'S	56	ST. MARY'S	48
1973	MEMORIAL	63	FERRIS	55
1974	LINCOLN	62	MEMORIAL	60
1975	HUDSON CATHOLIC	63	ST. ANTHONY	53
1976	SNYDER	61	N. BERGEN	51
1977	N. BERGEN	71	FERRIS	69
1978	SNYDER	64	N. BERGEN	56
1979	N. BERGEN	OVER	LINCOLN	(BY FORFEIT)
1980	ST. ANTHONY	85	SNYDER	62
1981	SNYDER	72	N. BERGEN	47
1982	ST. ANTHONY	40	SNYDER	36
1983	FERRIS	36	ST. ANTHONY	33
1984	ST. MARY	52	EMERSON	51 (4 OT)
1985	FERRIS	87	BAYONNE	76
1986	FERRIS	61	MARIST	46
1987	ST. ANTHONY	71	EMERSON	39
1988	ST. ANTHONY	91	BAYONNE	50
1989	MARIST	51	FERRIS	44
1990	SNYDER	56	MARIST	48
1991	MARIST	64	SNYDER	51
1992	MARIST	58	FERRIS	39
1993	MARIST	59	SNYDER	39
1994	MARIST	69	ST. MARY'S	65
1995	MARIST	62	FERRIS	44
1996	SNYDER	48	LINCOLN	46
1997	MARIST	48	N. BERGEN	46
1998	FERRIS	47	N. BERGEN	34
1999	MARIST	47	DICKINSON	45
2000	DICKINSON	61	EMERSON	34
2001	ST. PETER'S	66	MARIST	60
2002	DICKINSON	76	BAYONNE	60
2003	BAYONNE	76	MEMORIAL	38
2004	EMERSON	41	HUDSON CATHOLIC	38
2005	BAYONNE	41	ST. PETER'S	52
2006	N. BERGEN	63	BAYONNE	48
2007	LINCOLN	50	UNION HILL	46
2008	ST. PETER'S	48	UNION HILL	47
2009	ST. PETER'S	85	BAYONNE	50
2010	ST. PETER'S	81	N. BERGEN	65
2011	ST. PETER'S	76	MARIST	46
2012	HUDSON CATHOLIC	67	ST. PETER'S	54
2013	HUDSON CATHOLIC	56	ST. PETER'S	49
2014	HUDSON CATHOLIC	50	ST. PETER'S	47 (OT)
2015	HUDSON CATHOLIC	51	MARIST	48
2016	HUDSON CATHOLIC	71	ST. PETERS	55
2017	HUDSON CATHOLIC	48	ST. PETER'S	32
2018	HUDSON CATHOLIC	62	ST. PETER'S	52
2019	UNION CITY	64	MARIST	55
2020	ST. PETER'S	44	MARIST	41
2022	HUDSON CATHOLIC	60	ST. PETER'S	55
2023	ST. PETER'S	61	HUDSON CATHOLIC	46

HUDSON COUNTY CHAMPIONSHIP GAMES – GIRLS

Year	Winner	Score	Runner-up	Score	Year	Winner	Score	Runner-up	Score
1972	N. BERGEN	51	MEMORIAL	48	2003	BAYONNE	37	N. BERGEN	34
1973	N. BERGEN	56	MEMORIAL	35	2004	N. BERGEN	52	MARIST	51
1974	N. BERGEN	48	BAYONNE	42	2005	N. BERGEN	63	BAYONNE	52
1975	BAYONNE	78	N. BERGEN	34	2006	BAYONNE	45	N. BERGEN	32
1976	BAYONNE	60	ST. JOSEPH'S	28	2007	N. BERGEN	61	BAYONNE	44
1977	BAYONNE	66	MEMORIAL	54	2008	MARIST	52	BAYONNE	34
1978	MEMORIAL	58	BAYONNE	56	2009	BAYONNE	49	LINCOLN	40
1979	LINCOLN	48	ST. JOSEPH'S	36	2010	BAYONNE	39	LINCOLN	33
1980	BAYONNE	61	HOBOKEN	27	2011	BAYONNE	48	N. BERGEN	32
1981	LINCOLN	58	HOBOKEN	48	2012	LINCOLN	59	BAYONNE	51
1982	ST. ANTHONY	46	MEMORIAL	44	2013	LINCOLN	48	SECAUCUS	43
1983	ST. ANTHONY	52	MEMORIAL	38	2014	LINCOLN	46	BAYONNE	45
1984	BAYONNE	65	ST. ANTHONY	57	2015	SECAUCUS	54	LINCOLN	34
1985	ST. ANTHONY	57	BAYONNE	54	2016	BAYONNE	34	LINCOLN	27
1986	BAYONNE	38	ST. ANTHONY	33	2017	SECAUCUS	76	MARIST	50
1987	BAYONNE	51	HOLY FAMILY ACAD.	48	2018	LINCOLN	49	SECAUCUS	39
1988	BAYONNE	57	HOLY FAMILY ACAD.	36	2019	HUDSON CATHOLIC	43	LINCOLN	38
1989	BAYONNE	56	DICKINSON	49	2020	BAYONNE	46	HUDSON CATHOLIC	36
1990	BAYONNE	63	HOLY FAMILY	46	2022	BAYONNE	39	UNION CITY	23
1991	BAYONNE	62	SNYDER	35	2023	BAYONNE	53	SECAUCUS	46
1992	BAYONNE	35	HOBOKEN	28					
1993	FERRIS	44	SNYDER	21					
1994	FERRIS	54	ST. DOMINIC	50					
1995	BAYONNE	46	FERRIS	4					
1996	FERRIS	50	BAYONNE	38					
1997	BAYONNE	51	HOLY FAMILY ACAD.	34					
1998	MARIST	25	BAYONNE	24					
1999	MARIST	54	BAYONNE	47					
2000	ST. DOMINIC	61	BAYONNE	30					
2001	MARIST	55	N. BERGEN	53					
2002	BAYONNE	54	ST. DOMINIC	31					

NJSIAA BOYS BASKETBALL CHAMPIONSHIP HISTORY

HUDSON SCHOOLS IN CAPS AND BOLD

Year	Group IV Winner	Group IV Runner-up	Group III Winner	Group III Runner-up	Group II Winner	Group II Runner-up	Group II Winner	Group II Runner-up
1919	**UNION HILL**	Passaic	n/a		n/a		n/a	
1920	Passaic	Trenton	n/a		n/a		n/a	
1921	Passaic	Trenton	n/a		n/a		n/a	
1922	Passaic	Trenton	n/a		n/a		n/a	
1923	Passaic	Asbury Park	n/a		n/a		n/a	
1924	**HOBOKEN**	Trenton	Ridgefield Park	Glen Ridge	n/a		n/a	
1925	Passaic	**UNION HILL**	South Orange	Princeton	n/a		n/a	
1926	No Championship		Ridgefield Park	Princeton	n/a		n/a	
1927	Trenton	Passaic	Ridgefield Park	Roselle Park	n/a		n/a	
1928	Trenton	New Brunswick	Roselle Park	Garfield	n/a		n/a	
1929	Passaic	Atlantic City	Summit	**WEEHAWKEN**	n/a		n/a	
1930	New Brunswick	**UNION HILL**	Rahway	**WEEHAWKEN**	n/a		n/a	
1931	Jefferson	Neptune	Princeton	Caldwell	n/a		n/a	
1932	Trenton	South SideNewark	Carteret	**WEEHAWKEN**	n/a		n/a	
1933	Trenton	South SideNewark	**WEEHAWKEN**	Hamilton	Keyport	Cranford	n/a	
1934	Trenton	**UNION HILL**	Ridgefield Park	Woodbury	Carteret	Ramsey	n/a	
1935	Trenton	New Brunswick	Hamilton	Ridgefield Park	Bogota	Cranford	n/a	
1936	Asbury Park	**EMERSON**	West Orange	Millville	Cranford	Merchantville	n/a	
1937	Bloomfield	Asbury Park	Bound Brook	**WEEHAWKEN**	Princeton	Bogota	n/a	
1938	New Brunswick	Memorial (West NY)	**WEEHAWKEN**	Rutherford	Princeton	Atlantic Highlands	n/a	
1939	**MEMORIAL (WEST NY)**	Bloomfield	Lodi	South River	South Amboy	Wildwood	n/a	
1940	East Orange	**MEMORIAL (WEST NY)**	Rutherford	Bound Brook	Wildwood	Bogota	n/a	
1941	Asbury Park	**MEMORIAL (WEST NY)**	Cliffside Park	Bound Brook	Wildwood	Pompton Lakes	n/a	
1943	Asbury Park	Trenton	Cliffside Park	Merchantville	**WEEHAWKEN**	Highland Park	Dunellen	Egg Harbor
1944	New Brunswick	Camden	Ridgefield Park	Rahway	Bogota	Lakewood	Glen Ridge	Dumont
1945	Camden	**UNION HILL**	Hackensack	North Plainfield	Roselle Park	Carteret	Bergenfield	Hightstown
1946	Jefferson	Central (Newark)	Cliffside Park	Woodrow Wilson	**WEEHAWKEN**	Verona	Dunellen	Keyport
1947	Central (Newark)	**UNION HILL**	Englewood	Springfield Reg.	Merchantville	**WEEHAWKEN**	Fort Lee	Dunellen
1948	Orange	Atlantic City	Cliffside Park	Edison	Highland Park	**WEEHAWKEN**	Atlantic Highlands	Verona
1949	West Orange	**EMERSON**	Woodrow Wilson	Hillside	Neptune	Millburn	Fort Lee	Wildwood

1950	EMERSON	Central (Newark)	Springfield Regional	UNION HILL	n/a		Roselle Park	North Arlington
1951	BAYONNE	Jefferson	Englewood	Woodrow Wilson	Westwood	Ocean City	Sayreville	Verona
1952	Jefferson	EMERSON	Hackensack	Princeton	Roselle Park	Burlington City	Sayreville	Dunellen
1953	Bloomfield	Jefferson	Hamilton Twp.	Linden	WEEHAWKEN	Red Bank	North Arlington	Riverside
1954	Jefferson	Bloomfield	Cliffside Park	Linden	WEEHAWKEN	Sayreville	Riverside	Park Ridge
1955	UNION HILL	New Brunswick	Cliffside Park	Springfield	WEEHAWKEN	Palmyra	Ocean City	North Arlington
1956	UNION HILL	Trenton	Cranford	Penns Grove	Palmyra	Roselle Park	N. Arlington	Bordentown

	Group IV		Group III		Group II		Group I	
Year	Winner	Runner-up	Winner	Runner-up	Winner	Runner-up	Winner	Runner-up
1957	Bloomfield	Trenton	Bound Brook	Hillside	Verona	Ocean City	N. Arlington	Wildwood
1958	Bloomfield	Linden	Moorestown	West Side Newark	Clifford J. Scott	Highland Park	Glen Ridge	Dunellen
1959	Camden	Weequahic	Moorestown	Englewood	Riverside	North Arlington	Dunellen	Glen Ridge
1960	Camden	Weequahic	Englewood	Moorestown	Ridgefield Park	Riverside	HARRISON	Dunellen
1961	Trenton	Camden	Englewood	Burlington Township	Abraham Clark	Moorestown	Wildwood	North Arlington
1962	Weequahic	Westfield	S. Side Newark	Neptune	Mt. W. Orange	South Plainfield	Mt. Lakes	Dunellen
1963	Central	Hillside	Audubon	Paramus	Salem	Mt. W. Orange	South Amboy	Wood-Ridge
1964	Central	Hillside	South Plainfield	Summit	Ocean City	North Arlington	Wildwood	Wallington
1965	BridgewaterRaritan	Bloomfield	South Side Newark	South Plainfield	Merchantville	Clifford J. Scott	New Providence	Wildwood
1966	Weequahic	Hackensack	MEMORIAL	Sterling	Burlington City	Roselle Park	Park Ridge	Williamstown
1967	Weequahic	Camden	Lakewood	WEEHAWKEN	Gloucester City	Shore	Leonia	Burlington Twp
1968	Perth Amboy	Neptune	Orange	Emerson Union	Abraham Clark	UNION HILL	S. Brunswick	East Rutherford
1969	East Orange	Perth Amboy	South Side	LINCOLN (JC)	Abraham Clark	UNION HILL	Mt. Lakes	Ridgefield
1970	Woodrow Wilson	East Orange	Long Branch	Orange	Haddon Heights	UNION HILL	East Rutherford	Burlington Township
1971	Bloomfield	Ewing	South Side Newark	Ocean Township	Cliffside Park	Haddon Heights	East Rutherford	Gloucester City
1972	Westfield	Triton Regional	East Orange	Lakewood	Vailsburg	Ocean City	Abraham Clark	Wildwood
1973	Weequahic (Newark)	Atlantic City	East Orange	Northern Burlington	Abraham Clark	Gateway Regional	Haddonfield	Orange
1974	East Orange	Neptune	Camden	MEMORIAL WNY	Pleasantville	Hillside	Orange	Burlington Township
1975	Woodbridge	Eastside-Paterson	Lakewood	East Orange	Englewood	Pleasantville	Clifford Scott	Glassboro

Year	Group IV Winner	Group IV Runner-up	Group III Winner	Group III Runner-up	Group II Winner	Group II Runner-up	Group I Winner	Group I Runner-up
1976	Plainfield	Neptune	East Orange	Woodrow Wilson	Abraham Clark	Pleasantville	Orange	Glassboro
1977	**NORTH BERGEN**	Camden	Long Branch	Ridgefield Park	Orange	Pleasantville	Abraham Clark	Glassboro
1978	Camden	Linden	Woodrow Wilson	Malcolm X Shabazz	Asbury Park	Lodi	Glassboro	Newark Tech (N 13th)
1979	Camden	**UNION HILL**	Malcolm X Shabazz	Long Branch	Orange	Pleasantville	Wood-Ridge	Wildwood
1980	Barringer Newark	Trenton	Long Branch	Weequahic	South River	Berkeley Heights	Clayton	Mahwah
1981	Neptune	Malcolm X Shabazz	Mainland Regional	Randolph	Clifford J. Scott	Salem	Glassboro	Verona
1982	Camden	Montclair	Cinnaminson	Linden	Clifford J. Scott	Salem	Abraham Clark	Bordentown
1983	Plainfield	Trenton	Phillipsburg	Ewing	Red Bank	Elmwood Park	Abraham Clark	New Brunswick
1984	Camden	JFK Paterson	Emerson Union City	Ewing	Abraham Clark	Asbury Park	New Brunswick	Mahwah
1985	Elizabeth	Camden	Woodrow Wilson	Rahway	Rutherford	Burlington City	Burlington Twp.	Bogota
1986	Camden	Montclair	Ewing	Clifford Scott	Salem	Central Newark	Florence	Glen Ridge
1987	Camden	JFK Paterson	BridgewaterRaritan	Malcolm X Shabazz	Asbury Park	Orange	Burlington Twp.	Newark Tech (N 13th)
1988	Elizabeth	Camden	BridgewaterRaritan	Malcolm X Shabazz	Orange	Delran	Glen Ridge	Burlington Township
1989	Elizabeth	Trenton	Eastern Regional	Sparta	BridgewaterRaritan	Abraham Clark	Haddonfield	Newark Tech (N 13th)
1990	Elizabeth	Trenton	Snyder Jersey City	JFK Iselin	Hillside	Middle Township	Bogota	Haddonfield
1991	Elizabeth	Camden	Clifford J. Scott	Woodrow Wilson	Delsea Regional	Hillside	Essex Co VT Market St	South River

Year	Group IV Winner	Group IV Runner-up	Group III Winner	Group III Runner-up	Group II Winner	Group II Runner-up	Group I Winner	Group I Runner-up
1992	Shawnee	Irvington	Ewing	Orange	Hillside	Middle Township	Burlington Twp.	Newark Tech (N 13th)
1993	Irvington	Shawnee	Red Bank Regional	Snyder Jersey City	Middle Township	Hillside	Perth Amboy VT	Cresskill
1994	Piscataway	Teaneck	Orange	Camden	Middle Township	Hillside	Glassboro	Cresskill
1995	Shawnee	Elizabeth	Malcolm X Shabazz	Rancocas Valley	Pleasantville	Boonton	Science Newark	Burlington City
1996	Shawnee	Teaneck	Rancocas Valley	Snyder Jersey City	Pleasantville	Dwight Morrow	Paulsboro	Science Newark
1997	Union	Atlantic City	Malcolm X Shabazz	Hamilton East	Long Branch	Dwight Morrow	Pitman	Science Newark

Year								
1998	Rancocas Valley	JFK Paterson	Long Branch	Parsippany	Holmdel	W Morris Mendham	Pitman	Bloomfield Tech
1999	Teaneck	Rancocas Valley	Parsippany	Lawrence	Holmdel	W. Morris Mendham	New Providence	Highland Park
2000	Linden	BridgewaterRaritan	Camden	Lawrence	W Morris Mendham	Haddonfield Mem.	Florence	Waldwick
2001	Shawnee	Passaic	Malcolm X Shabazz	Camden	Weequahic	Pleasantville	Florence	Cresskill
2002	East Side Newark	Shawnee	Neptune	Weequahic	Middle Township	Abraham Clark	Burlington City	Cresskill
2003	Teaneck	Trenton Central	Franklin	Cranford	Abraham Clark	Neptune	Bloomfield Tech	Paulsboro
2004	Lenape	Plainfield	Raritan	Manasquan	Haddonfield	Summit	Bloomfield Tech	Burlington City
2005	Atlantic City	Ridgewood	Malcolm X Shabazz	Camden	Haddonfield	Summit	Science Park	A.P. Schalick
2006	Linden	Atlantic City	Hamilton West	Malcolm X Shabazz	Haddonfield	Central Newark	Bloomfield Tech	LEAP Academy
2007	Linden	South Brunswick	Shawnee	Passaic Valley	Chatham	Haddonfield	Bloomfield Tech	CREATE Charter
2008	Rancocas Valley	Piscataway Lenape	Scotch PlFanwood	Timber Creek	**LINCOLN JERSEY CITY**	Collingswood	Science Park Newark	Salem
2009	Lenape	Eastside-Paterson	Neptune	Teaneck	Science Park	Camden	University	Asbury Park
2010	Cherokee	Plainfield	W Morris Mendham	Kingsway Woolwich	Malcolm X Shabazz	Pequannock	University	Woodbury
2011	Eastside (Paterson)	Rancocas Valley	Plainfield	Burlington Township	Central Newark	Ewing	Asbury Park	Jonathan Dayton
2012	Atlantic City	Elizabeth	Plainfield	Neptune	Ewing	Pascack ...	Asbury Park	University
2013	Atlantic City	Linden	East Side Newark	Camden	Newark Tech	BCIT Medford	Pt. Pleasant Beach	Jonathan Dayton
2014	Linden	Trenton	East Side Newark	Ewing	Newark Tech	Camden	Pitman	Bloomfield Tech
2015	Paterson Eastside	Cherry Hill East	Bergenfield	Ewing	Newark Tech	Camden	Paulsboro	University
2016	Linden	Atlantic City	Teaneck	Winslow	West Side	Camden	University	Paulsboro
2017	Linden	Shawnee	Teaneck	Ewing	West Side	Camden	Verona	Woodbury
2018	Shawnee	Newark East Side	Hamilton North	Chatham	Haddonfield	Rumson-FH	Woodbury	Cresskill
2019	Newark East Side	Freehold Twp	Moorestown	Ramapo	Haddonfield	West Side	New Providence	Burlington City

2020 — Group Finals Canceled due to COVID-19

	NORTH I REGIONAL CHAMPION	NORTH II REGIONAL CHAMPION	NORTH III REGIONAL CHAMPION	NORTH IV REGIONAL CHAMPION	SOUTH I REGIONAL CHAMPION	SOUTH II REGIONAL CHAMPION	SOUTH III REGIONAL CHAMPION	SOUTH IV REGIONAL CHAMPION
2020	Paterson Charter	*Canceled*	Irvington	Elizabeth	Burlington City	*Canceled*	Timber Creek	*Canceled*

2021	*COVID-19 Tournament Cancelled*

2022	Elizabeth	Marlboro	Woodrow Wilson	Ramapo	Camden	Newark Central	Paterson Charter	Burlington City

	NON-PUBLIC GROUP A		NON-PUBLIC GROUP B		NON-PUBLIC GROUP C	
Year	Winner	Runner-up	Winner	Runner-up	Winner	Runner-up
1934	Good Counsel Newark	St. Mary's Rutherford	n/a		n/a	
1935	St. Mary's Rutherford	St. Peter's New Brun.	n/a		n/a	
1936	St. Peter's New Brun.	Good Counsel Newark	n/a		n/a	
1937	St. Mary's Rutherford	St. Mary's Perth Amboy	n/a		n/a	
1938	Trenton Catholic	Good Counsel Newark	n/a		n/a	
1939	St. Peter's New Brun.	Immaculate Montclair	n/a		n/a	
1940	Good Counsel Newark	Camden Catholic	n/a		n/a	
1941	Camden Catholic	St. Patrick's Elizabeth	n/a		n/a	
1942	Camden Catholic	St. Joseph's WNY	n/a		n/a	
1943	St. Mary's Elizabeth	St. Peter's New Brun.	n/a		n/a	
1944	Don Bosco	Camden Catholic	n/a		n/a	
1945	St. Cecilia	Trenton Catholic	n/a		n/a	
1946	Trenton Catholic	Seton Hall	St. Joe's Paterson	Immaculate Montclair	n/a	
1947	Trenton Catholic	Seton Hall	ST. JOE'S WNY	St. Mary's Perth Amboy	St. Patrick's Elizabeth	St. Rose Belmar
1948	Trenton Catholic	St. Michael's	HOLY FAMILY	St. Mary's S. Amboy	St. Patrick's Elizabeth	St. Rose Belmar
1949	ST. PETER'S J.C.	Trenton Catholic	St. Rose Belmar	Immaculate Montclair	No Champion Named	
1950	Trenton Catholic	ST. PETER'S J.C.	ST. JOE'S WNY	Red Bank Catholic	No Champion Named	
1951	ST. PETER'S J.C.	Trenton Catholic	St. Mary's Elizabeth	St. Mary's S. Amboy	No Champion Named	
1952	ST. PETER'S J.C.	Trenton Catholic	St. Mary's Elizabeth	St. Rose Belmar	No Champion Named	
1953	ST. PETER'S J.C.	Trenton Catholic	St. Mary's Elizabeth	St. Mary's Perth Amboy	No Champion Named	
1954	ST. PETER'S J.C.	St. Peter's New Brun.	St. Mary's Elizabeth	St. Joe's Camden	No Champion Named	
1955	ST. PETER'S J.C.	Trenton Catholic	St. Mary's Elizabeth	Gloucester Catholic	HOLY FAMILY	Wildwood Catholic
1956	ST. PETER'S J.C.	St. Peter's New Brun.	ST. ALOYSIUS J.C.	St. Rose Belmar	HOLY FAMILY	Wildwood Catholic
1957	Trenton Catholic	ST. PETER'S J.C.	St. Mary's Elizabeth	Gloucester Catholic	ST. CECILIA KEARNY	Wildwood Catholic
1958	Trenton Catholic	Seton Hall	ST. ALOYSIUS J.C.	Gloucester Catholic	Wildwood Catholic	ST. CECILIA KEARNY
1959	ST. PETER'S J.C.	Trenton Catholic	ST. ALOYSIUS J.C.	Gloucester Catholic	ST. CECILIA KEARNY	Wildwood Catholic
1960	Trenton Catholic	ST. PETER'S J.C.	St. Mary's Elizabeth	St. Joe's Camden	Wildwood Catholic	ST. ANTHONY J.C.
1961	Seton Hall	Trenton Catholic	Bishop Eustace	HOLY FAMILY	St. Patrick's Elizabeth	St. Joe's Hammonton
1962	Bishop Eustace	ST. PETER'S J.C.	St. Rose Belmar	Immaculate Montclair	HOLY FAMILY	St. Joe's Hammonton
1963	Trenton Cathedral	Roselle Catholic	St. Rose Belmar	Phillipsburg Catholic	ST. CECILIA KEARNY	Wildwood Catholic
1964	Seton Hall	St. Joe's Camden	Gloucester Catholic	ST. ALOYSIUS J.C.	HOLY FAMILY	Wildwood Catholic
1965	Christian Brothers	Don Bosco	St. Michael's	St. Mary's Perth Amboy	HOLY FAMILY	Wildwood Catholic

Year						
1966	Don Bosco	Christian Brothers	St. Rose Belmar	Our Lady o/t Valley	St. Patrick's Elizabeth	Wildwood Catholic
1967	Trenton Cathedral	Seton Hall	**ST. MARY'S J.C.**	St. Peter's New Brun.	St. Patrick's Elizabeth	Sacred Heart
1968	Don Bosco	Trenton Cathedral	St. Peter's New Brun.	St. Mary's Elizabeth	**ST. ANTHONY'S J.C.**	Sacred Heart
1969	Bishop Eustace	St. Peter's J.C.	**ST. MARY'S J.C.**	Gloucester Catholic	**ST. ANTHONY'S J.C.**	St. Augustine
1970	Don Bosco	Christian Brothers	Gloucester Catholic	**ST. JOE'S WNY**	Our Lady o/t Valley	St. Joe's Toms River
1971	Christian Brothers	Essex Catholic	**ST. JOE'S WNY**	St. Rose Belmar	St. Patrick's Elizabeth	Sacred Heart

	NON-PUBLIC GROUP A		NON-PUBLIC GROUP B		NON-PUBLIC GROUP C	
Year	Winner	Runner-up	Winner	Runner-up	Winner	Runner-up
1972	Christian Brothers	**ST. PETER'S J.C.**	Gloucester Catholic	Paterson Catholic	**ST. MARY'S J.C.**	St. Patrick's
1973	Christian Brothers	**HUDSON CATHOLIC**	Bishop Eustace	Our Lady o/t Valley	**ST. ANTHONY J.C.**	St. Joe's Camden
1974	Essex Catholic	Camden Catholic	Bishop Eustace	Don Bosco	**ST. ANTHONY J.C.**	St. Joe's Camden
1975	Essex Catholic	Paul VI Haddonfield	Bishop Eustace	St. Cecilia Englewood	**ST. MARY'S J.C.**	Sacred Heart
1976	**HUDSON CATHOLIC**	Holy Spirit	Bishop Eustace	Don Bosco	**ST. ANTHONY J.C.**	Sacred Heart
1977	Essex Catholic	Red Bank Catholic	St. Rose Belmar	Our Lady o/t Valley	**ST. ANTHONY J.C.**	St. Joe's Camden
1978	Bergen Catholic	St. Anthony's Trenton	St. John Vianney	Our Lady o/t Valley	Immaculate Conc.	Sacred Heart
1979	Christian Brothers	Bergen Catholic	Our Lady o/t Valley	St. Joe's Toms River	Sacred Heart	**ST. ANTHONY J.C.**

Group C discontinued after 1979 Tournament				

	GROUP A		GROUP B	
Year	Winner	Runner-up	Winner	Runner-up
1980	Paul IV Haddonfield	**MARIST**	**ST. ANTHONY J.C.**	St. Mary's S. Amboy
1981	St. Joe's Toms River	St. Joe's Montvale	**ST. ANTHONY J.C.**	Wildwood Catholic
1982	McCorristin	Seton Hall	St. Augustine	Bayley-Ellard
1983	Paul IV Haddonfield	Immaculata Somerville	**ST. ANTHONY J.C.**	St. Peter's New Brun.
1984	Christian Brothers	**ST. PETER'S J.C.**	**ST. ANTHONY J.C.**	St. Peter's New Brun.
1985	Christian Brothers	Bergen Catholic	**ST. ANTHONY J.C.**	St. Peter's New Brun.
1986	Seton Hall	Christian Brothers	**ST. ANTHONY J.C.**	St. Augustine
1987	Union Catholic	Christian Brothers	**ST. ANTHONY J.C.**	St. Joe's Hammonton
1988	Paul IV Haddonfield	Bergen Catholic	**ST. ANTHONY J.C.**	Wildwood Catholic
1989	McCorristin	Bergen Catholic	**ST. ANTHONY J.C.**	St. Rose Belmar
1990	McCorristin	Seton Hall	**ST. ANTHONY J.C.**	St. Peter's New Brun.
1991	Seton Hall	McCorristin	**ST. ANTHONY J.C.**	Bishop Eustace
1992	Seton Hall	St. Joe's Metuchen	**MARIST**	Bishop Eustace
1993	Seton Hall	Camden Catholic	**ST. ANTHONY J.C.**	St. Augustine
1994	Bergen Catholic	Camden Catholic	Paterson Catholic	St. Augustine
1995	Christian Brothers	Bergen Catholic	**ST. ANTHONY J.C.**	St. Peter's New Brun.
1996	Seton Hall	Camden Catholic	**ST. ANTHONY J.C.**	Bishop Eustace
1997	Seton Hall	Bishop Eustace	**ST. ANTHONY J.C.**	St. Augustine
1998	Seton Hall	St. Joe's Metuchen	St. Patrick's	St. Augustine

Year	Winner	Runner-up	Winner	Runner-up
1999	Seton Hall	St. Joe's Metuchen	St. Augustine	St. Patrick's
2000	Seton Hall	Christian Brothers	St. Patrick's	St. Augustine
2001	Camden Catholic	Seton Hall	**ST. ANTHONY J.C.**	St. Augustine
2002	Bergen Catholic	St. Augustine	**ST. ANTHONY J.C.**	St. Rose Belmar
2003	Camden Catholic	Bergen Catholic	St. Patrick's	Cardinal McCarrick
2004	St. Augustine	Seton Hall	**ST. ANTHONY J.C.**	Red Bank Catholic
2005	Seton Hall	Christian Brothers	St. Patrick's	Cardinal McCarrick
2006	Seton Hall	Christian Brothers	St. Patrick's	Wildwood Catholic
2007	Seton Hall	Christian Brothers	St. Patrick's	Wildwood Catholic
2008	Immaculata Somerville	Camden Catholic	**ST. ANTHONY J.C.**	Trenton Catholic

	GROUP A		GROUP B	
Year	Winner	Runner-up	Winner	Runner-up
2009	Immaculata Somerville	Christian Brothers	St. Patrick's	Trenton Catholic
2010	Camden Catholic	**ST. PETER'S J.C.**	Trenton Catholic	**ST. ANTHONY J.C.**
2011	St. Augustine	Seton Hall	**ST. ANTHONY J.C.**	Cardinal McCarrick
2012	St. Joe's Metuchen	Seton Hall	**ST. ANTHONY J.C.**	Gill St. Bernard's
2013	St. Joe's Metuchen	**ST. PETER'S J.C.**	Roselle Catholic	**ST. ANTHONY J.C.**
2014	St. Joe's Metuchen	**ST. PETER'S J.C.**	Roselle Catholic	**ST. ANTHONY J.C.**
2015	Pope John XXIII	Christian Brothers	Roselle Catholic	**ST. ANTHONY J.C.**
2016	St. Augustine	Don Bosco	**ST. ANTHONY J.C.**	Roselle Catholic
2017	Don Bosco	St. Augustine	Patrick School	**HUDSON CATHOLIC**
2018	Don Bosco	Camden Catholic	Roselle Catholic	Ranney
2019	Bergen Catholic	Camden Catholic	Ranney	Roselle Catholic
2020 Non-Public Group Finals Canceled due to COVID-19				
2021	*COVID-19 Tournament Cancelled*			
2022	*Bergen Catholic*	*Rutgers Prep*	*Roselle Catholic*	*Trenton Catholic*

BOYS MOST CONSECUTIVE TITLES WON (3+)

9   **ST. ANTHONY JERSEY CITY** (1983-1991)

6   **ST. PETER'S JERSEY CITY** (1951-1956)

5   Seton Hall (1996-2000), St. Mary's Elizabeth (1951-1955)

4   Bishop Eustace Pennsauken (1973-1976), Elizabeth (1988-1991), Passaic (1920-1923), Trenton (1932-1935)

3   Bridgewater-Raritan West (1987-1989), Christian Brothers Academy (1971-1973), East Orange (1972-1974), Haddonfield (2004-2006), Roselle Catholic (2013-2015), Seton Hall (1991-1993), Seton Hall (2005 - 2007), **ST. ANTHONY JERSEY CITY** (1995-1997), St. Joseph Metuchen (2012-2014), Trenton Catholic (1946-1948), **WEEHAWKEN** (1953-1956), Wildwood (1940-1942)

BOYS TITLES WON

#	School	#	School	#	School	#	School	#	School
27	**ST. ANTHONY**	4	Jefferson	2	Bound Brook	1	Delran	1	Ranney
12	Camden	4	Neptune	2	Burlington City	1	Delsea Regional	1	Raritan
14	Seton Hall	4	New Brunswick	2	Carteret	1	Dumont	1	Ridgefield
14	Patrick School	4	Newark East Side	2	Cranford	1	Edison	1	Ridgewood
11	Abraham Clark	4	Plainfield	2	East Rutherford	1	Egg Harbor	1	Scotch Plains–Fanwood
9	Trenton	4	Roselle Park	2	Eastern	1	Elmwood Park	1	Shore
8	Christian Bros. Academy	4	Science (Newark)	2	Fort Lee	1	Essex Co. VT Market St.	1	South Orange
8	Orange	4	South Side (Newark)	2	Good Counsel	1	Franklin	1	Sparta
8	St. Mary's Elizabeth	4	**ST. MARY'S JC**	2	Hackensack	1	Garfield	1	St. John Vianney
8	**ST. PETER'S**	4	Teaneck	2	Hillside	1	Gateway Regional	1	St. Joe's Montvale
7	Ashbury Park	3	Atlantic City	2	Holmdel	1	Gill St. Bernard's	1	St. Joe's Paterson
7	Bishop Eustace	3	Bogota	2	Immaculata	1	Steinert	1	Sterling
7	Cliffside Park	3	Burlington Township	2	Lakewood	1	**HARRISON**	1	Timber Creek
7	Haddonfield	3	Dunellen	2	Lenape	1	Hightstown	1	Triton Regional
7	Trenton	3	East Side	2	Merchantville	1	**HOBOKEN**	1	Union Catholic
7	**WEEHAWKEN**	3	Essex Catholic	2	Mountain Lakes	1	Holy Spirit Absecon	1	Vailsburg Newark
6	Don Bosco	3	Ewing	2	Newark Tech	1	Immaculate Conception	1	Verona
6	East Orange	3	Florence	2	Ocean City	1	JFK Iselin	1	Waldwick
6	Elizabeth	3	Glassboro	2	Our Lady o/t Valley	1	Kingsway	1	Williamstown
6	**HOLY FAMILY**	3	Glen Ridge	2	Pitman	1	Lawrence	1	Winslow
6	Linden	3	Gloucester Catholic	2	Red Bank	1	LEAP Academy	1	Woodbridge
6	Malcolm X Shabazz	3	McCorristin	2	Riverside	1	Leonia	1	Woodbury
6	Passaic	3	**MEMORIAL WEST NY**	2	West Side	1	Mainland Regional		
6	Ridgefield Park	3	Middle Township	1	A.P. Schalick	1	Manasquan		
6	Shawnee	3	Moorestown	1	Audubon	1	Millville		
5	Bloomfield	3	New Providence	1	Barringer	1	No. Burlington		
5	Camden Catholic	3	No. Arlington	1	Bayley-Ellard Madison	1	**NORTH BERGEN**		
5	Clifford Scott	3	Paul VI	1	**BAYONNE**	1	No. Plainfield		
5	Englewood	3	Pleasantville	1	BCIT Medford	1	Ocean Township		
5	Long Branch	3	Princeton	1	Bergenfield	1	Pascack Hills		
5	St. Augustine	3	Rancocas Valley	1	Berkeley Heights	1	Passaic Valley		
5	St. Rose	3	Roselle Catholic	1	Bernardsville	1	Paterson Charter		
5	Weequahic	3	Rutherford	1	Boonton	1	Penns Grove		
5	Wildwood	3	**ST. ALOYSIUS**	1	Caldwell	1	Pequannock		
5	Woodrow Wilson	3	**ST. CECILIA**	1	Chatham	1	Perth Amboy VT		
4	Bergen Catholic	3	St. Joseph Metuchen	1	Cherokee	1	Phillipsburg		
4	Bloomfield Tech	3	St. Joseph West NY	1	Cinnaminson	1	Phillipsburg Catholic		
4	Bridgewater-Raritan	3	St. Peter's N. Brunswick	1	Clayton	1	Pompton Lakes		
4	Central	3	**UNION HILL**	1	Collingswood	1	Pt. Pleasant Lakes		
4	Hamilton	3	University	1	**CREATE CHARTER**	1	Randolph		

NJSIAA GIRLS BASKETBALL CHAMPIONSHIP HISTORY

HUDSON SCHOOLS IN CAPS AND BOLD

Year	Group IV Winner	Group IV Runner-up	Group III Winner	Group III Runner-up	Group II Winner	Group II Runner-up	Group I Winner	Group I Runner-up
1976	BridgewaterRaritan	**BAYONNE**	Asbury Park	Paramus Catholic	St. Rose Belmar	Lyndhurst	Gloucester Catholic	**ST ANTHONY JC**
1977	Nutley	Willingboro	Asbury Park	Paramus Catholic	St. Rose Belmar	Union Catholic	Gloucester Catholic	Mother Seton Reg.
1978	Willingboro	Columbia-Maplewood	Paramus Catholic	Edgewood Regional	Pleasantville	Lyndhurst	Gloucester Catholic	Mother Seton Reg.
1979	Columbia-Maplewood	Atlantic City	Paramus Catholic	Ocean City	St. Anthony Trenton	**HOLY FAMILY BAYONNE**	Gloucester Catholic	Eastern Christian
1980	East Orange	Atlantic City	Edgewood Regional	Pascack Valley	McCorristin	Union Catholic	Mater Dei	Benedictine Academy
1981	Atlantic City	Eastside-Paterson	Pascack Valley	Camden Catholic	Pleasantville	Queen of Peace	Gloucester Catholic	Benedictine Academy
1982	Atlantic City	Plainfield	Pascack Valley	N. Hunterdon	Clifford J. Scott	St. Rose Belmar	Gloucester Catholic	Morris Catholic
1983	Hamilton West	Plainfield	Malcolm X Shabazz	Sterling	Clifford J. Scott	Somerville	Keyport	New Providence
1984	Neptune	Plainfield	Clifford J. Scott	N. Hunterdon	Asbury Park	Whippany Park	Arthur P. Schalick	Wallkill Valley
1985	Irvington	Washington Twp.	N. Hunterdon	Malcolm X Shabazz	Sparta	Middle Township	H.G. Hoffman	New Providence
1986	Irvington	Hightstown	N. Hunterdon	Hanover Park	Collingswood	**HARRISON**	H.G. Hoffman	Waldwick
1987	Hightstown	Bloomfield	N. Hunterdon	W. Morris Mendham	Manasquan	Jefferson Twp.	H.G. Hoffman	Waldwick
1988	J.F. KennedyPaterson	Neptune Sr.	Hanover Park	Lakewood	Manasquan	Jefferson Twp.	H.G. Hoffman	Roselle Park
1989	Bloomfield	Neptune Sr.	Pascack Valley	Mainland Regional	Sterling	Glen Rock	H.G. Hoffman	University
1990	J.F. KennedyPaterson	Toms River East	Sparta	Pennsauken	Sterling	Boonton	Haddon Twp	North Warren
1991	Ridgewood	Piscataway	Clifford J. Scott	Egg Harbor	Harrison	Manasquan	Wildwood	Cresskill
1992	Linden	Piscataway	Egg Harbor	Pascack Valley	Jefferson Twp.	Middle Township	S. Hunterdon	Whippany Park
1993	Linden	East Brunswick	West Side Newark	Egg Harbor	Mahwah	Delran	Haddonfield Mem.	N. Warren
1994	Linden	Washington Twp.	Delsea Regional	Morris Knolls	Middle Township	Summit	Haddonfield Mem.	N. Warren
1995	West Milford	Washington Twp.	Middle Township	Sparta	Delran	Morris Hills	Keyport	Bogota
1996	Elizabeth	Toms River North	Woodrow Wilson	Malcolm X Shabazz	Pt. Pleasant Boro	Caldwell	Rumson FH	Bloomfield Tech
1997	Piscataway	Elizabeth	Woodrow Wilson	Warren Hills	Haddonfield Mem.	W. Morris Mendham	Burlington Twp.	Cresskill
1998	Columbia-Maplewood	Piscataway	Red Bank Regional	Sparta	W. Morris Mendham	Sterling	Haddonfield Mem.	Bloomfield Tech
1999	East Brunswick	Columbia-Maplewood	Ewing	Sparta	W. Morris Mendham	Sterling	Haddonfield Mem.	Bloomfield Tech

Year	Group IV Winner	Group IV Runner-up	Group III Winner	Group III Runner-up	Group II Winner	Group II Runner-up	Group I Winner	Group I Runner-up
2000	Toms River North	Bloomfield	Willingboro	Orange	Sterling	W. Morris Mendham	Wildwood	North Warren
2001	Columbia-Maplewood	Marlboro	Sparta	Toms River South	Sterling	Hanover Park	Wildwood	Mountain Lakes
2002	Trenton	Morristown	Willingboro	Malcolm X Shabazz	Rumson FH	Newton	Wildwood	Mountain Lakes
2003	Marlboro	E. Orange Campus	Malcolm X Shabazz	Willingboro	N. Burlington	Newton	Butler	Wildwood
2004	Eastside (Paterson)	Marlboro	Malcolm X Shabazz	Willingboro	Haddonfield Mem.	Chatham	Bloomfield Tech	Riverside
2005	Absegami	Montclair	Woodrow Wilson	N. Highlands	Pascack Valley	Rumson FH	Bloomfield Tech	Salem
2006	Absegami	**BAYONNE**	Malcolm X Shabazz	Monmouth Regional	Rumson FH	River Dell	Bloomfield Tech	Salem
2007	Trenton	Eastside-Paterson	Willingboro	S. Plainfield	Rumson FH	River Dell	University	Palmyra
2008	Trenton	J.F. KennedyPaterson	Malcolm X Shabazz	Ocean City	Pascack Valley	Rumson FH	University	Wildwood
2009	Colts Neck	Columbia	Malcolm X Shabazz	Neptune	Rumson FH	Chatham	Bloomfield Tech	Gloucester City

	Group IV		Group III		Group II		Group I	
Year	Winner	Runner-up	Winner	Runner-up	Winner	Runner-up	Winner	Runner-up
2010	N. Hunterdon	Eastern	Neptune	Pascack Valley	Malcolm X Shabazz	Chatham	New Providence	Florence
2011	Rancocas Valley	J.F. KennedyPaterson	Neptune	Teaneck	Malcolm X Shabazz	Pascack Hills	New Providence	Haddon Twp
2012	Jackson Memorial	N. Hunterdon	Manasquan	Teaneck	Malcolm X Shabazz	Pt. Pleasant Boro	Cedar Creek	Whippany Park
2013	Rancocas Valley	Eastside-Paterson	Ocean City	Jefferson	Malcolm X Shabazz	Willingboro	Pt. Pleasant Beach	Bloomfield Tech
2014	Eastside (Paterson)	Shawnee	Woodrow Wilson	W. Morris Central	Manasquan	Newton	Malcolm X Shabazz	Haddon Twp
2015	Franklin	Shawnee	Middletown South	Old Tappan	Manasquan	Westwood	New Providence	Haddon Twp
2016	Lenape	J.F. KennedyPaterson	NV Old Tappan	Middletown South	Manasquan	High Point	University	Bound Brook
2017	Franklin	Sayreville	Pascack Valley	Ocean City	Manasquan	High Point	Bound Brook	University
2018	Franklin	Toms River No.	NV Old Tappan	Ewing	Manasquan	Newark Tech	University	Bound Brook
2019	Franklin	Lenape	Mainland	Chatham	Manchester Twp	**LINCOLN**	University	Bound Brook

	Group Finals Canceled due to COVID-19							
2020	NORTH I REGIONAL CHAMPION	NORTH II REGIONAL CHAMPION	NORTH III REGIONAL CHAMPION	NORTH IV REGIONAL CHAMPION	SOUTH I REGIONAL CHAMPION	SOUTH II REGIONAL CHAMPION	SOUTH III REGIONAL CHAMPION	SOUTH IV REGIONAL CHAMPION
	Cresskill	**LINCOLN**	Ramapo	Franklin	Bound Brook	Manchester Twp.	Ocean City	Cherokee

Year								
2021	COVID-19 Tournament Cancelled							
2022	Westfield	Cherokee	Sparta	Mainland	Manasquan	Jefferson	University	Shore
2023	BAYONNE	Cherokee			New Providence	SECAUCUS		

	NON- PUBLIC GROUP A		NON-PUBLIC GROUP B	
Year	Winner	Runner-up	Winner	Runner-up
1983	St. Rose Belmar	Paramus Catholic	Gloucester Catholic	St. Anthony J.C.
1984	Paramus Catholic	Notre Dame	ST. ANTHONY J.C.	Wildwood Catholic
1985	Paramus Catholic	Bishop Ahr	St. Peter's	ST. ANTHONY J.C.
1986	Paramus Catholic	Paul VI Haddonfield	Morris Catholic	Mater Dei
1987	Union Catholic	McCorristin	Immaculata	Immaculate Montclair
1988	Union Catholic	Notre Dame	Bishop Eustace	Immaculate Montclair
1989	Union Catholic	Paul VI Haddonfield	Bishop Eustace	Immaculate Montclair
1990	St. John Vianney	Academy o/t Holy Angels	Mater Dei	Immaculate Montclair
1991	St. John Vianney	Immaculata Somerville	St. Peter's	Immaculate Montclair
1992	St. John Vianney	Queen of Peace	St. Peter's	DePaul Diocesan
1993	St. John Vianney	Paramus Catholic	St. Rose Belmar	DePaul Diocesan
1994	St. John Vianney	Immaculata Somerville	Mt. St. Dominic	St. Rose Belmar
1995	Notre Dame	Immaculate Heart	St. John Vianney	Mt. St. Dominic
1996	Notre Dame	Paramus Catholic	Red Bank Catholic	DePaul Diocesan
1997	St. John Vianney	Paramus Catholic	Red Bank Catholic	ST. ANTHONY J.C.
1998	St. John Vianney	Pope John XXIII	St. Rose Belmar	MARIST
1999	St. John Vianney	Immaculate Heart	Paterson Catholic	St. Joe's Hammonton
2000	Red Bank Catholic	Immaculate Heart	St. Rose Belmar	MARIST
2001	Red Bank Catholic	Paramus Catholic	MARIST	Sacred Heart
2002	Immaculate Heart	Red Bank Catholic	Bishop Eustace	Morris Catholic

	NON- PUBLIC GROUP A		NON-PUBLIC GROUP B	
Year	Winner	Runner-up	Winner	Runner-up
2003	St. John Vianney	Immaculate Somerville	Sacred Heart	Morris Catholic
2004	Red Bank Catholic	Immaculate Heart	Morris Catholic	St. Rose Belmar
2005	St. John Vianney	Roselle Catholic	Sacred Heart	Morris Catholic
2006	Camden Catholic	Immaculate Heart	Morris Catholic	Trenton Catholic
2007	Red Bank Catholic	Morris Catholic	Trenton Catholic	ST. ANTHONY J.C.
2008	St. John Vianney	Morris Catholic	Trenton Catholic	MARIST
2009	St. John Vianney	Immaculate Heart	Paterson Catholic	Bishop Eustace
2010	St. John Vianney	Immaculate Heart	Trenton Catholic	Gill St. Bernard's

2011	St. John Vianney	DePaul Catholic	Trenton Catholic	Gill St. Bernard's
2012	St. Rose Belmar	Immaculate Heart	Gill St. Bernard's	Morris Catholic
2013	Red Bank Catholic	Immaculate Heart	Paramus Catholic	Morris Catholic
2014	Immaculate Heart	St. John Vianney	St. Rose	Morris Catholic
2015	St. John Vianney	Immaculate Heart	St. Rose	Immaculate-Lodi
2016	St. John Vianney	Immaculate Heart	Rutgers Prep	Saddle River Day
2017	Red Bank Catholic	Immaculate Heart	Rutgers Prep	Queen of Peace
2018	Saint Rose	Immaculate Heart	Saddle River Day	Rutgers Prep
2019	Saint Rose	Immaculate Heart	Saddle River Day	Trenton Catholic
2020	Group Finals Canceled due to COVID-19			
	NON-PUBLIC NORTH A SECTIONAL CHAMPION	NON-PUBLIC NORTH B SECTIONAL CHAMPION	NON-PUBLIC SOUTH A SECTIONAL CHAMPION	NON-PUBLIC SOUTH B SECTIONAL CHAMPION
	Immaculate Heart Academy	Saddle River Day	Saint John Vianney	Trenton Catholic Academy
2021	COVID-19 Tournament Cancelled			
2022	St. John Vianney	Immaculate Heart	Rutgers Prep	Saddle River Day

HUDSON SCHOOLS IN CAPS AND BOLD

GIRLS TITLES WON

17	St. John Vianney	2	Atlantic City	1	Egg Harbor
12	St. Rose Belmar	2	Eastside Paterson	1	Elizabeth
11	Malcolm Shabazz	2	Immaculate Heart	1	Ewing
8	Manasquan	2	Irvington	1	Gill St. Bernard's
8	Red Bank Catholic	2	JFK Paterson	1	Haddon Twp
7	Gloucester Catholic	2	Keyport	1	Hamilton West
6	Pascack Valley	2	Mater Dei	1	Hanover Park
6	Haddonfield Memorial	2	Middle Township	**1**	**HARRISON**
6	University	2	New Providence	1	Hightstown
5	H.G. Hoffman	2	NV Old Tappan	1	Immaculata
5	Paramus Catholic	2	Notre Dame	1	Jackson Memorial
5	Rumson–Fair Haven	2	Paterson Catholic	1	Jefferson Township
5	Trenton Catholic	2	Rancocas Valley	1	Lenape
4	Bloomfield Tech	2	Sacred Heart	1	Mahwah
4	Clifford J. Scott	2	Saddle River Day	1	Mainland
4	No. Hunterdon	**2**	**ST. ANTHONY**	1	Manchester Twp
4	Sparta	2	W. Morris Mendham	**1**	**MARIST**
4	Sterling	1	Arthur P. Schalick	1	Marlboro
4	Wildwood	**1**	**BAYONNE**	1	McCorristin
4	Willingboro	1	Bloomfield	1	Mt. St. Dominic
4	Woodrow Wilson	1	Bound Brook	1	No. Burlington
3	Asbury Park	1	Bridgewater Raritan	1	Nutley
3	Bishop Eustace	1	Burlington Twp	1	Ocean City
3	Columbia	1	Butler	1	Piscataway
3	Franklin	1	Camden Catholic	1	Pleasantville
3	Linden	1	Cedar Creek	1	Pt. Pleasant Beach
3	Morris Catholic	1	Collingswood	1	Red Bank Regional
3	Neptune	1	Colts Neck	1	Ridgewood
3	Rutgers Prep	1	Delran	1	South Hunterdon
3	St. Peter's	1	Delsea Regional	1	West Milford
3	Trenton	1	East Brunswick	1	West Side
3	Union	1	East Orange	1	Westfield
2	Absegami	1	Edgewood Regional		

GIRLS MOST CONSECUTIVE TITLES

6   **St. John Vianney** (1990–1995)

5   **H.G. Hoffman S. Amboy** (1985–1989), **Malcom X Shabazz** (2010–2014)

4   **Gloucester Catholic** (1976–1979), **Manasquan** (2014–2017)

3   **Clifford Scott East Orange** (1982–1984), **Paramus Catholic** (1984–1986), **Union Catholic** (1987–1989), **Linden** (1992–1994), **Haddonfield Memorial** (1997–1999), **Bloomfield Tech** (2004–2006), **Franklin** (2017–2019)

2   **St. Rose** (2014–2015) (2018–2019), **St. John Vianney** (2015–2016), **Rutgers Prep** (2016–2017), **University** (2016–2017), **Saddle River Day** (2018–2019)

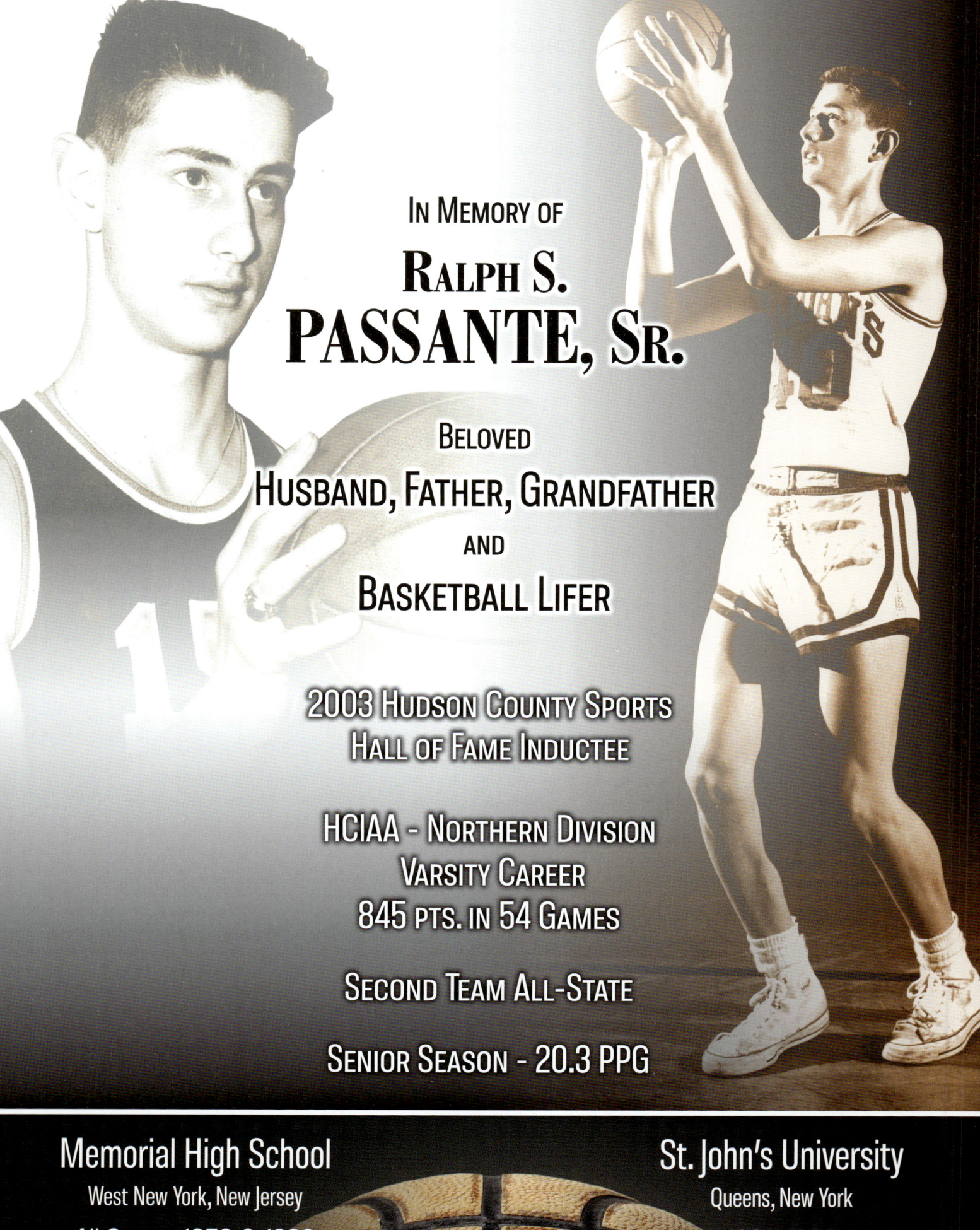

IN MEMORY OF
RALPH S. PASSANTE, SR.

BELOVED
HUSBAND, FATHER, GRANDFATHER
AND
BASKETBALL LIFER

2003 HUDSON COUNTY SPORTS
HALL OF FAME INDUCTEE

HCIAA - NORTHERN DIVISION
VARSITY CAREER
845 PTS. IN 54 GAMES

SECOND TEAM ALL-STATE

SENIOR SEASON - 20.3 PPG

Memorial High School
West New York, New Jersey
All County 1959 & 1960

St. John's University
Queens, New York
1961-1963

TEAM WALKER

Improving the quality of life for the children of Jersey City

ABOUT
Team Walker »

Team Walker is a 501(c)(3) organization located in the heart of Jersey City, New Jersey, that offers academic, recreation and athletic programs that provide safe and constructive alternatives to the negative influences that plague inner-city throughout the year to Jersey City kids in addition to community outreach programs for families and seniors. Founded in 1996 by former St. Anthony and Seton Hall Pirates basketball star Jerry Walker and his brother, Jasper Walker. The Walker brothers designed Team Walker around the youth programs they experienced while growing up, continuing the legacy of youth programs started by their grandfather, James "Pop" Curry that provided a foundation of dedication, determination, and discipline, the "3 D's." The Walker brothers modeled the 3 D's throughout their adult lives and credit their life success to these programs, which propelled Jerry's success in basketball and Jasper's on Wall Street. Team Walker passes this foundation onto today's Jersey City youth.

TEAM WALKER PROVIDES

Education

Physical Health

Mental Health

Vocational Training

Life Skills

Mentorship

GED Assistance

Weatherization Education

Energy Assistance Programs

Special Needs

Team Walker's
MISSION

Team Walker's mission is to improve the quality of life for the children of Jersey City through academic and recreation programs that empower the children's minds, bodies and souls. With access to positive role models, hard-won accomplishments in combination with a heightened awareness of their capabilities, the children have the opportunity to improve their quality of life significantly.

STAY UP TO DATE WITH TEAM WALKER

TeamWalker.org

 @TeamWalkerJC

 @TeamWalkerJC

 @TeamWalkerJerseyCity

Dan Finn Classic

Proud

"To have brought the best of high school basketball
to Hudson County and the Jersey City Armory"

Rewarding

"To bring educational, charitble, and humanitarian
relief to hundreds of people"

CONNELL FOLEY

Connell Foley was founded on the goal of providing outstanding legal counsel while maintaining a firm culture predicated on client service and teamwork.

Today, we gather to pay tribute to the remarkable honorees of Hudson County Hoops, each a testament to the indomitable spirit of this community. Among them, Elnardo J. Webster Sr. stands as a towering figure, transcending his legendary status in basketball to become a beacon of inspiration for us all.

As the Connell Foley team, we are humbled to sponsor this tribute, recognizing the profound impact these individuals have had on our lives and this cherished community. Elnardo Sr.'s dedication to education and unwavering belief in the transformative power of community servantry continue to resonate deeply with us.

Today, we honor not only Elnardo J. Webster Sr. but all the honorees of Hudson County Hoops, whose contributions have enriched our community in immeasurable ways.

With heartfelt gratitude,

The Connell Foley Team

Elnardo J. Webster Jr., Partner
ewebster@connellfoley.com
www.connellfoley.com

NJCU BASKETBALL
PRIDE. LEGACY. CHAMPIONS.

NJCU
MEN'S & WOMEN'S
BASKETBALL

15 NJAC CHAMPIONSHIPS

22 NCAA TOURNAMENT APPEARANCES

2 NCAA FINAL FOUR APPEARANCES

9 ALL-AMERICANS

WWW.NJCUGOTHICKNIGHTS.COM